CHECKOUT

THE STEP-BY-STEP, 7C METHOD TO BUILD A DOMINANT ECOMMERCE BRAND

NEIL VERMA
REN MOULTON

eBrandBuilders

CHECKOUT

THE STEP-BY-STEP, 7C METHOD TO BUILD A DOMINANT ECOMMERCE BRAND

eBrandBuilders
125-720 King Street West, Suite 2000
Toronto, ON M5V 3S5

Printed in the United States of America

Publisher's Cataloging-in-Publication data
Verma, Neil with Moulton, Ren.
Checkout: The Step-by-Step, 7C Method to Build a Dominant eCommerce Brand, Neil Verma with Ren Moulton.

1. The main category of the book — Books > Business & Money > Marketing & Sales First Edition

Dedication

Neil:
To my Mom. A constant source of inspiration, love and life.
To my Dad. An epitome of selflessness, positivity, and strong work ethic.

Acknowledgements

Thank you to our editor, Sinead Donohoe, for her attention to detail, and the constant reminders to diversify our vocabulary and avoid repeating the same words over and over.
Thanks to Kate Trotsenko, our designer, who exercised her creativity and for being extremely patient with our never-ending changes.

TABLE OF CONTENTS

INTRODUCTION

Who Am I to Teach You About eCommerce Branding?

Growing up, I always had a fascination some may call an obsession, with brands: the unique personalities behind them and their role in my life. It intrigued me that there were people and things that were somehow universally appealing yet cut from a unique pattern. Then it wasn't a surprise to friends or family when I focused on business and branding in college and later got an MBA in eCommerce Leadership. Nor was it a surprise to anyone that my first gig out of graduate school would be as a corporate banker and brand consultant.

This was part of my "5-year plan" at the time, after which I'd go out on my own: I just wasn't sure how. Of course, that 5-year plan turned into 6, 7, and then 10 years, but I had established a strong groove working for some of the biggest corporate brands in the world, managing $100 million businesses.

Leaving My Corporate Years Behind

I excelled in this role, helping ensure customers came back again and again, week after week, month after month. But of course, once you get good at something and form a repeatable system, it starts getting mechanical.

But.

I had an itch: an itch to build something from scratch.

To develop a business without the bureaucracy.

To make a difference.

With a core interest in brand and digital strategy, an MBA, and after building the digital strategy for several Canadian financial institutions, eCommerce was a natural calling. I jumped into the fray, head first, thinking I had established multi-million-dollar businesses, how tough could this be? And as I'm academically inclined, I took a few courses, thinking I would be well on my way to tasting immediate success. I remember the day I pushed back from my comfy Herman Miller chair, walked into HR with a smile on my face with a freshly printed letter of resignation. My confidence and excitement brimmed over as I walked out the front doors, 20 floors down, to an appropriately springy day.

6 months later, I chalked up my first eCommerce fail.

12 months later, my second.

At the time, my mantra 18 hours a day, 7 days a week, became 3 simple letters: "W...T... F?"

A year before I had total control: I was bonusing out to the tune of a new house in Toronto after 3 years, a summer house in 6, and soon my salary was just gravy. I was a respected "master" of brand and digital strategy in the business community at large, but 12 months out on my own and I had literally gone from "Real Kobe Beef" to "Ramen." I had no strategy. I was crouched in a corner reacting day-in-day-out, batting shiny objects like a meth-addicted tabby cat. I remember the many "aha's" I exclaimed aloud to myself as I discovered the tools that would surely change my fate: a new Facebook Ad technique, a Shopify theme optimized for conversions, a new Messenger marketing template, among others.

Of course, this was all still punctuated by my "WTF" mantra at the end of each of those days!

And while these tools proved to be useful, and should be used by any eCommerce maven, I found it all meant nothing. None of it moved the needle because I didn't have an identified CORE. A central purpose. Differentiated meaning. In other words: I didn't have a real brand.

I watched as other eCommerce businesses proved themselves in under a year, generating upwards of $1, 2, 3, and 5 million in revenue: what did other eCommerce entrepreneurs have that I lacked? I used the same marketing tactics as they did, and yet, they'd generate millions of unique page views while I was having trouble getting Facebook click-throughs on, in my opinion, some of the best advertising and offers in the broader industry.

But I've never been a quitter.

My eCommerce Branding Revelation

I dusted myself off, now easier than ever, as I'd traded in my Brooks Brothers suits for stretchy-waist tracksuits, which doubled conveniently as pajamas for the many nights I found it easier just to nap in the office. Then, I went back to the basics. I reminded myself that regardless of the nature of the business, customers buy for the same reasons. Buying psychology remains the same, whether it's a 401K package or a custom tooled, Corinthian leather bag. I had a store with unique products and marketing, but I needed to establish a (new) brand strategy.

But as I started taking a more formal and focused look at branding for eCommerce, I noticed two very distinct buckets of error. Anything even tangentially referring to eCommerce branding was incorrect or incomplete regarding actual branding tenets and laws. And the handful of eCommerce companies recognized for their branding either stumbled upon their methods from trial and error and a lot of expensive rework and learning or had outside firms, funded by a Series B, do the branding work from the "outside." The insight that seemed to be missing was that while the core laws of branding are consistent and universal, the specific implementation steps and processes are different and must be adapted to eCommerce. And the more I dug for any logical and well thought out approach to eCommerce branding, the less I found. I realized I'd have to figure out and develop my system in that vacuum.

Which is what I did.

First, I spent 12 months analyzing over 200+ Direct-to-Consumer (DTC) companies (some which I would say qualified as brands or near-brands), companies that had a real impact over the last 3 years. I analyzed their various evolutionary inflections and what worked. I also looked at what I had been taught about traditional branding methods, which worked everywhere else but didn't seem to work in eCommerce. I essentially went through every tool in my brander's toolbox and had to determine which ones were viable or usable in eCommerce, what the new eCommerce brand tools were, and what traditional tools could be adapted and applied to eCommerce that had never been used before.

hims STITCH FIX

chubbies MeUndies

BOMBAS

Tortuga® MACK WELDON

HARRY'S quip

brooklinen AWAY

allbirds ROTHY'S EVERLANE

I discovered most successful eCom brands were built around a core principle which then emanated through everything they did: from marketing to product development, to operations, to customer experience. These were not randomly assembled brands that achieved fluke success, even if early on various frameworks or individual tactics had been tested only to be quickly discarded and replaced. What emerged was that for all of these successful brands, there was *eventually* a systematic framework with a strong core around which everything else grew. While many of these systems remained incomplete, they worked, and it was obvious what subsystems were common across all of the top eCommerce brands. But to make order an actionable system that was practical and logical, I knew I had to break it down and define the individual elements which built on each other until a powerful result was achieved.

As I pieced these various elements together, it became the 7C framework, with each "C" addressing a critical aspect of eCommerce brand building:

1. Core
2. Customer
3. Community
4. Competition
5. Creatives
6. Content
7. Channel

It was from this framework that I founded and built my next eCommerce business, and within 11 months, I grew the business and was able to sell it for a tidy 7-figure sum.

"Third time's a charm," you might say, but for me, my third business only succeeded because of the 7C framework. This is the same framework that I started using for our consulting clients to take them from a mediocre to a mainstream brand. And just like my (3rd) eCommerce company...it worked for them, too. Every time.

My Inspiration for Providing the 7C System

You can see a thread throughout most of this history: struggle, repetition, iteration, realization, systematization, then repeatability to mastery... then boredom! While I love the consulting work and clients, there is a capacity ceiling, and I can't personally reach more than a few dozen new eCommerce companies and CEO/Founders a year. The only way to spread the word throughout the broader eCommerce community is by making this knowledge directly available as a standalone 7C text and coaching classes to positively impact thousands from the bounty of my own hard-fought learning.

Despite the success I've had adopting brand strategy as the underlying foundation of my eCommerce businesses, I know there remains prevalent systematic issues, myths, and misconceptions related to branding throughout the eCommerce world. If anything, I was an exemplar to the rule.

I am often shocked to see how diluted and misconstrued the term branding is in the eCommerce community. I know branding tends to be viewed as an unnecessary expense, something you do once you hit a certain clip or procure outside funding. But as I got deeper into the community, the fallacies around branding became more pronounced.

Here were some of my observations:

- Entrepreneurs often point to their logo or packaging, confusing creative design with branding.
- The sheer laziness of most digital marketing today. It's preoccupied with short-term tactics driven by FOMO to pump up conversions. Without branding, this campaign-obsessed mindset traps entrepreneurs in the death spiral of price wars, and ignores the importance of creating demand, not just capturing it.
- This situation only creates desperation, heightening the importance of every dollar. Meaning you never have the ability to balance marketing with the long-term methods that create customer relationships that increase their lifetime value, and multiplies retention, driving down your acquisition costs.
- There's a deficiency in patience in most eCommerce entrepreneurs. Even though we know organic users are more valuable long-term than paid users, pursuing paid customers is so much easier and faster in the short-term. As a result, branding – which is the best way to secure reliable, steady income and profitable growth – is totally ignored.

Why

"Ask Why"
Do you hear yellow detonations in mid-autumn?
From what does the hummingbird dangle its glittering symmetry?
Is 4 always 4 for everybody?
Are all 7s equal?
What's the name of the flower that flies from bird to bird?
-   Pablo Neruda, from <u>The Book of Questions</u>

eBB's "Why"

As an eCommerce entrepreneur, I encountered many fellow retailers who struggled with branding. Too often, these struggles weren't due to a lack of ability or resources, but mistaken beliefs and fallacies about the importance of brand and the branding process. Later, after I exited my eCommerce companies, I found myself wanting to contribute to the eCommerce community. Knowing the success I had achieved with the branding system I had used in my own businesses, and combined with the impression that many of my fellow entrepreneurs were grappling with branding, this ultimately inspired my vision to educate and guide other eCommerce retailers to use the power of branding to help them build their scalable businesses.

I then created eBrandBuilders.com (eBB), the platform through which I'd deliver my message. Today, eBrandBuilders is an online community that supports eCommerce entrepreneurs to thrive. This community is our tribe, and their success enhances the power and joy in our own circle.

Of the many tools and resources we provide at eBB, our flagship offering is our 7-week digital coaching program called eBrandcubator, and it's the only total brand construction program designed specifically for eCommerce entrepreneurs. The intensive 7-week session involves educating, training, and mentoring eCommerce entrepreneurs and taking them from being product hustlers to brand masters.

If you're interested in learning more, you can find further details by visiting ebrandbuilders.com/ebrandcubator.

The book you have in your hands is the core of our approach, and it provides an accessible stepping-stone to the world of eCommerce branding.

The Primary Goals of this Book
(aka What's In It for You)

I recently visited Amazon.com and did a quick search for "branding" books. There were over 9,643 individual entries, not to mention the hundreds of other books covering the various sub-practices of branding. Clearly, there's a lot of knowledge and expertise about branding out there. The problem is that among these thousands of results, almost all of these books take a traditional approach. They tend to be academic and overly theoretical, and none are specifically tailored to address the unique methods and specific tools needed to brand in the eCommerce space.

The advantage of this book is that I'm one of you, and I understand there's a strong overlap between eCommerce and digital marketing. Meaning, eCommerce entrepreneurs are comfortable with blueprints, workshops, guides, courses, and case studies. I've applied these learning frameworks throughout this book to give you a tangible, step-by-step methodology. This book is structured using the 7C's, the approach I developed over the years working with our consulting clients and in my eCommerce ventures. Each chapter details one of the 7C's, starting with the broader conceptual theory behind the C before going into actual implementation.

The practical side of the 7C approach takes multiple avenues:

The book features the proprietary, 1-page eBrandBuilders 7C Canvas. This page should be used as a landmark to develop and document your strategy as you progress through each phase.

As you read along, we will also be building the brand strategy for Meniml, a men's skincare brand created to demonstrate through example, and step-by-step, how to build an eCommerce brand that resonates with consumers.

We also use real-world, practical examples and case studies from other best-in-class Direct to Consumer (DTC) brands whose mastery of individual steps or concepts are illuminating.

The goal of this book is to provide you with a concrete, how-to plan to help you learn everything you need to know about developing a highly successful eCommerce brand: all in plain English. After going through this process, you should:

- Be strategic rather than over-reliant on tactics.
- Be able to increase your paid traffic campaigns by 3-5x, giving you a stronger foundation for your brand.
- Achieve greater cohesion and clarity among your team.
- Be closer than ever to reaching the much-coveted 7-8 figure mark.
- Be a brand master, rather than a product hustler.

I would add one caveat, however. While eBB team and I are always available to answer any questions, and a more formal consultation through the 7-week coaching program eBrandcubator (ebrandbuilders.com/

ebrandcubator), you'll get the most value out of this book if you act on each step outlined as you go along. Your comprehension will truly soar once you get your hands dirty and begin building your brand with our framework as your guide.

The core purpose of this book is to spread this message farther and wider: branding should not be an afterthought. Your brand strategy can, and should, extend beyond visual assets to be your organization's corporate strategy. Looking at the most highly valued corporations today, all of them first built a compelling brand, cultivated a loyal following, attracted premium talent, and built significant equity. eCommerce isn't just following a similar growth pattern, it's also evolving into a standalone industry: consider the $1 billion valuation of Dollar Shave Club, the acquisition of Tuft & Needle by an offline competitor, and Gordon Gekko sized acquisitions like PetSmart's $3.35 billion purchase of Chewy.com.

NOTABLE eCOMMERCE TRANSACTIONS

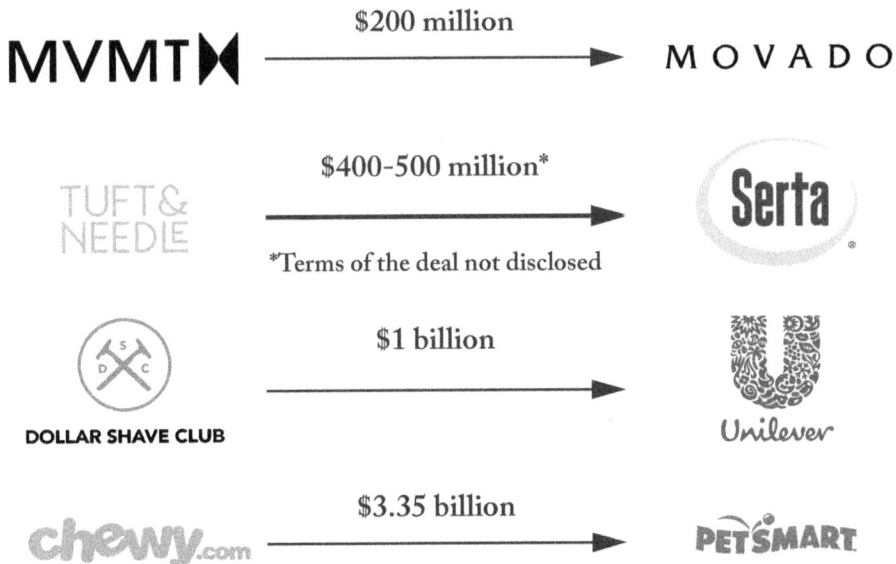

MVMT◀ —— $200 million ——▶ M O V A D O

TUFT & NEEDLE —— $400-500 million* ——▶ Serta

*Terms of the deal not disclosed

DOLLAR SHAVE CLUB —— $1 billion ——▶ Unilever

chewy.com —— $3.35 billion ——▶ PETSMART

Who Should Read this Book?

This book is for you if:

You're a struggling eCommerce owner stuck in a rut. Day to day, you're absorbed in chasing the magic-bullet solutions toted by gurus online. You hustle every day for sales, churning out offer-led ad campaigns, but your business never seems to grow, because you don't understand that what you've been taught is "right," is actually undermining the value customers place on your brand.

You're a new eCommerce owner, but you want to build a solid foundation from the start. You understand the value of branding and want to build your business from the inside-out, the right way, from day one.

You're a traditional, but struggling, brick-and-mortar brand leader. You'd like to emulate the success of newer eCom entrants into your space, but you're prepared to tackle the real issues. You're not just interested in changing your logo, you're ready to take stock of your current situation, make a cultural shift, align internal systems and processes, change your decision-making criteria, and focus on digital-first.

You're like us: you crave the education, direction, and support to build a highly successful eCommerce business. Whether you're looking to turbo charge your standalone store or build a synergistic portfolio of eCom properties, you want the knowledge and strategies to take your business to the next level.

BRANDING BASICS, BRANDER BASICS

Products versus Brands

There are more products in the world than producers or consumers. That is, there are more products in the world than the seven billion people who use them.

Amazon alone sells upwards of 606 million products: with an average of 1.3 million new products added every day.[1] Most of these products are commodities, which is neither good nor bad, though it does mean that many of these products are non-exclusive or interchangeable.

What this means for companies creating and/or manufacturing and selling these products is that competition in each category and sub-category is primarily based on price. And as we know from core business strategy, only one company can win in each category using the price-leader position: think Walmart.

Target, for instance, doesn't compete with Walmart on price, but on the strength of their in-house brands and custom branded products, for which it charges a premium. This is also why we shouldn't be surprised to hear about large and small companies with dominant revenues in their spaces suddenly facing bankruptcy or takeover. Companies grow through profitability, not revenue, and many unbranded, multi-million-dollar companies file for bankruptcy every year.

These economic truths explain why branding, selling emotions and meanings above the basic utility of a product alone, is - or should be - a key competitive asset for any company trying to make its way through the sea of competitive noise, and rise above the tooth-and-claw tactical competition.

To further explain: products perform a function. Early in the multi-community market life-cycle, most core products were unique. Today, in a mature marketplace, almost every category or sub-category is replete with competitor products offering similar functions. Branding today is as much a factor of survival as it is of (category relative) growth.

Brands offer emotions: they fulfill wants in addition to needs. As such, people fall in love with brands, not products. And while products perform a job, brands perform with purpose. For example, I may need a smartphone to make and receive calls, email, surf the web for information, and listen to music. And all smartphones (the product), have these same core functions. I can get a smartphone online or at literally hundreds of other places in my city, from phone service carrier outlets to electronics stores to mass merchants including Walmart and Target. On top of this, the actual phone function can be carried out through multiple carriers, those same carriers available for all major smartphone brands. The smartphone's core, embedded function as a phone, is in itself commoditized.

But I go to my local Apple store, its own experience, and always buy an iPhone: in fact, I have personally bought 8 iPhones over the last 10 years. It's the brand I trust. I feel good using it and know a human being will be there to help me with any problems (and it certainly doesn't hurt that that human is also a "Genius!").

iPhone is the brand in this case and visiting an Apple Store and using the phone is the emotional payoff I get from that brand. Associating with other iPhone users is an added community endorsement and belonging factor.

iPhone keeps me constantly connected in the way I feel most comfortable. If I want to access the latest apps, I know iOS is usually the first choice for developers. If I want to buy music, iTunes always has what I want. But it's integrated and easy, and like the Apple Store (offline), I like the iTunes experience: Apple is consistent across all of its "fixed" touchpoints. In fact, when I interact with iPhone, I am getting a whole constellation of Apple-supported brands in one: commonly referred to as its ecosystem.

Remember: product equals function. Brand equals emotion.

I'll stop here because I intend to point out how commodity products are basically at parity with each other. They perform the same jobs and fulfill the same needs. Brands are what differentiate the products because of the unique feeling they impart. Which, as we will demonstrate is the "EVP" or Emotional Value Proposition a brand brings in addition to the UVP, or Unique Value Proposition a product provides.

Brands are Multi-Generational: Products, like Humans, Eventually Die

Products, also, are more static than brands, especially physical products that are manufactured and can require a 2-year cycle to implement any market-desired change, upgrade, or addition. While a brand's core should never change, it can still evolve with its consumer base, and frankly has to. When a brand loses favor and doesn't change with its core customers' changing needs and wants, it is subject to two reactions:

1. *It loses significant market share:* these brands are typically plagued by increasingly steep, off-price promotions, which only further devalue the brand. Although promotions can temporarily stave-off a downward spiral, they end up increasing the velocity of their downfall after this initial stall.
2. *Inertia:* when a company ignores market feedback, it will soon find itself preparing for bankruptcy or becomes vulnerable to competitor acquisition.

Because branding, at large, is all-encompassing and impacts a company's operations, culture, and creates significantly valuable intangible assets, it's not surprising it has been defined in multiple ways. As this book is specifically focused on brand building for eCommerce properties, I'll first borrow a definition of branding from an eCommerce founder whose business represents 44 cents on every eCom dollar spent in the US today.[2]

According to Amazon's Jeff Bezos: "Branding is what people say when you leave the room."

This definition certainly speaks to all three elements of branding I alluded to earlier: it's all-encompassing, an end to end influence, and of course, addresses the abstract aspect of branding.

eBrandBuilders', core definition is:

A brand is the premium that you're willing to pay for a similar product.

- Neil, eBB

This premium reflects attributes including emotional appeal, perceived benefits, and elevated status.

Brands Versus Products: The Brass Tacks

1. Brands outlive products.

Brands convey a uniform quality, credibility, and experience. Brands are valuable, and many companies put the value of their brand on their balance sheet. For instance, when Kraft bought Cadbury for $19.5 billion, what did they buy? *The chocolate? The factories? The recipes? The candy makers?* No, they bought the brands.

2. Branding is fundamental.

Branding is basic. Branding is essential. And branding builds incredible value for companies and corporations.

3. Branding simplifies choice.

Walk down the cereal aisle alone: there are over 130 different types of cereals to choose from. Some are gluten-free, some are meant for weight loss, some are loaded with sugar, and some have higher protein content. Others are purely meant to appeal to our taste buds: be it cinnamon, honey, or raisins. Shapes vary, too. Add in the multiple choices for the type of milk you're going to use and the simple act of having breakfast is transformed into an overwhelming myriad of choices. If having breakfast presents a person with an immense amount of choice, what about the rest of the day?

4. Brands provide a stable asset.

Products might fail, companies are bought and sold, technologies change daily, but strong brands carry on through all these changes.

5. Brands provide economic value.

The value of organizations is divided into two areas: intangible and tangible assets. Brands are intangible assets. A study of organizations in the S&P 500 Index showed that over 30-years period, between 1975 and 2003, the overall corporate value of intangible assets increased from 17% to 80%.[3]

6. Brands set expectations.

We live in a world based on promises. The car dealer's mechanic promises to do a thorough job, checking and rechecking the car to make sure it's safe. Cafeterias promise to provide fresh coffee brewed in a clean environment.

In the eCommerce space, where DTC largely resides, branding is crucial. In the absence of any physical interaction, with no ability to touch, feel, or try a physical product, branding is what maintains the tangible cord of connection between a seller and buyer.

The eCommerce Buyer's Journey

To understand this better, let's follow the buyer's journey over a 7 day window and through 7 interactions. This represents a typical journey, and, yes, we are obsessed with "7s," as our framework happens to be complete with 7 steps, but this is a happy coincidence.

Phase 1: Product Awareness

Wednesday (Day 1). Angela takes her kids to their soccer game, and as the kids hit the field, she sets up her fold-out chair next to the other parents. She wants to be social, but at the same time, the sun is glaring down on her, making her uncomfortable. She decides not to move, as she'd rather chat with others, but it suddenly dawns on her: what if she could find a chair that has a built-in shade?

Phase 2: Solution Awareness

Thursday (Day 2). Finding a chair with an adjustable shade is still on Angela's mind. She mentions it to Frank, her husband, and he mentions he has seen people bring them to previous games. Now, Angela is intrigued. After putting the kids to sleep, she Google's "chair with shade." Well, Frank was right for a change, she murmurs, these do exist! She sees several ads for various brands, priced upwards of $45. And as she scrolls down on the page, she sees that they are available on Amazon, Home Depot, Lowes, and more. Pretty much everyone has them, and she wonders why she wasn't aware of them. Angela clicks on a few other sites - Target, Renetto, and more, but wanting to make the right decision, decides that she is going to do further research sometime over lunch tomorrow.

Phase 3: Brand Awareness: Identify & Secure Credibility

Friday (Day 3). At lunch the next day, Angela opens her laptop to first post some pictures on Facebook from a recent family vacation. But after logging in, she sees images of the same chair from last night in her newsfeed. Savvy marketers have retargeted her! Angela clicks on the ad, which leads to a blog post on "8 Cool Products You Need this Summer," hosted on renetto.com. She reads the post and finds it informative, and of course, it features the same folding chair with a built-in canopy she had browsed the night before. She then starts clicking through the rest of the site: she watches a few of their videos showing the chair in use and then visits the "About" page. It's here that she learns Renetto are the "inventors and creators of the Original Canopy chair," and they hold numerous patents for it as well. She also discovers it's their product that's sold at Target, Dicks Sporting Goods and other retailers. Running short on time, she thinks she will decide by tomorrow to have the chair in time for next week's soccer games.

Phase 4: The Purchase Decision

Saturday (Day 4). Early Saturday morning, with the kids now gone with Frank for their karate lessons, Angela gets back to her search. She decides to check out the reviews and other similar products. She does the same search for "chair with shade," and this time new brands are displayed: Kelsyus, Kamp-Rite, and Quik Shade. She checks them out, reads the reviews on the retailer websites and Amazon, and picks another contender to Renetto, Kelsyus, due to its strong reviews, build quality, and color options.

Next, Angela Google's "Kelysyus vs. Renetto" and finds there is a question posted in the FAQ section of renetto.com. She learns that "although the Renetto canopy chair and Kelsyus canopy chair are of the same patented innovation and design, we use the Kelsyus brand as a budget-conscious option." She also learns that as a result, the Renetto brand offers a much stronger build, greater color options, higher capacity, and a larger canopy. How intriguing, she thinks, that the two brands she narrowed her search to, are manufactured by the same company!

As she is exiting the site, a pop-up offering 20% off your entire order with a promo code appears, and as she has pretty much decided to go with Renetto, it's now a no-brainer since there's only a $20 price difference left between the two chair brands.

Just to reaffirm her decision, she does a quick search for "Renetto," and there she finds links to two posts that clinch the deal. One from Gizmodo and the other from Wirecutter, with titles that say "The Best Portable Chair."

Decision made.

Armed with her credit card, she heads back to renetto.com and places an order for two canopied chairs: one for her in pink, her favorite color, with a matching canopy and footrest, and a blue set for Frank. She uses her promo code and selects the fastest shipping option. The entire experience is seamless, and it's done!

Within a few minutes, she receives a welcome email. The email is well-designed, personalized, and lets her know that she will receive another email with her tracking number when her order is ready to be shipped. And later that evening, she gets an email notifying her that her order has shipped, along with a shipping confirmation number. The days of waiting for a week to have an item delivered are certainly over, she thinks.

Phase 5: Brand Moment of Truth

Tuesday (Day 5). Mid-day on Tuesday, Angela receives an email confirming her order was delivered. She is excited to unbox, and both she and Frank set up the chairs after they put the kids to bed. She is impressed with the overall build, loves the hot pink color, and is excited that she can finally stay out of the sun.

Phase 6: Brand Ambassador/Referral

Wednesday (Day 6). Back from work, and after having dinner with her family, Angela is now ready for the weekly soccer game. The chair is loaded in the SUV, and when she reaches the field, she is excited to make great use of her new chair. She heads straight for where all her friends are sitting and places the chair right smack in the middle of all the action. As she starts

CUSTOMER JOURNEY MAP

	Day 1	Day 2	Day 3	Day 4	Day 5	Day 6	Day 7
Buyer Stage	Problem Aware	Solution Aware	Brand Aware	Purchase	Post-Purchase	Delivery/ Usage	Feedback
Touchpoints	Word-of-Mouth	Ads, Landing Pages, Search, Socials, Site	Blogs, Influencers	Site, Chat/ Call	Site, Email	Chat/Call	Email, Tools
Brand Goal	Show up	Educate	Build Trust	Seamless Checkout	Allay Buyer Remorse	Brand Moment of Truth	Elicit +ve feedback.
Feeling	Is there such a product?	What product will best meet my needs?	Would this offer the best value?	Is buying a simple process?	Will it ship & arrive on time?	I hope it looks exactly like the pictures	This is what I needed and I need to share

watching her kids and makes conversation with the other soccer parents, she can't help but think that this is the best $100 purchase she has ever made!

Phase 7: Repeat Post-Purchase Brand Touch (Reinforcement)

Friday (Day 7). As Angela checks her personal email in the middle of the day, she sees a message from Renetto. The email is short and sweet, checking to see if she has been able to use the chair, and if so, could she click on the link to leave a review. Angela doesn't think twice and takes a few minutes to type a praising review for her chair and Renetto.

While each of these phases has a different brand life-cycle descriptor, each one details a specific point when the consumer interacts with the brand. These instances are referred to as "brand touchpoints."

The average number of touchpoints a typical brand is responsible for has expanded with the rise of social media and eCommerce. Touchpoints include your website, store, point of sale, phone system, marketing and transactional emails, online help center, social media accounts, service and support teams, and much, much more: from word-of-mouth referrals to street teams, to branded applications.

To smoothly lead a customer through the buyer's journey, like Angela's experience with Renetto in our story, a brand must present a consistent message and voice across all its touchpoints. You may have heard this advice before, but it's often ignored by mega-budget brands that splatter hundreds of touchpoints out into the mediasphere to "get more awareness" than their competitors. This approach only generates a lot of wasteful noise, but for upstarts, consistency is now demanded by consumers who are already overburdened by market signals from the moment they wake up. A staggering 87% of consumers expect the customer experience to be consistent across all channels and devices used to interact with brands, and 60% of millennials expect a coherent experience from brands whether they interact online, in-store, or via phone.[4]

Brand Agnostic? Really?!

As consumers, we are now linked to the brands in our community and world. Remember the neat personal expression Pins from the '80s? (Ok, maybe only through rerun viewings of Fast Times at Ridgemont High or Sixteen Candles, but trust us, it was a self-expression movement). Well, the best, and thus longest living brands, have been defined to such a fine point that they are clearly understood by most people in their day-to-day lives. We may not even realize it, but we are promotional vehicles for the brands we love, whether it's the can of soda we're carrying, the athletic jersey we're wearing, or the Persols® or Raybans® we're rocking: we are presenting these brands to the world. Whether or not we are conscious of it, by association, these brands have become part of our identity, what we represent to the world as far as who we are.

This even applies to people who claim they aren't "into" brands, or do not see brands as part of their *personal brand*. They claim to be hyper-rational consumers, driven only by utility and price. And we are all consumers: we've just upgraded from free-range meat, pond water, and mammoth-wool robes.

Sure, there was a short-lived consumer-packaged-goods (CPG) company, called Brandless, who sold plainly packaged, high-end staples for $3. Although their failure was due more to a failed business model, their approach to branding was smart. "We're unapologetically redefining what it means to be a brand," said Tina Sharkey, co-founder and CEO of Brandless in an interview with Fast Company.

But this "head in the sand" attitude of being brand agnostic, and I am speaking from personal experience, is represented by a high percentage of people running eCommerce stores, who when asked about branding in their own business equation, respond: "We realize that branding is crucial, but presently we have more pressing matters." Or, "We just want to launch first on Amazon, see what kind of traction we have, and then look at branding."

If that *is* the case, without the work of branding, how do you answer any of these questions?

1. *Who* is your customer?
2. *How* are you differentiating from your competitors?
3. *Does* your visual identity have any meaning?
4. *How* did you select your brand touchpoints?

To these agnostics, I say: if they had a solid branding strategy they could avoid a slew of hiccups and issues considered "par for the course" for many other eCommerce entrepreneurs. Much of the hustle and pivoting that's expected as part of the life of an entrepreneur is often completely unnecessary drama.

Branding is at the core of business strategy or should be. This is especially true of eCommerce ventures as their origin typically sees its founder, or co-founders, seeking to address a genuine need, solve a real problem, or challenge the status quo. And each of these intentions directly addresses "why" those founders started the business in the first place. Realizing and defining this, "why," which we call your *brand purpose*, is the onset of the branding conversation.

To a large degree, brands can control the narrative, shape the perception, steer the communication, and influence the messaging, but ultimately, the customer is calling the shots. In a digitally connected social world, one tweet, post, or video can either put your company on a pedestal or have you running for cover.

And if you aren't controlling this conversation, and think that branding is frivolous, or just "nice to have," think again. You *will* be branded, even if you are not engaging in deliberate brand building.

Take a look at the telecom companies - the Sprints, Comcasts or CenturyLinks of the world. Almost everyone can share a negative experience from their interactions with them. The companies themselves are not attempting to be part of the conversation, induce positive associations, or make efforts to change the overall course of this perception. Instead, they are branded (in this case, as if with a Scarlet Letter) *every second*.

As depicted, the concerns for any company, pre-branded or branded, should be that if you do not have a brand in place, you will leave it up to your competitors and the market to define it for you. Keep the core tenet of existentialism in mind: *you* are responsible for making every decision and *not* deciding *is a decision* that has an impact. For the poorly branded, of course, a direct competitor with a concerted focus on branding can more easily usurp your customers.

Enough brand equity will help you brush off any untoward incident, and with the proper leverage, brand equity can ensure you come out stronger and convey a much deeper position if anything goes amiss.

With the onset of the COVID pandemic, profound economic anxiety is resetting the meaning of brand equity. Although eCommerce has seen a surge of new customers, the crisis has reshuffled everyone's priorities, and frankly, entrepreneurs can no longer rely on offer-driven campaigns. For instance, shortly after government assistance started reaching consumers, Costco promoted the sale of a big screen TV for $1,200, exactly the amount paid out. The move was met with immediate backlash, and Costco lost trust by appearing predatory.

But uncertainty actually makes brand building easier. Consumer interest in direct sales in these moments is low, which challenges businesses to return to their roots as a way to solve customer problems with empathy and serve the community. Consumers are also more receptive to purpose-driven messaging, so the leverage of organic methods increases.

Although generating organic conversations is more challenging than gaining paid conversions, it's the brands that have an "always on" presence that will feel accessible to consumers on their terms. Availability builds a trusted relationship with customers, which becomes the cornerstone of brand equity. But it doesn't mean you're trading in results. Branding ensures your business emerges from uncertainty with lifelong customers who have competitive immunity, because you've created equity that's a reliable emotional preference for your brand.

THE EBB 7C MODEL

The 7C Framework is an Inside-Outside Model

Engineering a brand does not start with external brand signals like the logo, brand name, and taglines. Although these visual elements are critical pieces of brand identity, they are part of a brand's external face, which we'll cover in the Creatives section.

However, not unlike building a new home, the first step is to begin with the inside. The foundation of your brand connecting to and understanding the deep "Why" your business exists. This reason gives shape, coherence, and meaning to everything your brand does.

Like a Russian doll, we'll start at the center of your brand's heart, your core values, and work our way outwards layer by layer until you're ready to design the external elements of your brand like your logo and brand colors which then represent this deeper meaning. Having a firm grasp on your brand's core will also allow you to effectively execute more meaningful digital marketing initiatives.

Brand strategies built from the outside-in are typically shaped by competitive pressures, taking cues from the surrounding market. By contrast, with the inside-out model, you leverage your core strengths, your passion, and your brand purpose to create a compelling brand.

By starting from the inside, you logically build upon each following component so that you automatically have coherence between all the parts.

While the 7C's - Core, Customer, Community, Competition, Creatives, Content, and Channel - are not new, they are the most important parts of your eCom business. But they must work *together*. There is no single thing that needs attention. A successful strategy depends on an interwoven set of circumstances amongst all 7 of these pillars in your business. Many smart, talented, and (previously) successful entrepreneurs have fallen to the many traps that can show up in these 7 different areas of your business because you've probably never been shown *how* to make all 7C's work together. Until you have this kind of holistic strategy, all the amazing tools available to us today won't be optimized to explode your business's growth and build a formidable brand.

THE 7C CANVAS

◆ CORE
WHY DO YOU EXIST? PURPOSE.

essence

WHAT DO YOU STAND FOR? VALUES.

CUSTOMER
WHO'S YOUR AUDIENCE?

HOW DOES YOUR PRODUCT ELEVATE?

COMMUNITY
WHAT CULTURAL GROUP DO WE IDENTIFY WITH?

COMPETITION
HOW ARE YOU UNIQUE?

CREATIVES

NAMING

COLORS

+

TYPOGRAPHY

LOGO

PACKAGING

CONTENT
STORY OF THE BRAND

BRAND STORIES

CHANNEL
YOUR BRAND TOUCHPOINTS
OWNED CHANNELS

SHARED CHANNELS

PAID CHANNELS

The depiction of the 7C's is aptly placed in the eBrandBuilders' proprietary framework, the 7C Canvas, available for download at ebrandbuilders.com/checkout.

This one-page strategy canvas serves as a roadmap to steer your brand's future direction, increases team efficiency *and* effectiveness by helping them deeply understand your brand strategy and vision. It also facilitates the on-boarding of new hires and easily communicates brand expectations.

Meniml Case Study

Each "C" is addressed in its own chapter and will be "completed" in the 7C Canvas via a case study building a men's skincare brand, Meniml. The academic concepts, hundreds of best-in-class eCommerce examples, and execution via Meniml will enable faster retention, real-life practicality (an ode to my case study MBA days), and, most importantly, help you build and complete the 7C Canvas for your brand.

For our Meniml case study, the first step was to decide on a product category for our example brand. Based on predetermined filters, we narrowed the product categories, from an initial list of 20, down to a shortlist of 3, and finally to 1.

The final selection of men's skincare was based on adopting these filters:

Demonstrated Brand Power: What are consumers really buying when they buy a face cream? Scents that last a few hours or face creams that can't be seen once applied are neither straightforwardly utilitarian products, like food or computers, nor status-symbol luxuries, like expensive watches or designer jeans. Why do consumers pay so much for products whose ingredients are well known to represent only a small proportion of the retail price?

Explained Distribution Merits: Distribution in the age of the Internet doesn't mean just a sales channel. It means addressing every brand element, each of which can help the product spread. This might be packaging worth Instagramming, a tight community of die-hard fans, conversation-starting content, or a beautifully photographable store. Beauty is well-positioned to lead experimentation in modern brand building, as it is an inherently experiential category. It is open to new technologies and is currently in high demand.

Displayed Market Potential: Online shoppers spent $25.7 billion US on beauty and personal care products globally, according to ARC. This category is forecast to reach $100 billion US by 2025, growing at a CAGR of 18.6% from 2018.[5]

Caveat: The selection of this category is not implying by any means that these criteria have to be met to apply the 7C framework or its branding principles. The 7C framework can be applied across all product lines for all physical products. We have used these screening filters to enable us to better explain various branding concepts that otherwise would be amiss with a more straightforward product. In other words, it's a self-induced layer of complexity that you will not have to overcome as you are building your brand strategy.

It's a Brand New Day

This leads us to a follow-up question: if branding is necessary, "when is the right time to brand?" This is a question that clients constantly ask me at conferences and in our coaching sessions. Tongue in cheek, I respond: "It's a *brand*-new day."

Of course, I'm suggesting that now is as good a time as any to become a real brander, and since *every day* is a brand-new day, branding needs to become a habit, a lifestyle, and a skill you are always perfecting.

Now, here's your CTA: flip the page and let's start building your dominant eCommerce brand.

1.0
CORE

1.0 CORE

Introduction: The Changing Consumer

Consumers are no longer simply looking for products and services. As technology continues to evolve at a breakneck pace, coupled with the increasing complexities of globalization, unethical corporate behavior has become all too common. Consumers now want to do business specifically with brands that care about social welfare, fair trade, and who demonstrate a higher purpose. When customers say they're looking for healthier choices, they aren't just talking about more natural ingredients in the foods they buy; they're talking about brands that offer products that are good for all brand stakeholders: customers, employees, vendors, and the environment.

Millennials, in particular, are a generation that craves *ethics-based businesses*, and as they vote with their wallets, they're demanding their brands share their values. They want leader brands that are overtly striving to make a positive social impact. They want leader brands that own up to their mistakes and are transparent and responsible. Brands who can embody these qualities will be trusted, seen as authentic, and become dominant players in the market.

Brand Purpose

What Is "Brand Purpose?"

A brand purpose is a brand's "why:" why it exists, for whom it exists, and what it will do. It is also the most significant part of a brand to its advocates, as consumers today are more concerned with why a brand exists than what it does.

In this climate, the best way to engage consumers is to have an "inside-out" strategy, which is driven by your brand purpose. But this can't just be any initiative or set of principles. To truly resonate with consumers, your brand's purpose must be the true core of your brand, and you must know how to demonstrate the relevance of your purpose in your customers' daily lives.

In fact, to underline the importance of purpose, we'd say it's one of the defining differences between a brand and a product. For example, take the Charity Water brand. Their actual product tastes like other bottled water, and it's similarly hydrating, but Charity Water donates water to villages in need for every bottle of water they sell. Their brand purpose is to help supply the world with hydration, their product costs the same or more than what a consumer could buy at their local grocery store, but simply due to their purpose, Charity Water has sold several million dollars of bottled water to consumers while also donating over 100 tons of drinking water to those in need.

Business writer Simon Sinek[6] uses the concept of "The Golden Circle" to illustrate why every person and brand should start by focusing on their purpose, their why.

THE GOLDEN CIRCLE

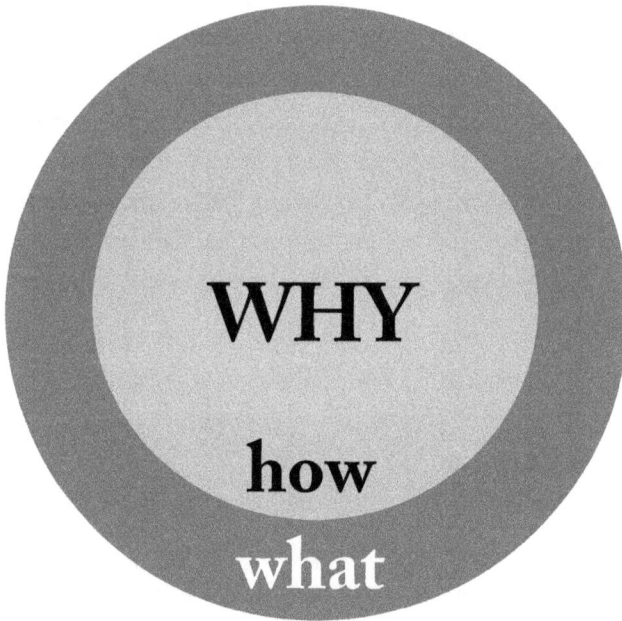

Source: Source: Sinek, Simon (2009). Start With Why. Portfolio.

WHY. At the center of the circle is your brand's "why" and while your business' mission or overarching goal may be making a profit, the purpose driving your brand, and its stakeholders, is the deeper reason your business exists. Your purpose propels you and your team forward, keeps everyone committed and focused day-to-day, and informs the decisions that are right for your brand and thus for your customers. Purpose also brings greater clarity and direction: it provides materials and fuel for your brand strategy, voice, and culture. With a clear brand purpose, you have a better sense of what product offerings fit your brand's persona, and the brand experience can be crafted around this changeless aspect. *Purpose is transformative: it can turn a product into an expression of your intentions, beliefs, and ideals.*

However, a brand's purpose is not necessarily cause-marketing, as it is specific to the difference an individual company seeks to make in the world. This may manifest as a simple vision, for instance, the goal of hims, an online subscription service for medication and wellness products for men, is "helping you understand that having an issue isn't weird. Not dealing with it is weird."

Likewise, Flex, a feminine hygiene product, has a grand, global vision to "[work] towards a world where every woman loves her body."

Moving out from the center, *"HOW"* defines specifically how your business operates in pursuit of its goals. It's more operational than purpose but is driven in part or whole by the purpose itself, which precedes it. Examples include a unique value proposition or a unique delivery system.

The outside ring of the circle is *"WHAT"* your company does. It literally describes your brand's products and services, what you tangibly offer your consumers.

Brand purpose, ideally, is a shared belief system among everyone in a company, the compass or specific rules for the organization as to what behavior is acceptable and what is not. As Daniel Pink has revealed in his seminal classic on motivation, <u>Drive</u>, people, including employees, are not driven by monetary rewards but by "intrinsics," a sense of higher *purpose*, pursuing that purpose, and the feeling of being highly competent in their roles. As we've evolved, so have our motivations, which is why the "carrot and stick" approach, still rampant in larger corporate environments, is backfiring. It's also why startups have been able to poach great talent at a fraction of their former salary. While most consider "brand" and its purpose as a key sales-driver with customers, we'd like to highlight the less understood and discuss the positive effect it has on a company and its people. As Daniel Pink explains:

"As humans formed more complex societies, bumping up against strangers and needing to cooperate to get things done, an operating system based purely on the biological drive was inadequate. In fact, sometimes, we needed ways to restrain this drive—to prevent me from swiping your dinner and you from stealing my spouse. And so in a feat of remarkable cultural engineering, we slowly replaced the existing version with one more compatible with how we'd now begun working and living. At the core of this new and improved operating system was a revised and more accurate assumption: humans are more than the sum of our biological urges. That first drive still mattered—no doubt about that—but it didn't fully account for who we are. We also had a second drive—to seek reward and avoid punishment more broadly. And it was from this insight that a new operating system—call it Motivation 2.0—arose...[7]

"Despite its greater sophistication and higher aspirations, Motivation 2.0 still wasn't exactly ennobling. It suggested that, in the end, human beings aren't much different from livestock."[8]

What does "intrinsic" mean to the individual? We'll quote one of the lead Linux engineers & creators, who left the corporate engineering trough and spent several years at zero pay while working as an open-source engineer:

"*Enjoyment*-based intrinsic motivation, namely how creative a person *feels* when working on the project, is the *strongest* and most pervasive driver."[9]

This is the *turbo-boosting* motivation a genuine brand purpose can instill with the "inside" members of its tribe.

Benefits of Brand Purpose

While purpose-driven brands are motivated by more than profits, this doesn't mean purpose offers no financial upside. In fact, because consumers increasingly see their buying choices as ways to express their values and ethics, *real purpose can be profitable.*

Purpose can also be a powerful differentiator from competitors without a purpose outside of selling products, but it also helps you stand out as purpose overtly affects your decisions and actions positively.

As a competitive differentiator? Take the example of two restaurants on the same block, which may very well be in your neighborhood, town, or city. Both serve the same style and quality of food and have similar stellar service, but one place is committed to using local, organic ingredients to support neighborhood farmers and agriculture. This restaurant will easily attract customers based simply on this practice. This is a purpose that differentiates and *sells*.

When you place your purpose at the heart of your everyday operations, your purpose becomes the common ground that attracts talent and consumers who share your vision. This foundation of conviction also helps you retain that talent because they'll feel like their work is meaningful and that they are making an important difference in the world.

Purpose also keeps customers coming back to you. Having a clear purpose helps increase brand adoption as it provides a context to spark meaningful conversations with your customers (and prospects) through direct and social channels. This clarity of vision will engage like-minded consumers and build loyalty. The relationship you create with customers will be more authentic, and as a result, simpler and more natural for you and your employees.

What if, to be authentic, your brand's purpose may anger some people? This is not a bad thing. In fact, most of the brands that are referred to as "iconic" today built a rallying and rabid brand fan base because they were fighting the status quo. If a brand is serious about taking on the status quo, it will definitely spawn enemies.

Big companies are often known for their conservatism. They often feel "too big to fail" and take on a sense of paranoia, worrying that even the slightest upset will scare customers away. This is not to say there are no examples of huge corporations sticking their necks out for a controversial cause: Nike, for instance, has always toyed with the borderline shocking and confrontational as part of their competitive spirit. Recently they have waded into the realm of politics, and this bravery has been largely rewarded.

In three recent ad campaigns, Nike has featured athletes whose reputations have been in some way tarnished. Nike then positions these setbacks as simply another challenge along the path to greatness.

The first in this series features Tiger Woods. Following a painful adultery scandal, Nike stuck by him and learned something: that outrage subsides, and the American public has an enormous capacity for forgiveness. Woods is back on the PGA Tour, his lucrative relationship with Nike untouched. They celebrated Tigers' first win in 5 years with a brilliant new ad:

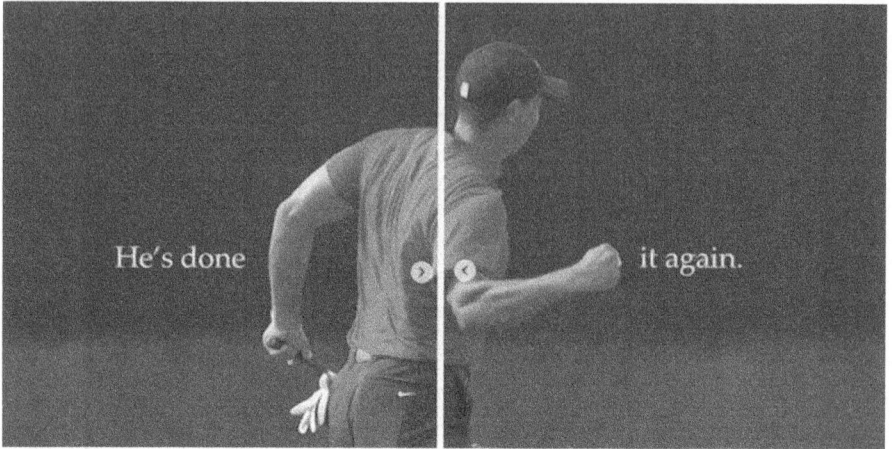

The next ad is Nike's response to the French Open's controversial decision to ban Serena Williams' catsuit. Nike drew inspiration from Serena Williams' assertion that the outfit made her feel like a "warrior princess:"

Nike's third controversial ad features former NFL quarterback Colin Kaepernick who became a national figure when, in 2016, he began kneeling for the United States national anthem before the start of NFL games to protest against racial injustice in the United States. The backlash was intense, reaching even the White House, and recently, Kaepernick settled a collusion lawsuit against the NFL. The ads featuring Kaepernick include the words "Believe in something. Even if it means sacrificing everything." This campaign is remarkable as it goes beyond simply sticking by its tribe to making a bold *political stance.*

Nike could have faced a ton of backlash, both from the public and their shareholders or Board of Directors, for backing these fallen stars. Many other corporate brand sponsors dropped them, but Nike stuck it out with them. Instead of drowning in a backlash, by being the only brand left standing, the public embraced the campaign and the stars once again.

You don't, however, need to be a billion-dollar brand to take a real stand. You just need the courage to stick by your convictions. Know that when the dust settles, for every enemy you may have made, your brand tribe will have at least doubled, and brand loyalty will have also soared.

Examples from eCommerce

We'll use Harry's as an example of an eCommerce brand with a clear purpose. Although it may not be immediately obvious based on their product offerings, Harry's really is a brand that wears its heart on its sleeve (or technically on its "face," so to speak).

Harry's is a shaving supplies company, and the majority of its customers are men. Its purpose, however, is not to "supply a simpler, less expensive, but thorough shaving experience."

Harry's stated purpose is, rather, to:

"Help guys navigate what it means to be a man today."

Is this unique and compelling? With today's social focus on the female and non-gendered side of the spectrum, for men today, it *is* a compelling purpose. In addition, this purpose has very little to do with shaving, except of course, that most adult men shave, but women do too.

Harry's also demonstrates transparency in how they prioritize their vendor partnerships, a process totally aligned with their purpose statement:

We make products for all men, thoughtfully.

We believe that you shouldn't have to compromise when it comes to the products you use, so ours are designed to be effective and to provide a great experience. Our team of more than 800 engineers, designers, craftsmen, and chemists make our products from the finest materials and ingredients to ensure they perform as well as they possibly can.

Indeed, while a company's mission may be focused on what the company accomplishes for its internal stakeholders, purpose specifically addresses what a brand seeks to do for the wider community and world.

To clarify, we've broken down the 3 elements of a great purpose: your brand's why, how, and what. We've also discussed the most important role of brand purpose, which is to address what the world needs.

Locating Your Brand Purpose

How does one go about determining their brand's purpose? From experience with over a hundred brands, both big and small, the purpose is strongest when it's uncovered, not when it's "created." If you are your company's founder, you may already be living the purpose as you are in touch with the deep reason you started your business. But if you can't put your finger on your purpose off the top of your head, here are some strategies to uncover it.

- Go back to the origins of the company. Why did the founders start the business?
- Do a brand audit: highlight your brand's strengths, unique capabilities, and the common praise you receive from customers. Do a side-by-side comparison of all these elements to see if you can identify a pattern that defines how your brand serves your community.
- Next, ask your employees why they were attracted to the company when they joined. What do they see as unique to the brand, and what, if anything, makes them proud to be associated with the business?
- Ask your outside stakeholders (such as partners, vendors, service providers, investors, board members, etc.) a similar set of questions to determine what they see as unique and valuable and what benefits they've seen from being involved with your company.

Remember, not all brand purposes have to be global and epic to be strong and important. For example, the local restaurant we mentioned before? Their use of local ingredients was just one part of their broader local purpose, which was to "transport our customers at least once a month outside their day-to-day existence, and elevate the entire neighborhood for all stakeholders, from farmer to farmhand." The importance and relevance of their purpose is specifically a reflection of their community. Your brand's world may only be a neighborhood, but it can be epic in its home turf.

Similarly, the benefits of a purpose, while its breadth may be national, maybe less ambitious, but no less important. Urban Outfitters, which has a deeply loyal brand following, states its purpose is simply to be a "provocateur."

Take your time thinking about this, and don't be surprised if your biggest issue turns out being *which* purpose to choose. Every brand has a purpose.

Every company has a brand. These are atomic truths. You need only focus on the unique good your brand can offer.

Which of course, we'll help you with. While we can't tell you what your brand's specific, unique purpose is, we can show you how to craft a stellar structure for your purpose statement, bring greater clarity to your brand's vision, and then help you share it with the world.

Meniml's Purpose

At the heart of Meniml's "why" was "who." The skincare category is dominated by brands aimed at women, and while there are several product lines made for men, they are under-served. Certainly, this has a lot to do with the association skincare has with beauty and femininity, and until recently, this meant that beyond the basics needed to shave, men didn't view skincare as necessary or "masculine."

For us, part of the decision to create a men's skincare brand was motivated by the desire to help men find a more inclusive definition of masculinity. In the past, there has always been a dominant ideal of masculine identity and behavior. For example, 20 years ago, the ideal man was the "corporate warrior," but this model fell out of favor as corporate greed and corruption created an ethically murky picture of the corporate man. Today, this model has been defanged altogether. Although corruption is still associated with the corporate world, we tend to see the average corporate man as nothing more than a stuffed shirt.

Of course, it's always been more complex than that: the ideal model of masculinity has typically been defined generationally. And when one model has its day in the sun, another is emerging with the younger generation. In addition, counterculture has always existed, so where there's a dominant model, a defiant type stands in contrast. This model has changed as well, for instance, hippies, punks, and grunge have at various times offered an opt-out of the dominant model – even if they weren't exclusively male-centered identities.

Today, the gender roles and stereotypes that inform all these models no longer hold the same social power they once did. Nor are they necessarily relevant to how men feel about themselves. Without a socially dominant model for the "ideal man" today, men are free to define their role with no expectation as to whether it should resemble more traditional models or not.

BRAND PURPOSE
Triangulating your brand purpose

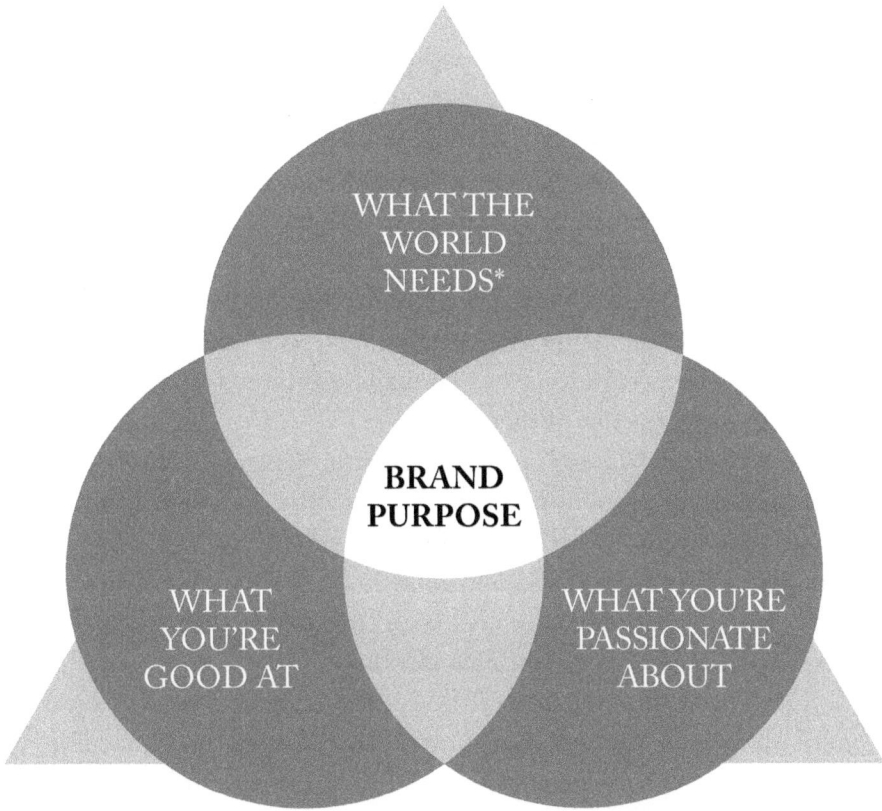

WHAT THE
WORLD
NEEDS*

BRAND
PURPOSE

WHAT
YOU'RE
GOOD AT

WHAT YOU'RE
PASSIONATE
ABOUT

*Want versus need. The world needs food, clothing, shelter, love and connection. Needs are not Wants. A person who lives in Siberia needs a thick winter jacket in the winter to survive, though they may want it to fit their personal style, or in eagle-skin leather to fit current fashion trends as outside-esteem.

This freedom is a good thing, but the fact remains that as essentially tribal animals, we still long to find a tribe to identify with and share experiences. The downside to the lack of a dominant model is that it has left a lot of men feeling tribeless and rudderless.

In this void, several competing models of masculinity have emerged, but none has quite caught on as an anchoring identity. For example, 3 of the main male subcultures relevant to a skincare brand are metrosexuals, lumbersexuals, and warriors. Metrosexuals embrace qualities and rituals traditionally associated with femininity, especially when it comes to beauty and cosmetics. Lumbersexuals, or "mountain men," are interested in the essentials of grooming and maintenance only. And warriors, who embrace a primal definition of masculinity, largely reject the need for men to worry about beauty or grooming.

Each of these 3 subcultures has vibrant communities with their own sets of rituals, interests, luminaries, and writers. And while most men will identify with aspects of at least 1 or even all 3 of these models, many don't fully identify with any one of them.

This was the gap Meniml sought to address. Being able to offer a more inclusive identity is relevant to a skincare brand because your identity has profound implications on self-care. Who you believe you are defines what you can and will do for yourself, and what you care about: for instance, this is exactly why skincare and cosmetics is an emerging male market since it's always been associated with feminine identity.

A quick note before we move forward: the organic process of creating Meniml developed the brand's purpose and a deep understanding of Meniml's customer simultaneously. As a result, purpose and customer for Meniml are tightly interwoven. As you might have noticed, the customer is our 2nd C and covered extensively in the next chapter. But, for the sake of clarity, we didn't want to overwhelm you with the detailed customer analysis process we went through before covering the underlying material. You'll find a detailed dive into the 3 male models covered briefly here as well as the precise model Meniml came to represent in the next chapter. For now, however, it's enough to understand that Meniml's primary purpose is to provide men with a more complete model of masculinity.

Meniml has a secondary purpose, as well. From our research, it was obvious that while many men do want to groom themselves, they largely do not, unlike most women, have an established self-care regimen. Providing a simpler, but everyday routine is thus another important purpose of Meniml. This is expressed in many ways, for instance, our straightforward packaging makes it clear what each product is and its necessity in a daily routine. In labeling as well, each product clearly states the order of how and when it should be used. Formulations also reflect this intent. Consider that most women's beauty brands "over-SKU:" that is, in an effort to both compete and add revenue in every possible area, many women's beauty products create extra steps. For example, a shampoo could easily contain a conditioner, but these are typically split out into 2 separate products to be used one after the other. The same goes for body moisturizers, sun protection, and even facial moisturizers and razor burn care. For Meniml, splitting those out into 4 products just adds steps to a regimen that could be far simpler for men who previously had little to no regimen. If at the center of "minimization" for men is "simplifying," then we've interpreted "simple" across multiple realms.

Combining these intentions, we distilled Meniml's purpose:

To offer a new, complete model for today's man. Meniml seeks to bring together thousands of factionalized "men," providing examples and models that their fathers, social peers, and role models could not. Meniml also makes it easy to take pride in grooming, with a simple to follow regimen and products that are sized and organized to make that regimen clear.

Now it's time for *you* to complete your brand purpose statement. To aid in completing your Brand Purpose Statement, I am going to simplify it even further and provide the following sentence structure (that we have used for Meniml too) to craft your own Brand Purpose statement:

BRAND PURPOSE

Why Your Brand Uniquely Exists; what Future State it Wants to Promote in the World.

Our Brand exists...

To [help/make]
ACTION

Our
WHO (CUSTOMER)

[More/To Be]
CUSTOMER IMPROVEMENT

[changed state]

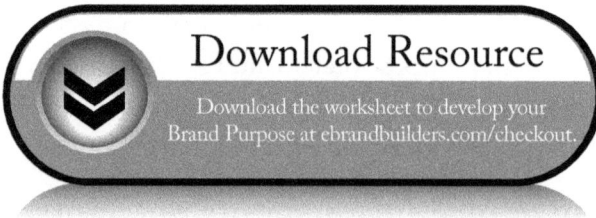

Download Resource

Download the worksheet to develop your
Brand Purpose at ebrandbuilders.com/checkout.

Now that we have crafted Meniml's Purpose statement, I will go ahead and place it in the 7C Canvas.

MENIML 7C CANVAS

⬡ CORE

WHY DO YOU EXIST? PURPOSE.

To offer a new, complete model for today's man. Meniml seeks to bring together thousands of factionalized "men," providing examples and models that their own fathers, social peers, and role models could not.

essence

WHAT DO YOU STAND FOR? VALUES.

💬 CUSTOMER

WHO'S YOUR AUDIENCE?

HOW DOES YOUR PRODUCT ELEVATE?

👥 COMMUNITY

WHAT CULTURAL GROUP DO WE IDENTIFY WITH?

⊙ CREATIVES

NAMING

LOGO

COLORS

+

TYPOGRAPHY

PACKAGING

◉ COMPETITION

HOW ARE YOU UNIQUE?

☰ CONTENT

STORY OF THE BRAND

BRAND STORIES

🖼 CHANNEL

YOUR BRAND TOUCHPOINTS

OWNED CHANNELS

SHARED CHANNELS

PAID CHANNELS

Brand Values

What Brand Values Are and Why You Need Them

Your brand's values are the foundation of your company's identity. These values define who you serve, the problems you solve, and the principles that guide your decision making in the pursuit of your purpose. These are the core, bottom-line beliefs that your brand stands for and defends.

Brand isn't just a visual identity: it's behavior and attitude, a commitment to certain ideals that define who you are. Values are the "North Star" that guide your conduct regardless of the goal you're pursuing, and they keep the overall direction of your brand honest and accountable to something other than profits (and sometimes at their expense).

Honoring your brand values is the cornerstone of customer loyalty. Customers admire brands that act in accordance with who they say they are. Deep bonds are forged with these brands because values give your brand a human touch and directly impact how consumers perceive the authenticity and emotional appeal of your brand.

One great example is Chubbies, a retro-inspired DTC brand of men's shorts that wears their values on their sleeves. Chubbies proudly post their values on their site, and opening with "We believe in the weekend," they offer a passionate slacker's credo (see opposite page).

But values are worthless on paper. They need to guide your real-life decisions. In June 2020, the "Stop Hate for Profit" movement started to gain steam online. It's a coalition between civil rights groups, the NAACP, the Anti-Defamation League (ADL), and Color of Change. Inspired by the global protests following the death of George Floyd at the hands of police, the campaign focused on holding Facebook and its CEO, Mark Zuckerberg, accountable for all the misinformation and hate speech circulating unchecked on the platform.

Although Facebook has come under fire for these issues before, they've been able to get away with nothing more than lip service to being more responsible. "Stop Hate for Profit," however, seems poised to change that, as 200+ brands joined the campaign and agreed to stop all advertising on Facebook for the month of July and potentially beyond.

Welcome to Chubbies. Here is what we believe.

We believe in the weekend

We believe that **"short shorts"** is a redundancy

We believe in **swim trunks, swim shorts, bathing suits, swim suits** or whatever the heck else you wanna call 'em because we believe that if you've got a pair of those on, well, you must be doing something right

We believe in the right your quads have to a life of freedom and sunshine

We believe in comfort

We believe in our fathers - they led the way; we are but revolutionaries standing on the shoulders of amazingly mustachio'd giants in proper length shorts

We believe **sweat shorts** are the greatest innovation in lounging since hammock cup holders were invented in the early 1780s

And we damn sure believe in Friday at Five

Onward to the Weekend >

-Team Chubbies

Pioneers signing on to the campaign included brands known to be purpose-driven, like Unilever, Ben and Jerry's, Patagonia, and Lululemon. In their announcements, all of them quotes their brand values as their motivation. For instance, Lululemon explained "We believe we all have a responsibility to create a truly inclusive society," a phrase that might seem like a platitude if the act of halting advertising, and the potential profit loss that will come with it, didn't signal their commitment.

Seeing as 98% of Facebook's $70 billion in revenue comes from advertising, it didn't take long for them to announce they would submit to an audit of their hate-speech policies by the Media Rating Council.

It's a testament to the power of brand values when they're taken seriously. And it's precisely why purpose-driven brands are winning with consumers, because customers appreciate the authority brands have to standup, work together, and leverage their power to force positive change.

Keep in Mind:

Every brand must be careful to ensure they are crafting a single set of core values to create a sense of transparency and build trust. When your values are also true reflections of what you stand for and are willing to fight for, then your values will resonate with consumers and likewise inspire your team.

Bridge the gap between the company and brand values by ensuring your core values are honored from the inside out: core values should be the same for employees as well as customers. You may ask, as an eCommerce retailer, "how can the Chubbies team get everything done if their core focus is the weekend and comfort? Aren't these values for customers more than the internal team at the company?" We'd suggest that these values are shared by many brands, including Patagonia, who encourage their team to take long lunch breaks, go surfing or biking, and work only 4 days a week. Despite their more leisurely approach, and perhaps *because* of it, Patagonia remains a hugely profitable, premium, and mass brand. And this is precisely what we mean by "inside-out" values: values only feel genuine when they're an honest reflection of your company culture.

Here's another example: Tortuga sells backpacks online specifically designed for city travel. Tortuga, like Chubbies, is another "personal freedom" brand, and while they do not contradict Chubbies' credo, they prioritize their values very differently:

Our Values

Work On Our Terms	Scratch Our Own Itch	Prioritize the Customer	Build and Improve Systems
We are a distributed team. Everyone sets their own hours and chooses where to live and work.	We created our first product because we needed it. Every product that we make must solve a problem for city travelers. We will never slap our logo on a "me too" product just for the cash.	If you have a problem, we'll do everything in our power to fix it. When you contact us, you are always speaking directly to a person with the authority and ability to solve your problem.	We use software and systems to help our team focus on what matters: product and people.

"Work on their Terms" and "Build and Improve Systems" are very different from loving weekends and short-shorts, but still part of Tortuga's focus on achieving personal freedom.

Tortuga and Chubbies may both be brands seeking personal freedom, but they each pursue this ideal with very different values. Likewise, Tortuga is a bag company, but comparing them to another bag company, Leader Bag, as depicted on the next page, whose core values include love and kindness, and again, we see how values help clearly define your brand. Note that differentiation is founded in locating and prioritizing your brand's top values. In other words, Chubbies, Tortuga, and Leader Bag are complementary, that is, they all have a similar ethos, but their specific top values make them clearly different from one another. *Different but not contradictory.*

Selling products is almost the last thing brands do, as the most successful brands are using products to sell ideas, their personality, and their core beliefs. Having this human heart at the center of your brand will also powerfully attract your ideal target customers. These are the customers that share your worldview and believe in what you are doing and trying to achieve. A relationship formed around shared values goes beyond a transaction and is a deeply felt connection to your brand. When customers feel like your brand understands them, they feel respected and heard, and

About Our Values

LOVE	PEACE	WISDOM	SOLIDARITY	KINDNESS
We try to live with love in our hearts. It's the most basic, important universal core value to feel und to spread.	We embrace respect, collaboration and resolution. We strive for peace inside and out.	We work to keep learning and growing, to understand health, the environment and to promote prosperity.	We endorse trust, fellowship and standing among all others as our equals.	When we promote kindness, we promote all human values, including empathy, respect and love.

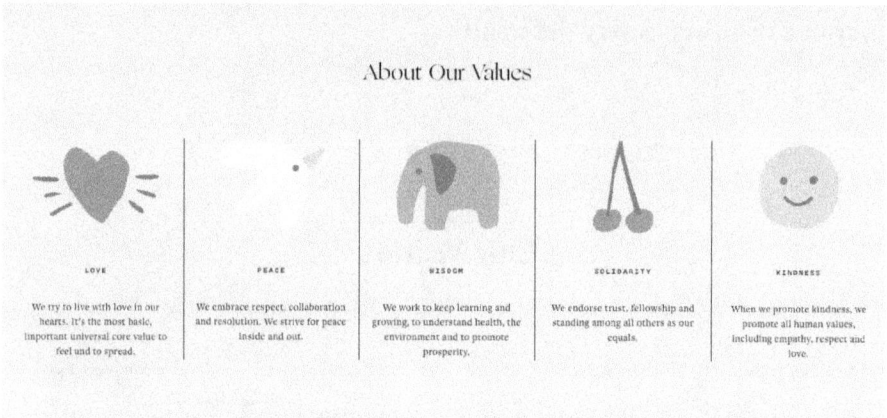

your brand becomes a familiar, friendly face, a source of comfort, and part of the customer's identity.

However, you must realize that your values are a timeless quality of your brand, and they should never change.

While, of course, your brand messaging and product offerings will adapt over time, the fundamental way you approach and practice business should remain defined by these bedrock values. Changing values sends the message that you're insincere and never cared for your stated beliefs. Make sure your values are genuine reflections of your identity, and that you're willing to go to battle to defend them.

How to Come Up with Your Brand Values

To find your brand's "North Star" values, start with your brand purpose and explore why you're in business. Ask yourself the following questions and be sure to write down your answers:

- *What* value are you seeking to create beyond profits?
- *What* are your brand's priorities?
- *What* ethical lines are you unwilling to cross?
- *What* inspires and drives your brand?
- *What* principles will keep you on track in a crisis?
- *Do* any of your answers overlap?

You'll likely come up with a long list while going through these questions, but limit your final list to 3 core values to define your brand vs. competitors.

By choosing 3 from 50+, you make your stand. Then, prioritize that list into your top value, and then second and third in order of importance.

As a counter-example, to explain this disciplining of your choices, have you ever seen a corporate site with a dozen values listed? You've probably noticed the values are tepid, vague, and redundant. This laundry list is usually symptomatic of trying to value everything in an attempt to appeal to everyone, but ultimately, they aren't truly valuing anything. Your customers will know this, even if just intuitively, but it's just as important to make sure your brand followers (yourself and your employees as an example), *live* your brand values and adhere to them in real life. And without a top 3, and top 1 of 3, you'll find it impossible to have any consistent focus.

However, avoid empty words and descriptors like "transparent," and "authentic." Many organizations define broad values like "teamwork," "accountability," and "friendly service."

But nearly every brand claims to have these qualities, so they're table stakes, not deep values. Besides, they are too vague to mean anything of substance to employees and customers alike. Remember, too, because values are powerful differentiators, focus on values that will help you stand out. Look for specific values that your brand can own that no one else can offer with the same passion and conviction.

Make sure, too, that your values are actionable. They need to be able to guide how your business operates. 'Authentic,' for instance, isn't a value, it's a symptom of acting in accordance with what you say you believe in. Likewise, don't list "integrity." Instead, describe *how* your brand builds and demonstrates integrity. Being admired isn't a value either: you want to zero-in on the characteristics that inspire admiration.

Above all, whatever values you choose, they must be principles that are genuinely meaningful to you and your team: otherwise, they'll just be wallpaper.

Meniml Analysis

Sometimes it's helpful while figuring out who you are (as a brand or a human) to determine who and what you are not. As we touched on in the discussion on purpose, every new men's brand segment values "masculinity," but each brand has a very different framework or concept for what masculinity means.

As a value, masculinity tends to be an extension of our personal ideals of "manliness." In terms of defining Meniml's values, it's therefore critical to narrow our vision of masculinity, and it is, therefore, helpful to compare the varying concepts of masculinity valued by other men's "subcultures."

For example, Meniml values masculine strength, but it's not the blind aggression of the "Warrior." Instead, Meniml sees strength as independence of thought and spirit. Meniml's masculinity is not a zero-sum game in the sense that he doesn't see winning and losing as defining a man's worth. Our model (which we cover in the next chapter, Customer) isn't an attempt to protest other subcultures, but simply to offer a currently missing niche. Our man is open-minded toward other models, and both identifies with some aspects while disagreeing with others: he appreciates guidance, but forges his own path. This encapsulated our first value: "Independence."

Next, while Meniml is a men's beauty brand, unlike metrosexuals, we do not associate with traditional women's Health and Beauty Care (HBC) in its promise of "feminine beauty," which, with cosmetics, is "additive." Meniml, meanwhile, expresses an honest love for a natural style, and cleanliness-based grooming. Meniml's concept of self-care is closer to maintaining and expressing natural handsomeness versus "beautifying." Maintenance is closer to the ethos of the lumbersexual except for a Meniml man, but it's more than grooming one's beard. This is captured with the value "Style-Cleanliness." This is also a step up from the "Warrior" ethos, where some of its luminaries even question the "weakening civilization" of hiding a man's scent through the use of soap!

Finally, another Meniml value is "Self-Respect." This is tied to both independence of thought and style as pride in self. The Meniml man respects passions and interests: a man can be "strong" if dedicated to their craft, and true to themselves, whether it is as a writer, or programmer, or construction foreman. With self-respect comes dignity, and for Meniml, that can come through dedication and love for *any* craft as long as there is a commitment and focus on achieving some level of mastery in that field. This is also a unique "value add" to the community we want to build through the brand as we cross subcultures and even generations to bring men together as peers around these shared values.

Here we have gone ahead and entered the three Brand Values for our Case Study. Now it's your turn to craft the brand values for your brand.

MENIML 7C CANVAS

◈ CORE

WHY DO YOU EXIST? PURPOSE.

To offer a new, complete model for today's man. Meniml seeks to bring together thousands of factionalized "men," providing examples and models that their own fathers, social peers, and role models could not.

essence

WHAT DO YOU STAND FOR? VALUES.

- Independence
- Style – Cleanliness
- Self–Respect

✆ CUSTOMER
WHO'S YOUR AUDIENCE?

HOW DOES YOUR PRODUCT ELEVATE?

⚹ COMMUNITY
WHAT CULTURAL GROUP DO WE IDENTIFY WITH?

◉ COMPETITION
HOW ARE YOU UNIQUE?

◎ CREATIVES

NAMING

LOGO

COLORS

TYPOGRAPHY

PACKAGING

☰ CONTENT
STORY OF THE BRAND

BRAND STORIES

◪ CHANNEL
YOUR BRAND TOUCHPOINTS
OWNED CHANNELS

SHARED CHANNELS

PAID CHANNELS

A Quick Note

Before we move on to brand essence, I wanted to comment on how we've structured the 7C system. Specifically, why we begin with your brand's core. One reason is that it's the natural starting point of many eCommerce entrepreneurs.

Consider these 2 common stories:

In many situations, eCommerce founders start a business to scratch their own itch. Meaning, they're developing products to solve a problem they're experiencing. The result is a business that has a laser-focus on what it's trying to achieve and the greater good it's creating.

It's also common for eCommerce companies to take the D2C route, whose very business model cuts out the middleman to deliver greater simplicity and value to customers.

In both of these instances, founders have a head-start in building a brand with purpose and strong values. Therefore, it makes sense to complete this process by precisely distilling this core before moving forward.

However, there's also a strong argument to begin, instead, with a deep competitive analysis and the customer work we cover in the next section, particularly if you're working with an established business. These are obviously important steps, and they're all covered here.

One of the dangers of focusing on your competitors too early in the process – especially if you're just starting out – is that you're more likely to get trapped chasing trends and spending all your resources just trying to keep up. Your brand should be informed by competitors, but not controlled by them.

There are 2 major advantages in defining your brand's core upfront. First, your brand's purpose and values are self-determined, and to ensure they're authentic and unique to your brand, they should be formed away from the undue influence of what competitors are doing.

Second, having a clear direction of purpose and values will narrow your focus going forward. It will guard against analysis paralysis when it comes to finding relevant customer segments and prevent you from trying to appeal to too general an audience.

Brand essence is an integral part of your brand's core, but it's not as self-contained as your brand purpose. As you'll see in this section, essence takes the customer experience into account. As such, understanding your audience and your competitors can lend important insights to the essence process.

Our recommendation, though, is that you work through the 7C's in order. But while we describe essence as the "timeless" quality of your brand, don't get stuck here thinking you have to make the perfect selection out of the gate. Instead, once you've completed your brand work through C4: Competition, feel free to come back to C1 and make any adjustments if needed.

Of course, if you've been in business for a while, you may choose to skip ahead. That's fine, too; we want to give you the freedom to adapt this process to your needs. But in almost all cases, we do still advise that you go through the steps in order.

Don't worry – we'll remind you after C4 to come back.

THE 7C SYSTEM

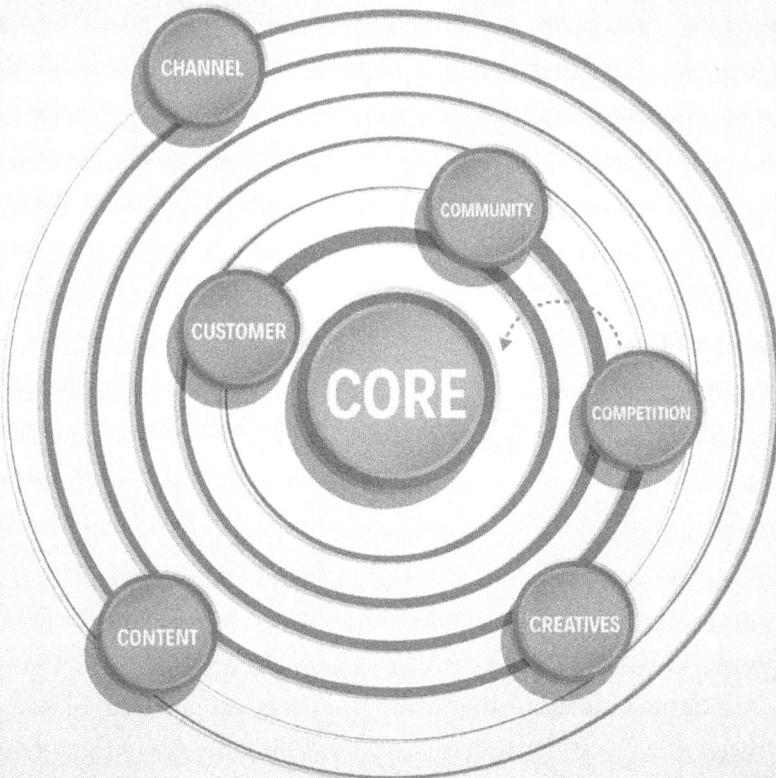

Brand Essence

Your brand's essence is the soul of your brand. Essence is the core value, idea, or emotional benefit that consumers associate with your products and services. Your essence thus defines the role your brand plays in the lives of consumers: it's the emotional experience consumers can count on your brand to deliver with every interaction. Your essence is the point where all the elements of your brand intersect, and it captures the absolute core of who you are in the shortest, cleanest way.

In one to three words, essence captures the identity of your brand, what you stand for, and the brand experience you offer. It is wholly unique to you, and it represents the intangible emotional experience customers cannot find with any other brand. It's thus the emotional heart of your brand's story, and this brand "DNA" is the heart of your brand's strategy; it also shapes your brand's messaging and brand extensions. This essence is a timeless quality to your brand, and while *how* you deliver this essence may change, the essence itself is set in stone.

Barkbox, for example, doesn't just sell dog toys and treats, they offer customers a tangible way to express their love for their dogs and create meaningful conversations among pet-owners. This love for pets, is therefore, their essence. Likewise, when you buy an Apple product, you're not just buying cutting edge, innovative technology, you're buying the essence of "thinking differently," and you're challenging the status quo.

Elements of Brand Essence

While your stated brand essence is simple and often represented by one or two words, there are several elements you must keep in mind when seeking to define your own.

Above all, your essence needs to reflect the experience of your audience. On the one hand, your essence will attract consumers, but it must also be directly related to what they feel when they interact with your brand. This builds trust as consumers directly experience that your brand follows through on its promise. This doesn't mean your essence can't be aspirational, but it must be believable and align with your brand experience. For example, Coca-Cola's essence is "refreshing," and certainly the hiss of carbonation when you open one, and its association with being ice cold, all conjure images and feelings of being refreshed on a hot summer's day.

Essence distills the intangible emotional response your brand evokes in your customers and the stronger that emotional response, the more deeply your essence will resonate. The Denver Broncos, for instance, have nurtured a community-first mindset that only uses football and sport as a foundation for

their role as a unifier. This essence appeals to deep, tribal emotions and creates a sense of belonging that elevates the Broncos beyond a football team and transforms them into a central element of their fans' identity.

You also want your essence to be unique to your brand. Essence is a true asset when your brand "owns" a specific emotional benefit, and it becomes a powerful differentiator. Ford, for instance, whose essence is "Tough," is going to attract a much different audience than a Ferrari, whose essence is "Passion."

However, the emotional benefit at the heart of your brand essence *must* be delivered consistently. If customers don't experience your essence in every brand interaction, it's not going to stick, and it will erode trust. This is why you must be careful to *uncover* your essence from the real products and services you offer, rather than choosing something that simply sounds appealing. Essence must be directly related to your brand experience if it's going to feel real. Likewise, your essence must be sustainable enough to resonate in any current or planned brand extension, for example, if Barkbox decided to ever expand into offering products for cats, they've already created such a strong essence around the love of dogs, that convincing consumers they stand for the love of pets would feel like a natural evolution of their brand.

Finding Your Brand's Essence

To find your brand's essence, I recommend using the process of "laddering." The process entails exploring your brand's features and benefits and distilling the emotional resonance these benefits create in consumers, and that identifies your brand. You begin with your brand's attributes and extrapolate their functional benefits; you then mine these functional elements for the implied emotional benefits. From product attribute, to functional benefit, to emotional benefit, to essential meaning. In this process, you move from the practical elements and functions of your *products* to the role your *brand* fills in the lives of consumers.

Ideally, an essence can be described in one word, and a brand then owns that word in its category. An essence, however, is not a tagline, or a promise statement, like "Just Do It." This is unquestionably a great tagline, but it's just under Nike's essence, which is "achieving greatness," as they are a motivational brand.

Indeed, the single word "motivate" is an ideal word for Nike's essence.

To illustrate laddering for an essence, we'll use a mainstream digitally native brand, which makes each step more obvious given its extreme exposure.

Laddering to Essence

Some markets are remarkably predictable. Most famously, former Federal Reserve chairman, Alan Greenspan, coined the term "The Men's Underwear Index." Greenspan's theory is that because men's underwear is generally seen as a necessity, sales figures tend to be constant. In fact, he argues these underwear sales are so reliable the numbers can be used to measure the health of the economy. If men's underwear sales dip, it usually indicates a slumping economy.

But in true eCommerce fashion, MeUndies, an online underwear brand, is shaking up this previously boring category and challenging the traditional wisdom that underwear can't be a luxury.

Central to the MeUndies revolution is redefining why and how consumers buy underwear. Let's see how we would use the process of laddering to generate its brand essence.

Product Attributes:

- Made with a material called "micro modal," which is harvested by grinding up Beachwood trees into a fine pulp, running that pulp through machinery, then using a carbon-neutral method to extract the fibers.
- And the waistband. Oh, lord almighty, the waistband. According to MeUndies, it's made from "a blend of Italian fibers including polyester, nylon, and lycra, tightly woven to create a silky elastic that stays flat and smooth on the skin."

Functional Benefits:

- Comfortable (finest, softest material, softer than soft basics).
- Snugness.
- Support.

Emotional Benefits:

- "Imagine the smooth luxury of silk, the stretchiness of elastane, the breezy coolness of bamboo, and the structural support of cotton. Now imagine that magical fiber draped lovingly atop your nether regions."
- "Honest to god, walking around the office with these things swishing delicately under my jeans is a borderline sick pleasure

DERIVING *MeUndies* ESSENCE
(through laddering)

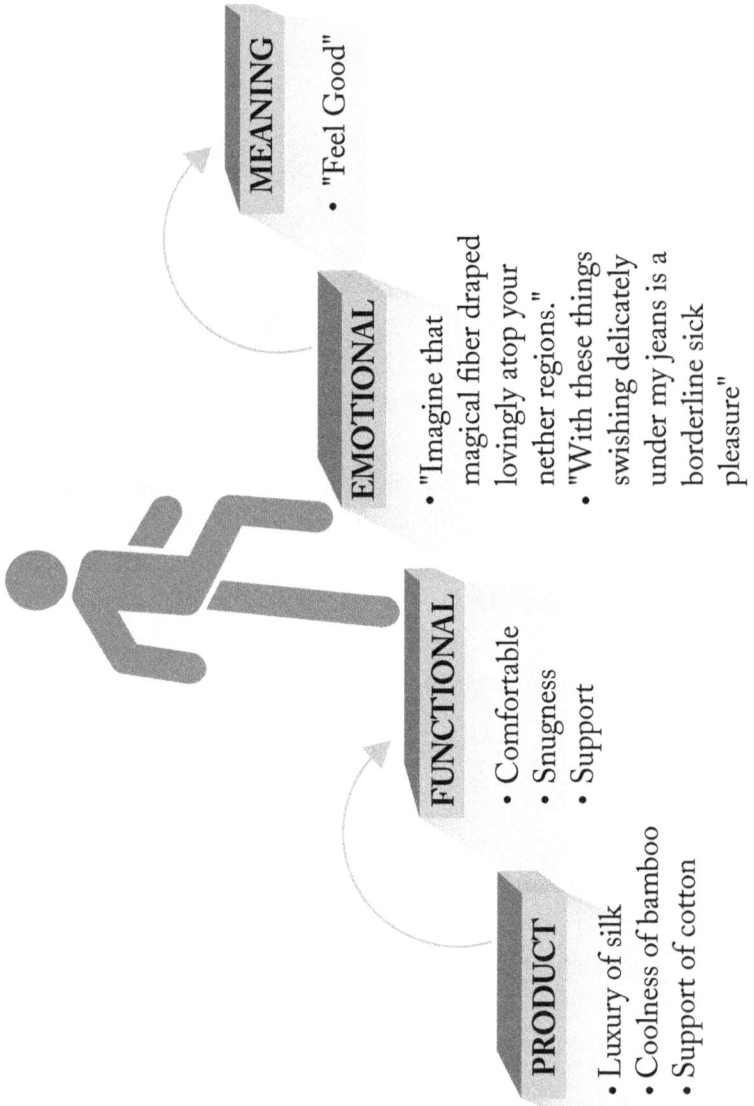

PRODUCT
- Luxury of silk
- Coolness of bamboo
- Support of cotton

FUNCTIONAL
- Comfortable
- Snugness
- Support

EMOTIONAL
- "Imagine that magical fiber draped lovingly atop your nether regions."
- "With these things swishing delicately under my jeans is a borderline sick pleasure"

MEANING
- "Feel Good"

that everyone should experience at least once. It feels like I'm breaching some kind of weird societal taboo."

- According to MeUndies CEO Bryan Lalezarian, in an interview with Forbes: "At MeUndies, our mission is to inspire confidence and individuality through fun and comfortable underwear, because when you feel good, anything is possible. It's almost about redefining what sexy means. When you think about the legacy brands in our space, "sexy" tends to be a little bit more superficial, or visual. Whereas in our view, sexiness is being who you are and owning it and being confident."[10]

From the Product, Functional, and Emotional benefits we can construe that the Essential Meaning, The Brand Essence is "Feel Good". A brand essence that fills a role in the lives of consumers.

Essence versus Tagline and ESP (Emotional Selling Proposition)

Taglines are a short "pitch" for your brand that typically embeds the brand promise, purpose, ESP or EVP (emotional value proposition). An essence is typically (or ideally) captured in one, if not two words and it may not even be overtly stated outside the walls of your company. It is often a litmus test to quickly confirm whether any particular brand element, including marketing, is "on-brand."

We'll use eCommerce women's underwear brand Third Love as an example, as they have a great, condensed tagline: "To Each Her Own." Not only is it short and memorable, but it meets the criteria of communicating the emotional benefit (the ESP, or EVP), and is also close to, but not specifically, its "essence."

Meniml Analysis

Determining the essence for Meniml required the same thought process as reconsidering "what is a man" in today's world. Laddering for whom is the obvious question.

But, as we detailed earlier, Meniml's purpose goes far beyond providing simple, high-quality men's grooming products. It even extends beyond the emotional pleasure of "simplicity and ease," knowing the basic product bundle is complete and simple to choose and use. But, as a culture-leading brand, part of the "simplification" is in providing one clearly defined model for what is man, that appeals to members of every individual male faction (be it metro, lumber, even warrior).

Meniml seeks to include all concepts of masculinity in one simple model. We arrived at this model by first identifying a gap in the market between metro, lumber, and warrior. As we discuss at length in the next chapter, the specific model we chose combines strength, intelligence, self-sufficiency, and independence. Since there are no words used today in popular culture to describe this specific but unique mix, we'll use one from history that is perfect: "Dashing." Dashing is ideal as it's a word as specific and unique as the Meniml brand itself.

Here's how we'd ladder to that:

- Product Attribute: High-quality grooming products based on natural and organic ingredients, with a "female pleasing" but male-neutral brand scent.
- Functional Benefit: Prideful male grooming, made simple by self-organizing product selection sized to need and numbered by regimental sequence.
- Emotional Benefit: Unabashedly and ruggedly handsome, minimized time to care, looking good while feeling good.
- Essence: "Dashing"

I will now go ahead and place the Brand Essence for Meniml in the 7C Canvas.

It's over to you now to build the brand essence for your eCommerce store, and I would recommend using the process of laddering as it allows you to proceed in a structured manner.

As a final note, before you move on to the next C, we hope you've found this first section on your brand's Core enlightening, and that it's given you a solid place to start. But, if you still feel like you need individualized guidance, or that you want a deeper dive into your brand's core, you can easily reach out to us via our Facebook group at facebook.com/groups/ecommercebrandbuilders.

MENIML 7C CANVAS

⬡ CORE

WHY DO YOU EXIST? PURPOSE.

To offer a new, complete model for today's man. Meniml seeks to bring together thousands of factionalized "men," providing examples and models that their own fathers, social peers, and role models could not.

essence
DASHING

WHAT DO YOU STAND FOR? VALUES.

- Independence
- Style – Cleanliness
- Self - Respect

👥 CUSTOMER

WHO'S YOUR AUDIENCE?

HOW DOES YOUR PRODUCT ELEVATE?

👥 COMMUNITY

WHAT CULTURAL GROUP DO WE IDENTIFY WITH?

🎯 COMPETITION

HOW ARE YOU UNIQUE?

◎ CREATIVES

NAMING

LOGO

COLORS

TYPOGRAPHY

PACKAGING

▤ CONTENT

STORY OF THE BRAND

BRAND STORIES

📷 CHANNEL

YOUR BRAND TOUCHPOINTS
OWNED CHANNELS

SHARED CHANNELS

PAID CHANNELS

2.0

CUSTOMER

2.0 CUSTOMER

Who Is Your Customer

"The purpose of any business is to create customers" - Peter Drucker, the most cited business guru of all time.

Peter Drucker's wisdom still applies today, 30 years after he spoke those words. Applied to branding, the update would simply be: "the purpose of any brand is to enhance the personal lives of customers (self-actualization), and to improve the world through the service it provides to its core audience."

To highlight the importance of the customer, we'll introduce yet another nugget of brand wisdom, perhaps you've heard it before: "Companies don't own their brands, their customers do." But what does this really mean? In the context of this chapter, it means by understanding your target customer first, you then have a powerful and accurate compass to help you find and emphasize the core, unique elements of your brand to target them specifically. Technically, no company "builds" their brand, as brands exist to fill the gap in a specific group of people's lives.

Your core, target audience and customer base, therefore, creates your brand. This is why it is paramount that you understand the hearts and minds of your customers. We use the brand persona tool to create a comprehensive profile, or prototype, of your target customer, which identifies all their interests, demographics, and needs. Once you have it fleshed out, everything else becomes very clear.

As an analogy, top performers and public speakers often follow similar wisdom. When you're in front of an audience, the trick is not to focus on the entire group, but to find one person in the audience you connect to and then focus on them the entire time. This person gets you, and they get your message. By focusing on them alone, you ensure you'll resonate with a tribe of like-minded people. Amateur speakers allow their adrenaline and nerves to be spiked by the stragglers checking their phones, frowning, or not paying attention. But you could change your speech or presentation a hundred times, and it wouldn't make a difference. They just aren't your audience, and they never will be. As such, move on and focus on who matters.

Consider the Unique Buying State of Your Customers

Traditional marketing tends to focus on the selling proposition of products: here, brands make a rational appeal to consumers based on why their products are superior and how they compare to those of the competition. However, according to cognitive expert Edward de Bono, marketers would find more meaningful success by instead focusing on the "UBS," the Unique Buying State of their customers. This style of marketing places the emotional state and experiences of customers at the core of a brand's appeal. These brands don't just offer a transaction, they promise a relationship, a memorable and reliable connection made possible through their products.

A great example of an eCommerce company whose product itself focuses on its customer's buying state is Peloton. They could have used a product mentality and focused on the higher quality and features of their bikes, but instead, they decided to go beyond that. Peloton understands that when you go to a gym to exercise, nobody leaves talking about their bikes. Rather, people talk about the exercise routine, the instructor, and so forth.

Peloton leveraged this thought process by providing exercise routines to at-home bikers. They then extended to offering live biking sessions, bringing together their large community of bikers and fans. Thereby understanding the unique buying state of the customer to build "a relationship, a memorable and reliable connection made possible through their products."

Branding Starts with Knowing Your Customer

Do a simple exercise. Ask your employees: "What does this company/brand mean to you?" You'll likely get several different answers. This incoherence often stems from confusion regarding who your customer is, and the service it provides for those consumers. Even if you have a clear picture of your customers, it may be that you haven't communicated it to your team. But, unfortunately, it's far too common that amidst all the hustle and bustle of work, people don't "go outside the walls" and spend time understanding, let alone meeting with their customers.

This is especially true in eCommerce where, unless you are focused on a very specific product category, the customer understanding is typically vague because interactions are filtered by a screen. But you *need* to establish a brand identity, as well as a model of your customer (your brand's "persona," which we discuss below), and the ROI of your marketing budget depends on the depth of that knowledge.

Imagine running a paid traffic campaign for luxury leather bags without knowing your customer. Who would you target? What age group? Where do they live? Why are they buying your brand? Who, or what else have they researched? What's important to them? Where do they shop? These data points are just the tip of the information-iceberg for what you should know about your customer.

Without knowing the specifics of your customer, how do you know what to communicate to them? What pain points to push and resolve? What tone of voice to use? *Where* to market? Hopefully, you're getting a clearer picture of how knowing who your customer is allows you to focus and power your business.

I love this example from Free People, who sell free-spirited bohemian fashion for women, and describe their customer as:

> A 26-year-old girl... smart, creative, confident and comfortable in all aspects of her being, free and adventurous, sweet to tough, tomboy to romantic. A girl who likes to keep busy and push life to its limits, with traveling and hanging out and everything in between. Who loves Donovan as much as she loves The Dears, and can't resist petting any dog that passes her by on the street.
>
> *free people*

That is the level of understanding you need to have about your ideal customer, and the biggest tool in the brander's toolbox is finding that "one" person amidst the rabble and noise who will model your brand persona. We'll help you develop this persona with an exercise later in this chapter.

Solid Brands Always Focus on the Customer

To brand more effectively, it's important to realize that your customers are in the driver's seat. They alone hold the power to purchase your products and services, so you would do well to recognize customers as your greatest asset.

When your brand experience aligns with your promise and advertising, customers will become your brand promoters and cheerleaders, recommending your brand to their networks, friends, and family. Amazon excels at this with its mission to be "the world's most customer-centric company." They realized the power of customers to control the success of their brand as their reviews and word-of-mouth recommendations are the most powerful form of marketing a brand can hope for. Neglecting customers, meanwhile, can spell the end as word of negative experiences spreads extremely quickly through a customer's network.

Realizing this at its inception, Amazon started by brainstorming about great service, and what makes one brand's service stand out from others. They zeroed in on the specialized service you get from a hotel concierge: they greet you, recognize repeat customers, provide personalized recommendations, help customers make plans and reservations, and look up any information or resource customers need to enjoy their stay.

Amazon thus decided to adopt a "concierge mentality" to inform their brand experience. Their platform, therefore, empowers customers to easily find everything they may want to buy online. Customers also trust that Amazon's prices are the lowest possible, at least perceptively, keeping them from looking elsewhere for what they need. To succeed these days, brands need to take Amazon's lead and focus more on their customers and how to better meet their expectations and delight them.

How to Understand Your Customer

Rather than being all things to all people, you want to make sure that you address who you want as a customer. Certainly, this would be a function of the nature of your product, its pricing, and its features/benefits. But within that, there is a subset of customers that you want to market your product to.

Let's say you wanted to introduce an economical bedding line for women, in the $200-$250 range for a set of sheets. Relative to well recognized high-end bedding brands, that's about half the price.

Start by asking yourself:

- *Which* women need this budget-friendly bedding line?
- *What* are they really buying? This goes beyond the bedding itself.
- *What* are their wants, needs, and desires?
- *What* segment of this bedding market is necessary to target to achieve our objectives?
- *What* type of women (age, income, marital status, number of children, work status) should we be directing our message?
- *What* are their pain points? Price factors in here, but what practical and emotional pain points do they also face?
- *How* does their problem make them feel?

This initial self-analysis will serve as a backdrop of who your target customer is, and as you conduct external research, this hypothesis will either be validated or new insights will move you in a different direction.

Research Methodology

Methods on a Low Budget

With New Customers

You should have some idea of the general community around your product, so you likely should be able to find a local spot where many of them will hang out, physical or digital. For example, if you're selling a skincare product, go to a beauty store, spa, or a hair salon.

In this initial recruitment phase, you will also find you'll start to understand the groupings or general sub-segments of consumers that are relevant to what you are doing. Find these insights by interviewing consumers and look out for the common interests within each sub-segment.

With Existing Customer Base

Reach out to your existing base of customers: send them a simple email asking for 15 minutes of their time over Skype/Zoom (video preferred) or phone (so you can get the textural meaning from their vocal tone and speech patterns). This barebones and direct method has worked very well for us. In fact, we like to do this at least once or twice per year, just to keep in practice and to make sure we've got our finger on the right pulse.

How many people do you need to talk with to paint an accurate picture? A baseline goal should be 20 if time permits. Or, you can put together a "customer day" with employees and colleagues and make it a fun contest (it's also an important group learning exercise!). If so, then 100 would be ideal. As an index, the bare minimum should be 10 as a base to be able to apply percentages with comparing data from one customer to the next, and the group as a whole.

Some caveats:

Beware of false positives from well-meaning contacts.

Make sure when you ask your personal network for input that you remind them to be as candid as possible and to leave their personal feelings about you aside.

One-on-ones are always more telling than groups. A major reason we stopped doing focus groups 5 years ago is a phenomenon called "groupthink." This is the tendency for groups of people to agree with the dominant opinion even if it clashes with their honest feelings.

Surveys are another way to reach out to your existing customer base using tools like surveymonkey.com. But I have always preferred a video-based Zoom call as it tends to be more personal and elicits longer form answers. If you do want to use surveys, make sure they are to supplement the information from a good round of face-to-face interviews, if anything, to back up that information.

Methods for Medium Budgets

Host a Wine and Cheese Party

This works great for both existing and new customers and is fun for you and your employees to boot. Unless you're focused on adult weight loss, or a youth market segment, wine and cheese parties can't be beaten for generating engaged and informal but detailed interaction. Send out invites to friends, as well as friends of friends, to visit your office or home and take your product for a test drive. Ask them to invite some of their friends, so you aren't in a closed feedback loop with those who you know are already positively biased towards your products and brand. Let them know that you'll cater take-out snacks and beverages in lieu of their time. The one requirement is that you get honest feedback. Make it a point that they provide blunt and brutally honest insights.

This is also why the "wine" in "Wine and Cheese Party" is so useful. Remember the old saying "In Vino Veritas" ("in wine there is truth").

Methods on a Higher Budget

Formal Market Research

On the opposite end of the cost spectrum is formal market research, which includes in-depth interviews, ethnographic studies, and focus groups, again for both existing and new customers. Professional focus groups can yield a tremendous amount of data, but they're relatively more expensive, and as mentioned, have a tendency to drive "groupthink." In addition, given most focus groups are paid, participants often hold back with the most valuable criticism of all: negative criticism.

Costs include recruitment and compensation of participants, facility rental, moderator and/or agency fees, and possible travel to multiple locations to get prospectives from different demographics.

Research Questions to Ask

Whatever research methodology that you undertake, here is a sample of questions to ask potential buyers, regardless of your research approach.

We'll use the bedding line for women we mentioned earlier to direct these questions. Our hope is these examples will give you insight into what you're ultimately trying to understand.

- *How* often do you purchase bedding-related products?
- *Where* do you typically purchase them?
- *What* other brands come to mind when you are thinking of bedding?
- *What* do you like about their products?
- *How* would you describe these brands, what comes to mind?
- *What* brands or products do you never buy when having to purchase an alternative?
- *Why?* (is it price, quality, convenience...you need to dig for perceptual reasons)
- *How* much do you typically spend on bedding in a year?
- *Do* your friends like the same brand(s)?
- *What* are your favorite books or movies (and why)?

- *What* are 3 of your favorite songs or brands?
- *What* clubs (if any) did you belong to in high school?
- *What* did you study in college?
- *What* are your favorite hobbies (sports, arts, recreation)?
- *What* are your favorite types of foods?
- *Where* would you move tomorrow if money were not a concern?
- *How* would you describe people using your favorite brand?
- *What* are your top 3 values (friends, achievement, money, etc.)?
- *What* top 3 qualities do you look for in your friends?
- *What* main words would you or your friends use to describe you?
- *Who* are your role models or heroes?
- *When* you are using this brand, is your main purpose:
  - Improving the quality of your sleep?
  - Beautifying your bedroom/home?
  - To find more durable, higher quality sheets?
  - To indulge in a little luxury without a luxury price?
  - To save money?

Remember, your brand will never appeal to everyone, but it will appeal deeply to a specific segment. *People buy from brands they like, but they buy for life from brands they love.*

Key Tool: The Customer Persona

Now, we are going to take all the information that we have researched and analyzed about our ideal customer and use it to craft a customer persona.

A customer persona is a "prototype" of a person who represents a brand's ideal and deeply engaged target customer. It's a composite of the elements and characteristics you've found repeating through your research by subjects that are obviously a fit for your brand.

The ideal customer model, this persona, should serve as a guiding principle for all of your brand work. It will provide you with a clear and pinpointed focus for developing your brand's story.

I like to think of the ideal customer persona as the profile of that single customer who will spend the most money with you over the longest time because he or she has so strongly bought into your brand experience.

Benefits of Having and Using a Customer Persona

Imagine creating and running paid traffic campaigns. You will know exactly which demographics to target, what motivates your buyer, what they're passionate about, and the most effective way to connect with them.

You will know what customer pain points to address in the ad copy, what language to use to sound like a trusted friend, strengthening your efforts by making your "lead magnet/bait" even tastier to your key audience.

It will reduce your marketing spend and save time by identifying where your customers spend their time so that you can be right where they are.

It ensures that you don't dilute your brand messaging or product offerings in an effort to appeal to everyone. If you do, then you virtually ensure that you appeal to no one. Heck! You will know what new products to introduce in your product mix.

Based on all the research, we can now craft a buyer persona.

Completing a Customer Persona

After you've spoken to enough customers and people who use the product, or that will try it out in exchange for an interview, try to write down a description of your ideal customer. This is where the creative part comes in.

Returning to the bedding sub-category...

Close your eyes and conjure up a vivid image of who the perfect person is to buy your brand. Conjure up an image of who that person is, and write down everything you can think of.

Demographics (Buyer statistical/group data):

- How old is your female customer?
- Married or single?
- Kids or no kids?
- What are her age and income?
- Where do they live?

Psychographics (Who the buyer is as an individual/on the inside: their feelings, beliefs, outlook). This corresponds to the bulk of questions that we just reviewed. It relates to our female customer's buying habits, hobbies, spending habits, values, personality traits, and lifestyles.

Here we have crafted a customer persona, with Sarah, for the Bedding Line:

SARAH: BEDDING BRAND'S PERSONA

"Happiness is homemade."
- Sarah

AGE: 36

ROLES: Ad Exec

FAMILY Married + 3 kids

LOCATION Atlanta, GA

HH INCOME $175K

CHARACTER: Resourceful, Susceptible to self doubt, Warm, Creative, Outgoing

GOALS

- To transform her bedroom into a tranquil retreat
- Loves to travel, hopes to bring the luxury of a hotel into her home
- Sheets durable enough to be washed normally
- Softness and comfort that feels like an indulgence

FRUSTRATIONS

- Doesn't want to pay $800 for luxury sheets
- Cheaper sheet sets fall apart quickly and come out of the washer full of wrinkles
- Most affordable sheet sets don't fit deeper mattresses

BRANDS

CLUB MONACO
ALLSAINTS Casper

MOTIVATIONS

High Quality at Reasonable price

Simple Clean patterns/designs

Environmentally friendly, ethically made

BIO

Sarah, mother to 3 young children with a 1-year-old Labradoodle, too, the house can get a bit chaotic, but it's home. It's important to her to create a beautiful, inviting space and she carefully decorates each room in her home. A fan of Marie Kondo, she keeps the house light on things but full of joy. Luxury to her doesn't mean luxury prices – she is a smart shopper.

Sarah has a busy schedule - working P/T, running her household & getting the kids to all their activities. She believes family should be together.

Her husband is a corporate exec with a busy schedule, but they treat themselves to a luxury vacation at least once a year. To bring some of this tranquility into her everyday life, Sarah believes their bedroom should be a serene retreat. She's looking to bring the comfort and relaxation of these vacations into her bedroom with hotel-like bedding.

PREFERRED CHANNELS

Facebook

Instagram

Pinterest

This snapshot of your customer is probably one of the most important tasks that you can undertake in building your eCommerce brand. And frankly, the success of your brand development and marketing efforts rests completely on conducting this analysis and after that, its completion.

Meniml's Customer Persona

Based on the above, how would we develop a persona for Meniml? What kind of man would Meniml appeal to? Up until now, we've only briefly discussed the subcultures of metrosexuals, lumbersexuals, and the warrior. We needed a model on which we could build our brand.

There is a cultural reference to a potential model from a short-lived but hugely impactful moment in the '60s. This trend followed the 1950's vision of masculinity as head of the household and breadwinner and preceded the hippie movement in the late '60s.

These men were independent, competent, and self-ruling but uninterested in controlling or ruling others. They were strong and defended their freedom, but they weren't aggressive. They were stoic, but enjoyed life and were unconcerned with the opinions of others. They were competitive in non-traditional "sports," but only in the name of fun and excitement, not conquering. They were also stylish and "well-groomed," but as a matter of personal pride, not vanity.

This was the British Mod scene, which still has a cultural impact today, even in its absence. It also had its icons, including Steve McQueen, who was just as comfortable as a rebel cop in Bullitt as he was a wealthy art thief and trickster in The Thomas Crown Affair. This is also the last time the adjective "dashing," Meniml's brand essence, was in contemporary vernacular.

Adapting this model for today, we call it the "Rebel Royal." And from here, we're better able to construct a customer persona. Here is how the rebel royal compares to other masculine subcultures in terms of what they're looking for in a skincare brand:

STRATEGIC SEGMENTATION
21st Century Male «Models» HBC

METROSEXUAL	LUMBERSEXUAL
• Makeup • Hair • Face • Body	• Beard
Relevant Archetypes:	Relevant Archetypes:
• Caregiver • Lover (Child)	• Pre-civil/primitive • Rebel
REBEL-ROYAL (DASHING)	**(TRIBAL) WARRIOR**
• Hair • Body • Face	
Relevant Archetypes:	Relevant Archetype:
• Ruler (King) with Rebel (Wizard) • Sage-Warrior	• Warrior

In providing a clear, relevant, and compelling modern "male model," with its own unique set of values and attributes, and a product set that helps its users organize and embed rituals, Meniml is an example of a brand with a purpose of providing an aspirational role model (exactly what Nike did at its inception).

Also, to help us further define the Meniml customer, we created visual "mood" boards to compare side-by-side the various male models. This isn't always necessary, but we did it here because it helped us confirm that we were truly fleshing out an existing gap in the market and that we'd be providing a relevant model for today's men.

Metrosexual Man

Lumbersexual

Modern Warrior

"Mod" & Rebel Royal

While you do need to understand targeting, this kind of *new* segmentation is typically only possible, or necessary, perhaps 2% of the time as marketers and branders have already segmented core markets for their own work, turning over many rocks for you. We've included this in this book solely for intellectual honesty. In the case of Meniml, this was something organic, but necessary. Hopefully, if you are focused on the men's market, this very segmentation may be beneficial to you.

Once we did this segmentation work, we looked more closely at what each model specifically looked for in a skincare brand. Metrosexuals are loyal to women's beauty brands, which is a world away from our simplified approach. Beard brands resonate heavily with lumbersexuals who tend not to use many other self-care products. Warriors, meanwhile, have limited to no interest in grooming overall.

This means the handful of existing/new men's grooming brands are "aiming at the middle," which is always aiming at nothing. As such, our persona, using the same template, is based on figuring out the gaps and also some of the unmet needs of men in grooming. It is unlikely you'll have to go to this length in your persona work, but hopefully, you can see our thought process here and how you might laser target your brand on a specific niche of customers.

Once we had narrowed our persona to the Mod-inspired Rebel Royal, we then got more specific. In addition to the basic demographics of our customer, we used the insights gained from our audience segmentation and mood board to dive deeper into our target customer's psychographics: his motivations for choosing skincare products, his goals for a skincare regimen, and his frustrations with the currently available solutions. As you can see below, we also include a short biography and the preferred channels and brands of our Rebel Royal, to further help us find him online and speak to him directly and effectively.

Here is Meniml's completed customer persona:

PERSONA: JACK | REBEL ROYAL

> "I TAKE CARE OF MYSELF, MY LADY, THE WORLD AROUND ME, AND ENJOY LIFE WHILE IGNORING EVERYTHING ELSE"
>
> - JACK

GOALS

- Taking care of self, which includes grooming
- Will pay a premium for high quality and expects products to do what they claim.
- Is proudly handsome, and naturally stylish, but not trend or beauty brand obsessed, so wants a simple offering of the essentials vs. having to pick single items.

FRUSTRATIONS

- Going beyond soap and water, but not having to buy "beauty" to get quality grooming.
- Garish men's (sub)brands; embarrassing (e.g. Christian Dior for Men).
- He has taste, but prefers his products understated.
- Having to spend time replenishing individual grooming products every month (shopping is a necessary function, not an event for him); prefers "man sized", group packaged, and auto-replenished.

AGE: 34

ROLES: traveler, writer/blogger, journalist

FAMILY: happy bachelor but likes women, loves independence

INCOME: $150K

CHARACTER: Adventurous, independently minded, but social and playful with friends. Believes life is meant to be enjoyed, to learn and explore, to make one's own way.

PERSONA: JACK   REBEL ROYAL

BIO:

Jack is an 80's baby yet born with a timeless cool. He was raised in Connecticut, his parents a longshoreman and a professor who'd met in Indiana. Always independent and curious, but more prone to acting and doing than reading, he - from an early age- engaged deeply with anything that interested him, from a stint one summer with a local circus, to busking and traveling his way across Europe each summer in between his English studies at Brown University. Since college, he's blogged, cheffed, worked (successfully) as a journalist, boxing trainer, and even tried his hand at motorcycle racing after dropping in at a local contest and winning its $1,000 prize. While he'd been considered a rebellious child, he always loved his parents, and was close with both Mom and Dad, but not dismayed at leaving home a year early for college. His friends comment on how stylish he is, which both surprises and embarrasses him. He just likes to keep himself groomed, and likes things he thinks look good on him. He's not a label fanatic. Just has good taste. He's lived in Brooklyn, Austin, Los Angeles, and even spent 3 years blogging remotely from Colorado.

FAVORITE BRANDS:

HELMUT LANG

MOTIVATIONS:

- Quality and efficacy
- Understated style
- Simplicity in use/availability
- Less energy spent in individual replenishment (and shopping)

CHANNELS:

- YouTube Vlogs, specifically: TMF Style, IAmAlphaM, Gentleman's Gazette, The Modest Man
- eZines including GQ
- Mobile advertising
- Prefers phone to text; uses email
- Word of mouth via friends
- Instagram as much as Facebook

The next step is to place the abridged version of Meniml's Customer Persona in the 7C Canvas.

Now it's your turn to complete the Buyer Persona form using the initial customer identifier data and feedback you've received. Don't worry about getting it perfect right out of the gate, either. This exercise gives you a place to start, and you can always make adjustments as you grow and learn more about your audience.

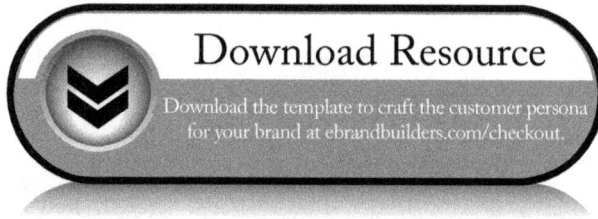

Download Resource

Download the template to craft the customer persona for your brand at ebrandbuilders.com/checkout.

We also always recommend adding a photo of whom you'd imagine your persona to look like. An easy hack, if you are having trouble finding the right photo, is to think of a celebrity that you think fits, exactly what we have done with Meniml, or a famous fictional character. They, or their writers and directors, have already done the work for you in developing this persona! This will help you imagine a specific person or character to "speak to" when crafting your message or writing your brand's story, which we'll delve into in the 6th C, Content.

Once you have the details completed in the persona form, you can transfer them over to your 7C Canvas while they're top of mind, and as you continue fleshing out your bigger brand picture.

MENIML 7C CANVAS

⬡ CORE

WHY DO YOU EXIST? PURPOSE.

To offer a new, complete model for today's man. Meniml seeks to bring together thousands of factorialized "men," providing examples and models that their own fathers, social peers, and role models could not.

essence
DASHING

WHAT DO YOU STAND FOR? VALUES.

- Independence
- Style – Cleanliness
- Self–Respect

👤 CUSTOMER

WHO'S YOUR AUDIENCE?

Jack is an 80's baby yet born with a timeless cool. Raised in Connecticut, always independent and curious, he engaged deeply with anything that interested him, from a stint one summer with a local circus, to busting and traveling his way across Europe each summer in between his English studies at Brown University. Since college, he's blogged, chefed, worked as a journalist, boxing trainer, and even tried his hand at motorcycle racing, after dropping in at a local contest and winning its $1,000 prize.

HOW DOES YOUR PRODUCT ELEVATE?

👥 COMMUNITY

WHAT CULTURAL GROUP DO WE IDENTIFY WITH?

⊙ COMPETITION

HOW ARE YOU UNIQUE?

◎ CREATIVES

NAMING

LOGO

COLORS

+

TYPOGRAPHY

PACKAGING

▤ CONTENT

STORY OF THE BRAND

BRAND STORIES

CHANNEL

YOUR BRAND TOUCHPOINTS

OWNED CHANNELS

SHARED CHANNELS

PAID CHANNELS

Help Your Customer Be Who They Want to Be

It's critical to know *who* your ideal customer is, but you can't stop there. The next step is to clearly define the role your brand plays in their life. When customers buy a product, they're not just buying that item's features and functional benefits: customers are also buying a better version of themselves. With a detailed customer persona, the next step is to understand who your customer is striving to be when they buy or use your brand. Likewise, knowing your brand's purpose, essence, and values, what identity would you like your brand to help customers achieve?

The psychographic work you did to create your customer persona is a great place to start to get a feel for what the answer to these questions might be. We may also ask these questions:

- *Why* are customers buying our products?
- *What* is the product's main purpose in their lives?
- *Who* are *you/customers* to want these things or this brand?

While you will begin to answer these questions as you establish your customer persona, you will need to dig deeper to understand the real reasons customers reach for your products. *It's not enough to find out who your customers are, you, as a brand, need also help them become the people they want to be.*

Instead of strategizing about how to improve and position your products, think about how to improve and position your customers. Truly successful innovations generate wealth for their users, not just their creators, and by wealth, we don't just mean monetary wealth. In branding, wealth can also be social, educational, physical, spiritual, as well as the traditional definition of capital.

The question, then, is, what is the highest good you can want and create for your customer?

The primary good that a company can offer its customers is empowerment. The best brand builders see greatness in their customers and figure out ways to enable it. How can a brand reach this pinnacle where they not only understand their customers, but also help them become what they aspire to be?

According to psychologist Abraham Maslow and his "Hierarchy of Needs," every human is typically focused on fulfilling their needs along the ladder of personal development, from basic survival to individuation. Maslow

MASLOW'S HIERARCHY OF NEEDS

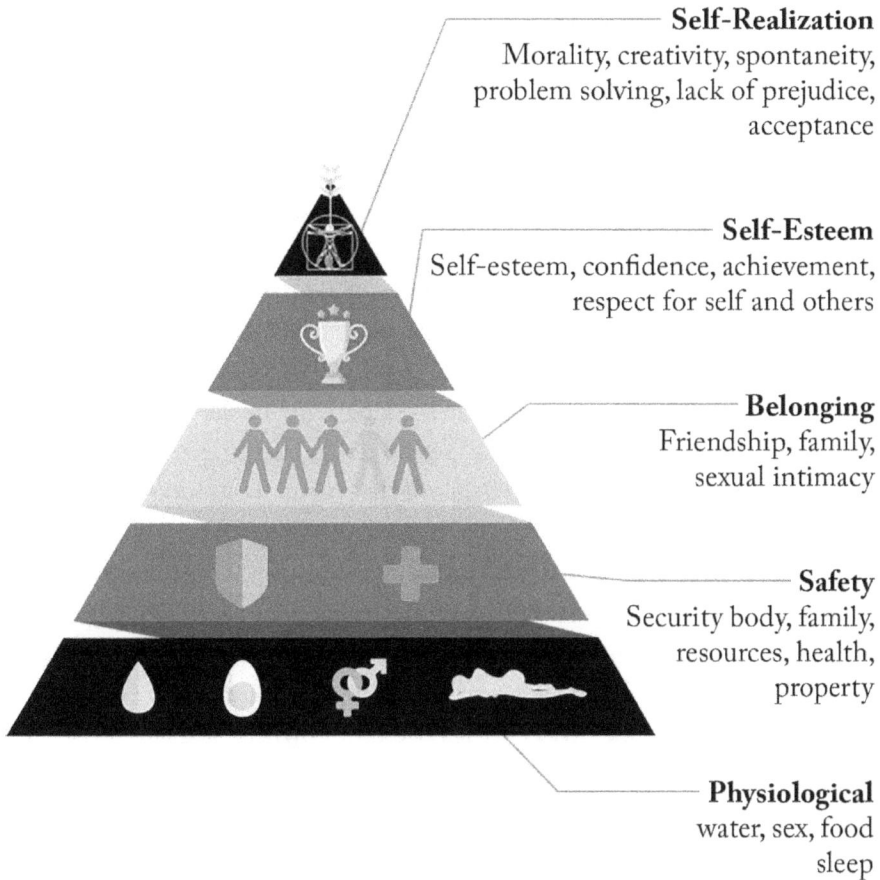

Self-Realization
Morality, creativity, spontaneity,
problem solving, lack of prejudice,
acceptance

Self-Esteem
Self-esteem, confidence, achievement,
respect for self and others

Belonging
Friendship, family,
sexual intimacy

Safety
Security body, family,
resources, health,
property

Physiological
water, sex, food
sleep

Source: Maslow, A.H. (1692). Toward a Psychology of Being. Princeton.

shaped his hierarchy like a pyramid with the theory that all humans must first solve the needs on the lower levels of the pyramid before moving to the upper levels. The most basic human needs—food, water, shelter, and air reside at the base, while loftier, more emotional needs tip at the top. Once a person is no longer worried about finding food and water, he or she can move up to solve the problem of safety. Once that person figures out safety, he or she can move up to love, and so on.

In separating "need" from "want," we'd suggest the following: actual *needs* define what humans need to *survive* (or as Maslow would say, the physiological needs to exist). And those needs can be broken down into two broad categories, sustenance and biological protection:

1. Water: a basic need because life as we know it cannot exist without it.
2. Oxygen: humans cannot survive without oxygen.
3. Internal Energy: this is needed to grow and maintain our physical bodies and internal core body temperature. This carbon-based energy comes from the food we eat.
4. External Energy: this energy comes from the sun. We humans must moderate this energy with clothing and shelter to maintain our internal core temperature.
5. Sleep: humans cannot go for very long without sleep which helps the human body repair itself and refreshes our energy levels.
6. Procreation: males and females of the species to reproduce in kind.
7. Communication: humankind must have some form of communication to survive, be it visual, oral, or tactile.

Wants and desires, on the other hand, are related to our craving for pleasure, comfort, self-esteem and self-actualization. Whether we find this in luxury items or tasty soda is a matter of personal taste. And wants vary specifically by individual groups (think BMW versus Mercedes owners or Coke versus 7UP drinkers). When people have what they need to survive, they move on to making friends and finding mates. When they're satisfied with their relationships, they focus on doing things they enjoy and improving their skills in things that interest them. First existence; then relatedness; then growth.

Distinguishing between want and need is more important to you as a brand than for the general population. The more your target segment connects with your brand, the more they will *want* your brand. And the better you communicate those connections through your brand messaging, the more attractive your offer will become to consumers.

In other words, if you're going to build a successful brand, it's necessary to understand what your customer segment most *wants* from your brand, and then use these specific desires to differentiate your brand from others. Appealing to these wants builds a "moat" between you and competitors who may consider moving into your space. Your brand purpose is to provide what your core segment wants, but *once you've proven you can do that, as long as your brand keeps its promise(s), consumers seldom defect to a competitor, due to the pain of excess choice and consideration.*

With this in mind, identify the wants or needs your customers are currently focused on and how they *prioritize* these motivations. Then, when positioning your brand in their lives, aim for one step above where they are today to help them move toward actualization.

To help you position your brand on the need/want pyramid, here are the primary questions you need to answer:

- *How* does the brand make customers feel?
- *How* does it advance the goals these customers have for their own lives?
- *How* does the brand help make customers a better person?

Brand Benefits Pyramid

Corresponding almost directly to Maslow's Hierarchy of Needs, the Brand Benefits Pyramid describes the wants and needs consumers are seeking to fulfill when they make a purchase decision. Be careful not to underestimate this process: *every* brand and product decision is deeply motivated by the drive to meet our needs and fulfill our desires. There are other similarities to Maslow's Hierarchy:

Just as the bottom of Maslow's Hierarchy describes the human need to support our basic survival. In the Brand Benefits Pyramid, the bottom rung of the ladder corresponds to the functional needs a brand's products offers, the thing a product does.

Upon fulfilling these base functional needs, consumers seek to find a product that also addresses the next level on the pyramid: a product's emotional benefits.

The final, and ultimate level on the Brand Benefits Pyramid addresses the self-actualization desires of customers.

Brands and products cannot fulfill a higher level of need without first addressing the lower, supportive needs.

Not all brands and products will rise to the level of providing self-actualization benefits, but to do so, they must also provide basic, functional benefits and emotional appeal.

BRAND BENEFITS PYRAMID

SELF ACTUALIZATION BENEFITS

EMOTIONAL/ESTEEM BENEFITS

FUNCTIONAL BENEFITS

To explain further, let's take the example of two DTC women's clothing brands, Everlane and MM.LaFleur.

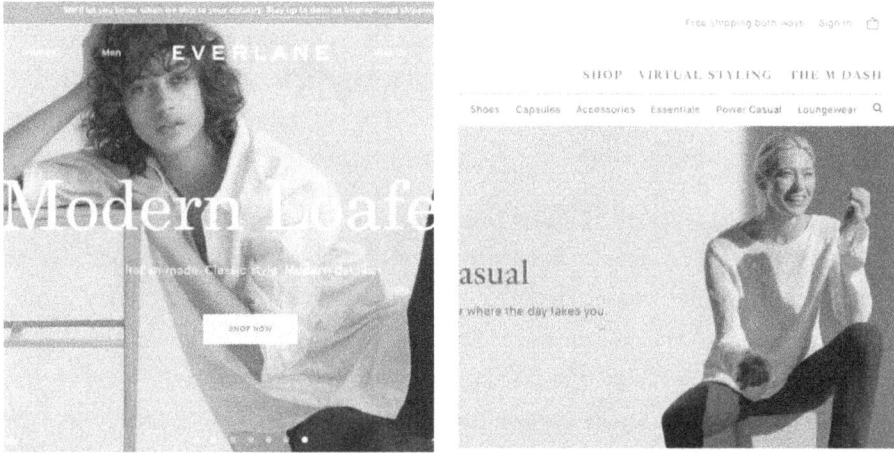

Functional Benefits

These utilitarian elements are important differentiators for brands competing in the same category. And while you cannot base the appeal of your brand on functional benefits, without them, your brand will lose market share. These functional elements, as mentioned, map directly to Maslow's physiological needs. Even if a brand is focused on the top of the pyramid in terms of its brand meaning, purpose, and promise, if its products aren't functional, the brand will not survive, let alone thrive.

Between Everlane and MM.LaFleur, these practical elements are similar and thus directly comparable to a consumer.

Everlane describes its functional benefits as exceptional quality, using the finest materials, products that are designed to last, and are essential and affordable. Whereas MM.LaFleur denotes their product's benefits as versatile, comfortable, machine-washable, and available within a convenient subscription model.

Emotional Benefits

Emotional benefits correspond to the next level on Maslow's Needs Hierarchy: safety, belonging, and affiliation and esteem desires. These benefits make customers feel like they're a member of the tribe and, therefore, secure.

In the brand benefits pyramid, these middle tiers describe how certain product features make customers *feel*. In branding, we refer to these as emotional benefits.

Everlane expresses their emotional benefits as a fashion-forward aesthetic, a minimalist ethos, and the rapid launch of new selections. On the other hand, MM.LaFleur classifies its emotional appeal as offering a unique look, form-fitting options, a timesaving model, and a sophisticated, luxurious style.

Self-Expressive (or Self-Actualizing) Benefits

Self-expressive benefits correspond with the top of the Hierarchy of Needs, Self-Actualization, and are at the top of the Brand Benefit Pyramid. These benefits assist customers in completing this statement: "When I buy, carry, use, wear, or drive this brand, I feel _____."

Everlane, for example, focuses on "shown quality," but "mid-level," or everyday style, similar to the Gap. But Everlane offers a unique level of transparency: showcasing exactly where their products are manufactured. Unlike most other clothing brands, especially "fast fashion" companies like Zara, who use factories in Asia, Everlane manufactures its products in Europe and the U.S. Everlane even highlights these "places of production" by including "Factories" among the top-links on their homepage. For an Everlane customer, while the actual clothing designs are modern, though not design-forward, the value of quality and craftsmanship at "everyday value" is front and center.

MM.LaFleur, contrarily, focuses specifically on "sophistication through detail, but minimalist design," all for the professional woman. It's a different form of traditionalism, pulling on all the associations and heritage of Japanese style and design. This is reflected in their use of language, for example, they have a "Bento" collection (a pre-packed lunch in a wooden box in Japan). In terms of self-expression, MM.LaFleur is "professional, high-end, curated," yet efficient and convenient.

EVERLANE VS. MM.LAFLEUR BRAND BENEFITS

Self-Expressive Benefits

- Ethically made
- Radical transparency

- Uses power of self-presentation and rethinks the shopping process altogether
- Creates a wardrobe for women who want to be seen and heard

Emotional Benefits

- Fashion forward aesthetic
- Minimalist
- Rapid new selection
- Choose what you pay model

- Personal stylist to curate
- Form fitting
- No worry what to wear
- Time saving
- Professional
- Sophisticated
- Luxurious

Functional Benefits

- Exceptional quality
- Finest material
- Designed to last
- Essentials
- Affordable

- Versatile
- Comfortable
- Machine washable
- Convenience (subscription)

Meniml's Brand Benefit Pyramid

Based on this approach, here is how we would craft the Brand Benefit Pyramid for Meniml.

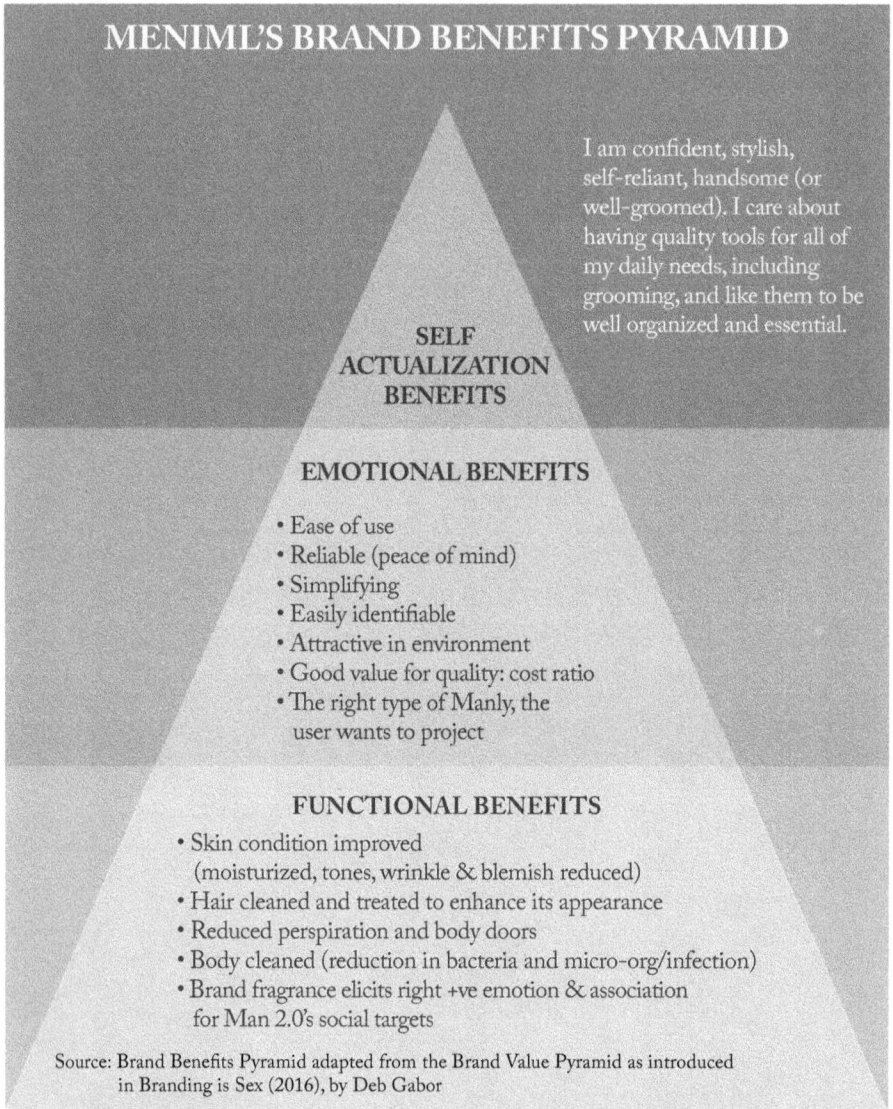

MENIML'S BRAND BENEFITS PYRAMID

I am confident, stylish, self-reliant, handsome (or well-groomed). I care about having quality tools for all of my daily needs, including grooming, and like them to be well organized and essential.

SELF ACTUALIZATION BENEFITS

EMOTIONAL BENEFITS

- Ease of use
- Reliable (peace of mind)
- Simplifying
- Easily identifiable
- Attractive in environment
- Good value for quality: cost ratio
- The right type of Manly, the user wants to project

FUNCTIONAL BENEFITS

- Skin condition improved (moisturized, tones, wrinkle & blemish reduced)
- Hair cleaned and treated to enhance its appearance
- Reduced perspiration and body doors
- Body cleaned (reduction in bacteria and micro-org/infection)
- Brand fragrance elicits right +ve emotion & association for Man 2.0's social targets

Source: Brand Benefits Pyramid adapted from the Brand Value Pyramid as introduced in Branding is Sex (2016), by Deb Gabor

To complete the analysis, we can now place the Meniml's Self Actualization benefits in the 7C Canvas.

MENIML 7C CANVAS

◈ CORE

WHY DO YOU EXIST? PURPOSE.

To offer a new, complete model for today's man, Meniml seeks to bring together thousands of factionalized "men," providing examples and models that their own fathers, social peers, and role models could not.

essence
DASHING

WHAT DO YOU STAND FOR? VALUES.

- Independence
- Style – Cleanliness
- Self-Respect

💬 CUSTOMER

WHO'S YOUR AUDIENCE?

Jack is an 80's baby yet born with a timeless cool. Raised in Connecticut, always independent and curious, he engaged deeply with anything that interested him, from a stint one summer with a local circus, to busting and traveling his way across Europe each summer in between his English studies at Brown University. Since college, he's blogged, chefed, worked as a journalist, boxing trainer, and even tried his hand at motorcycle racing after dropping in at a local contest and winning its $1,000 prize.

HOW DOES YOUR PRODUCT ELEVATE?

I am confident, stylish, self–reliant, handsome (or well–groomed). I care about having quality tools for all of my daily needs, including grooming, and like them to be well–organized and essential.

⚒ COMMUNITY

WHAT CULTURAL GROUP DO WE IDENTIFY WITH?

◉ CREATIVES

NAMING

LOGO

COLORS

PACKAGING

TYPOGRAPHY

▣◉ COMPETITION

HOW ARE YOU UNIQUE?

▤ CONTENT

STORY OF THE BRAND

BRAND STORIES

🖼 CHANNEL

YOUR BRAND TOUCHPOINTS
OWNED CHANNELS

SHARED CHANNELS

PAID CHANNELS

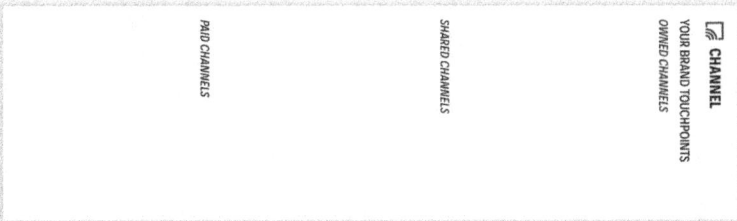

What Business Are You Really In?

Reaching the pinnacle of this pyramid, where customers are experiencing the self-actualization benefits of a brand, only happens when brands understand what business they are really in. Remember, the best brands get that customers aren't just buying products: they're buying a better version of themselves.

Traditional push-marketing no longer speaks to customers. Therefore, instead of trying to make overly rational appeals, use your brand to build emotional connections with customers. Although it's still critical to share the features and attributes of your products and services, you should constantly be framing these features in such a way that they support and define the emotional appeal of your brand. When your products feel emotionally relevant to the lives of consumers, your brand becomes an intimate part of their lives, not just something they buy. Not only does this inspire brand loyalty, but research also shows emotional ties are the best way to maximize customer value. These customers will visit your online store more often, buy more, be less sensitive to price, click on your Facebook ads, and open your emails.

To forge these emotional ties, your brand must tap into the fundamental motivations of your customers and aim to address their deep, usually unspoken, emotional desires. Consider what emotional wants your brand and products address. Much like your brand essence, the emotional quality of your brand experience and identity can serve as a differentiator from the competition if the emotional appeal of your brand is unique and resonates with consumers.

For instance, some particularly strong motivations include the desire to feel like you belong, the desire to succeed, the need to feel secure and safe, the desire to stand out and feel unique, the desire to feel free, the desire to be thrilled. Once you zero in on what motivator your brand naturally taps into, it's clearer how to shape your brand experience to make sure you're meeting these emotional desires. Remember, consumers rarely make wholly logical decisions about which brand to buy; instead, they choose based on how a brand makes them feel.

Virgin Airlines, for instance, understand that their real job isn't simply getting people from A to B safely, rather, they're seeking "to always provide you with an unforgettable experience that adds value to your trip." To

A (MOSTLY) ECOMMERCE FOUNDER POV

allbirds

Allbirds founders envisioned Allbirds as a sustainable material innovation company. Co-founder Joey Zwillinger says: "For us, it was about creating a brand that challenges the status quo and redefines what it means to make something better. We don't think of ourselves as a shoe company, Zwillinger added that the team is in the early stages of looking into apparel and other categories outside of shoes. "We think about ourselves as delivering simple, beautiful design with the aim of been comfortable and made with sustainable materials."

NIKE

The best example of all and one of the best jobs of marketing the universe has ever seen is Nike. Nike sells a commodity...Shoes. But when you think of Nike, you think of something different from a shoe company. In their ads, they don't ever talk about the product. They don't ever talk about their air soles and why they are better than Reebok's air soles. What does Nike do in their advertising? They honor great athletes, and they honor great athletics. That's who they are. Their purpose is to inspire the "everyday" athlete to greatness. Not thinking. Not worrying. Just DOING it.

BARK≤BOX

"We are not in the Product business, but in the joy business - which is the subject of loving a dog." Says Bark-Box. This brand perspective allows one to create a meaningful conversation with a small subset of your super customers. They create content to start the conversation with people and to have a conversation that's not about products.

make sure this emotional promise is kept, Virgin empowers their staff to make decisions on the spot if it improves the customer experience. This consistently kept promise for a great flight makes it more difficult for their flyers to settle for a lesser experience with another airline, but this great experience wouldn't be possible without the brand's true commitment to nurturing better relationships with customers.

Purchases are thus rarely based on reason and instead appeal to us based on the identity products help consumers create. Instead of focusing on how to position your products in a way that convinces consumers you have superior technology and design, think about who you can help your customers be when they choose your brand. When you can capture the soul of your customers, you create true wealth. This is the highest good you can serve, and you can get there by empowering your customers and keeping the customer relationship the center of your decisions and practices.

When you're in touch with your deeper purpose for being in business, you'll be clear about why and how you serve customers beyond seeking profits. Allowing this purpose to shape your brand's product lines, messaging, and personality will send a clear message that you care more about customer relationships than making a quick buck, creating fertile ground for deep bonds with your customers.

Meniml, for instance, strives to be a direct-to-consumer men's skincare brand, but what business are we really in? *(Hint: The answer to this question will always tie back to the Self Actualization benefit that you uncovered for your brand in the last chapter).*

On the surface, Meniml is in the men's grooming business. But, pun intended, beauty is only skin deep.

At Meniml, we aim to boost the confidence of men as they carry on with their daily personal and professional commitments looking and feeling great.

What business are *you* really in?

3.0

COMMUNITY

3.0 COMMUNITY

Why Your Brand Needs a Community

The rules for building brand awareness have shifted over the last few years. While eCommerce merchants could previously rely on social media and traditional digital marketing for all of their awareness building, these avenues are not as effective as they once were. Even the once robust vehicle of Facebook has lost its luster. There's more competition than ever, online as much as offline, and more brands are maneuvering for the same consumers. The best way to be heard through all the noise is to demonstrate that you care about more than sales and that you're interested in building genuine relationships between customers and your brand, as well as supporting relationships among customers. When you demonstrate to consumers that you're willing to listen and respond as a *human* brand, you begin to forge real connections with them. All of this is possible when you build a community for your customers to interact within.

We all want to be part of a tribe where we feel welcome, safe, and can contribute. This sense of belonging is integral to our identity, and the negative side effects of feeling isolated and secluded have been well proven.

In the hunter-gatherer stage in human history, being part of a tribe was even more serious, and we see the legacy today with people continually searching to reconnect with the phantom tribes imprinted in our genetic memory. Being excluded from the group used to mean your very life was in peril, as you'd be left on your own in the wilderness unprotected. These needs and fears linger in us, and the desire to belong is thus a deeply ingrained part of our nature, and while online connections aren't always a substitute for the real thing, they do still offer significant emotional benefits. Research has shown that social connections through Facebook offer some of the same positive perks as in-person interactions, like greater feelings of well-being. Creating an online community for your customers is, therefore, a powerful way to build a tribe and deeply bond customers to your brand.

Your 1,000 True Fans

As per Internet pundit Kevin Kelly:

"To be a successful creator, you don't need millions. You don't need millions of dollars or millions of customers, millions of clients or millions of fans. To make a living as a craftsperson, photographer, musician, designer, author, animator, app maker, entrepreneur, or inventor, you need only thousands of true fans."[11]

Who is a true fan? Someone that will buy anything your brand produces. They'll drive 200 miles to see a band, they'll buy multiple versions of your book, and they'll ask permission to "make the t-shirt" if you don't offer one they can buy. We've probably all been fanatical at one point of our lives or another, and today, great brands are the new rockstars for adults.

If you can generate 1,000 fans, the theory goes, you can support yourself from your fan base. You may not be able to afford your own jet or mansion, but you can absolutely make a sustainable living.

Building your brand community, thus, starts with this metric: aiming for your thousandth brand fanatic. The beauty of branding is its organic virality. Once you hit 1,000, those fans will carry your brand across the psychic mosh pit to the next 2,000, 3,000, 10,000 fans. This is the difference between branding and marketing.

How Do You Build Your Community for Your First Fans

Define the Purpose of Being Part of Your Community

First, define the purpose of being part of your community, and what it promises to someone who'd join it, be a part of it, and enforce its cultural ethics.

Focus on meeting the needs of your core audience and reflecting their interests and beliefs. Be sure you're in touch with what these biggest fans are passionate about, what their needs are, what they're concerned about, their motivations, and how they want to connect with you.

Once you have this understanding, you can actively shape your community to appeal to the heart of your ideal customers instead of trying to please everyone. You won't be able to thoroughly serve anyone if your community members don't feel like you're speaking directly to them and that you do "get" them. The key, then, to making your community a success is to purposefully serve this core audience first and foremost.

Community building is premised on the goals of the people your brand serves, not about your business goals. In fact, building a community is the major goal of any brand.

Utilize Grassroots Marketing

An example of successful grassroots marketing comes from Glossier, one of the trendiest direct-to-consumer beauty companies in the world. It evolved out of a popular blog, *Into the Gloss*, which harnessed the power of building relationships with women online and transferred that into a real-world love affair with the Glossier brand: 80% of Glossier's growth comes from peer-to-peer recommendations!

Glossier founder Emily Weiss started the cosmetics brand with a shockingly simple message: "Skin first, makeup second." In a TechCrunch interview, Weiss said, "I'd be sitting on their bathroom floors and squeezing tubes of creams and… discussing the big wide world of beauty, and I realized there was a disconnect between the leading beauty conglomerates and their customers." Though many women seemed to have an affinity for certain products, they didn't necessarily know anything about those brands' values, and most brands don't communicate these core beliefs in any way.

Weiss spied an opportunity to rectify this by "building a company around what women want, not just from a product perspective but from an engagement perspective, from a distribution perspective, and from a values perspective."[12] With this in mind, Glossier launched online in 2014 with just four products. They have since expanded to a full line of skincare, makeup, body, and fragrance products.

Glossier also set up a sales rep network where *every representative is given their own landing page* on the Glossier website, complete with their favorite products and a video introduction. The company now has approximately 500 active sales reps. When there are openings for positions within the company, Weiss will do weekly posts on her personal Instagram account (@ emilywweiss), called "Recruitment Monday." Glossier even set up a Slack group, for its top customers to be part of a group to discuss beauty, organize meet-ups, and share feedback on products.

Lastly, Glossier establishes trust and gives customers a sense of ownership by letting them shape and develop products. This helps generate curiosity and excitement before product launches, leading to higher customer loyalty.

This is the power of community: not only do you have a cult of fans; you also have the experts who love your products, an audience who wants to engage with you. They help you launch new products and spread the word on the brand. Consumer and enterprise brands are hungry for this type of engagement from their fans, but Glossier lives it through everything they do, and by simply and thoroughly listening and responding to their brand fanatics.

Build an Influencer Program

Hiring an influencer may be a good option if they're highly relevant to your core audience. Huckberry, an outdoor apparel and gear brand, took this approach and partnered with renowned photographer Chris Burkard who documented his outdoor adventures using their products. Also, on Burkard's website there's a link to Huckberry's page, citing it as his favorite gear.

It's always possible one of your community members is an influencer. This is the ideal candidate to be a "brand ambassador" because they're already honestly involved with and love your brand. Consumers can tell when an influencer is shilling for a paycheck, and when they're genuinely sharing something they love. Of course, if you do go outside your tribe, the first thing to do is make sure your prospective influencer gets a branded gift-pack before you even discuss working together.

Promote Your Facebook Group to Other Social Media Platforms

Focus a large chunk of your time on nurturing your early community, particularly those leading up to your first 1,000 members. Once you have this solid foundation, you can start sharing highlights and insights with the broader world through Facebook as a means of recruiting new members. You might also consider running paid traffic to gain new members, but be sure you're targeting the right people.

If you're trying to grow a massive community open to people outside of your customer base, outreach is an effective tactic. Identify relevant newsletters, publications, and blogs to share your community with. This works well for the influencer community, as well. We'll go into more detail on specific outreach tactics in the Channel chapter.

Decide Where Your Community Will Live

Though there are other tools and platforms you can use to create a community, here are some of our top picks: Slack is appropriate for the tech community; LinkedIn for reaching a broader corporate community; forums and Q&A boards work well for eCommerce stores selling physical products; and of course, Facebook is still the best "all segment" social platform, one that has built-in advertising should you choose to use it.

Engage Your Community

Perfect your hashtag creation skills. If your company doesn't have a hashtag, you're missing out on the ability to track and mobilize your community.

Statebags.com, for instance, chose the hashtag #GIVEBACKPACK at their launch to highlight the brand's commitment to donating bags to local children living in challenging environments.

Search for Ways to *Add More Value* to Your Customer's Engagement with Your Brand

Figure out a way to generate a sense of belonging among your followers and customers, which is the easiest and often most significant form of value-add you can provide. By becoming a tribal leader, you'll develop an especially deep relationship with the members who join and participate in your community. Marketing guru Seth Godin dedicated an entire book to this phenomenon, Tribes. Some of Godin's tips on tribe making:

Lead with something *interesting*. You can identify people and set the foundations, but *you need to get involved* in the community from the inside. Make sure you're monitoring the conversations in your community. If messages go unanswered or requests go ignored, *you will lose members*. Ergo, reply to threads, ask and answer questions, but balance this with backing off, listening, and letting the community engage.

Make Sure There are Unique Benefits to Being Part of Your Community

Having a healthy community of fans and customers means you have a direct line of communication with your most interested and engaged customers. This makes it easier to upsell and cross-sell products. They're also your best focus group, so get to know them better through direct conversations, interactions, feedback, and surveys. Always be open to hearing the needs, passions, and concerns of your core audience. The process of getting to know them never ends and staying in touch with them ensures your community is always growing in the right direction. If you succeed in making your base community feel understood, you'll create brand ambassadors, customers who are so inspired and impressed with your brand that they'll want to share it with others. Having this kind of grassroots potential is priceless, and they may even share ideas with you for posts or events.

Don't forget, however, that the glue that will hold your community together is the support and service you provide your members.

Meniml's Community Build

Our community of men sees our brand as a cultural rallying point. Unsatisfied with the combative tribes of lumbersexuals, metrosexuals, or warriors, but knowing they're more than sterilized stallions in corporate suits and ties, they look for relationships with other "modern classic" men who are self-reliant, tough but fun, curious but principled, confident, but vulnerable. In other words: "whole men." They don't want to sit around a sweat lodge hugging other men and crying, but they do want to feel a connection to others that can share a joke or have their back while living life to the fullest.

While developing a community is important to any successful brand, we saw it as core to instilling our "man values" while building awareness for Meniml across the country, then the world. As we wanted to introduce a new way of "being" for today's man, which in part also establishes how men interact socially, we wanted to go beyond looking at our online community and extend into real-world social interaction and community building through events to be replicated throughout the country. In addition, we looked at North America as our primary geographical market and focused on the top 10 "Meniml" Designated Market Areas (DMAs), which we define as urban, but with close proximity to outdoor recreational areas.

In part, this was inspired by Fit & Fly. Fit & Fly was initially a popular fashion blog that hit a major road bump while trying to sell some of the items they reviewed. It was not until they flipped the camera around and started putting together meet-ups in different cities, where founder and team would participate in bike rides and other healthy activities with their community, that they then cultivated sales. Fit & Fly sold products related to their event activities, and their community solidified behind the brand.

We, too, wanted to break down that "4th wall."

Looking at men, we wanted to cast a wide net, yet be clear about our own rallying cry, promise, and purpose because we saw Meniml as providing a much clearer and more usable model for "masculinity" in the modern age. Something that would attract self-identified lumbersexuals, some metrosexuals, and even some self-identified neo-warriors, all of whom value deeper bonds with other like-minded men, but who feel as if each of their subcultures is lacking something. Then, of course, there were the other men who had no cultural reference before Meniml.

We also felt, for an individualistic, ruggedly handsome, adventurous men's brand, focusing on urban areas first made sense. But choosing the right activities to host would be key.

At first, we considered doing massive barbecues. This option would be relatively simple, as renting flatbed/floats to bring the backyard into the edge of city centers requires relatively little set up. However, regardless of simplicity, this seemed too predictable and overdone, even a bit old fashioned.

We wanted a more active event, not limited to only hardcore athletes, but with an edge of adventure. On the other hand, seeing what "neo-warrior" groups were doing, such as Jack Donovan's "ranches," where men gather to fistfight, drink, and make fires, we wanted something with an edge, but certainly not as overtly aggressive. Meniml is, after all, about ruggedness *but sophistication*.

We then worked backwards from the top 5 potential geographical markets, areas with the highest male grooming purchases, but also cities with a rural feel, that were "on-value." These included San Francisco, Detroit, Brooklyn, Toronto, and Montreal.

We realized the perfect event – something that could be replicated, something that had legs on its own, which would attract men on its own merits, and truly provide something social and adventurous would be...

Urban scavenger hunts on mountain bikes.

In "packs," safer in cities, physically engaged, but requiring deductive skills and problem-solving more than bench strength and aerobic prowess, and certainly tribally bonding. We'd end each day both with awards (from a lifetime supply of Meniml products to on-hand masseuse treatment), and an outdoor bonfire and food.

And so began "Manimation 2019." Hashtag #DashingDudes

meniml manimati⚙n 2019

5 North American cities	50 invites per city + 1 friend

Puzzles based on history, lit and art	Urban mountain-bike friendly competition	Tribal celebration, food, clean-up and massage

This is an example of creatively rallying a brand community, and now we'll place Meniml's community efforts in the 7C Canvas.

Now it's your turn to review who your audience is and identify the community that will form your 1K true fans.

Now it's your turn to review who your audience is and identify the community that will form your "1K true fans." As we move into the 4th C, if you're feeling overwhelmed or are feeling like you need more 1-on-1 guidance to apply these concepts to your brand, because you're one of the first entrepreneurs to order this book, I'm offering a free, 45-minute coaching call for a short time. We can talk about anything you're having trouble with, and I can help you problem-solve for your business. Of course, these spots are limited, and will likely fill up quickly. To secure your spot visit ebrandcall.com.

MENIML 7C CANVAS

◆ CORE

WHY DO YOU EXIST? PURPOSE.

To offer a new, complete model for today's man. Meniml seeks to bring together thousands of factionalized "men," providing examples and models that their own fathers, social peers, and role models could not.

essence
DASHING

WHAT DO YOU STAND FOR? VALUES.

- Independence
- Style – Cleanliness
- Self-Respect

✿ CUSTOMER

WHO'S YOUR AUDIENCE?

Jack is an 80's baby yet born with a timeless cool. Raised in Connecticut, always independent and curious, he engaged deeply with anything that interested him, from a stint one summer with a local circus, to busting and traveling his way across Europe each summer in between his English studies at Brown University. Since college, he's blogged, cheffed, worked as a journalist, boxing trainer, and even tried his hand at motorcycle racing after dropping in at a local contest and winning its $1,000 prize.

HOW DOES YOUR PRODUCT ELEVATE?

I am confident, stylish, self-reliant, handsome (or well-groomed). I care about having quality tools for all of my daily needs, including grooming, and like them to be well-organized and essential.

⚔ COMMUNITY

WHAT CULTURAL GROUP DO WE IDENTIFY WITH?

Our community of men see our brand as a cultural rallying point. Unsatisfied with the corrosive tribes of lumbersexuals, metrosexuals, or aggro-jock warriors, but knowing they're more than sterilized stallions in corporate suits and ties, they look for relationships with other "modern classic" men, who are self-reliant, tough but fun, curious but principled, confident but vulnerable. In other words, "whole" men. They don't want to sit around a sweat lodge hugging other men and crying, but they do want to feel a connection to others.

◉ COMPETITION

HOW ARE YOU UNIQUE?

◎ CREATIVES

NAMING

LOGO

COLORS

TYPOGRAPHY

PACKAGING

▤ CONTENT

STORY OF THE BRAND

BRAND STORIES

▤ CHANNEL

YOUR BRAND TOUCHPOINTS

OWNED CHANNELS

SHARED CHANNELS

PAID CHANNELS

4.0

COMPETITION

4.0 COMPETITION

The Importance of Having Sole

Between 1975 and 2008, the number of products in the average supermarket swelled from an average of 8,948 to almost 47,000, according to the Food Marketing Institute.[13] To put this in perspective, consider that the average consumer faces the task of choosing between over *500* different soap products alone! Some are anti-bacterial, some are organic, some are French, some contain original sandalwood, some tout vitamin C & E, some are vegetable-based, some geared to vegans, some for sensitive skin, some have mango butter, some are gluten-free, and others are antimicrobial. And then, soap is just one of a series of separate products that make up a complete "beauty care/grooming" set for daily use. Compound this soap choice with the related choices (and decisions) for face wash, shampoo, conditioner, and scrub, and you can see why, for some, the simple act of preparing to take a shower can become paralyzing.

In the hyper-competitive world of CPG, this inundation of choice is one of the downsides of competition. And several prominent psychologists have cited this paralysis caused by too many choices as a modern disease, one that can lead to more serious anxiety and stress disorders in the long term. The new acronym to describe the root of this issue is "FOMO," or "Fear of Missing Out," but the damage of too much choice is composed of several key elements:[14]

When you choose one item, you're also *not* choosing other items that could be as good or better.

Greater choice makes us expend time imagining better options out there, so more options typically lead to greater regret.

Too many options can lead us to make *bad decisions*, instilling feelings of guilt, which can, in turn, lead to *paralysis of action* that extends to other aspects of our lives.

The decision-making process in the face of too much choice can waste several hours a week (the time we never get back), leaving less time to make the right decision.

Choosing between too many options can cause *decision fatigue*, which negatively affects the quality of future decisions, even the more consequential decisions that impact one's family or business.

Sculpting a well-defined brand relieves this decision-fatigue for consumers. Branding is "anti-competitive" in the sense that it separates a brand from other brands, and helps the right people choose it. With that said, the issue, and the opportunity, for you as a brander can be supported by this data, as reported by Mark Di Somma on the podcast <u>On Brand</u>:

"Only 25% of brands are seen as distinctive by customers. The rest blend into the mush. You have to build an understanding both inside your walls and outside of your walls. You have to build something people want to interact with. They should interact with your brand instead of just transacting."[15]

And this doesn't just apply to physical retail: in fact, the percentage of distinctiveness among eCommerce brands is even lower, just looking at the eCom "hot territories" of Amazon and Shopify.

In 2019, Amazon generated $53.76 billion in revenue from its third-party seller service, relative to $42.75 billion in the prior year.[16] As such, while this space is growing, so is the number of new, third party entrants into the space. 25% of all new entrants in the Fulfilment by Amazon (FBA) program are direct Chinese importers that were formerly (OEM) suppliers to North American eCommerce entrepreneurs.[17]

Shopify launched a new app, Shop, in April 2020[18] which will allow users to seamlessly browse and order from any store powered by the platform. Currently, users can only search by store name, rather than product type, but the step toward reshaping Shopify as a marketplace will make it harder for stores to maintain a distinct identity, particularly as separate from Shopify.

The good news is that eCommerce is expected to continue to grow faster than the rate of new entrants, especially following the onset of the COVID pandemic, which has accelerated eCommerce growth exponentially. Research by Kantar found that the number of people who do more than 50% of their shopping online has grown between 25-80%, and 6 in 10 consumers say they'll continue this long term.[19] However, consumer trust will play a bigger role in brand preference, and so your ability to take advantage of this growth will depend on strong, professional branding.

Which matters because increasingly, you'll be competing with professional brands. As stay-at-home orders have led to a surge in online orders, well-known offline brands are rapidly adopting digital-first thinking. Pepsi, for instance, who always relied on retail, built 2 new eCommerce delivery channels in 30 days. Pantryshop.com sells themed pantry kits including breakfast, snack, and post-workout options, and Snacks.com offers a range of Frito-Lay brands. The pandemic has created a massive influx of new online shoppers, but this change to consumer behavior will only make competition brand driven.

To become a true master brander, you must evolve beyond the focus on features, and even benefits, into unique communities, meanings, and emotions. Gone are the days when brands competed with better, cheaper, and faster mousetraps "online," stealing share from brick-and-mortar. But this is a good thing for *you*.

Let us explain…

Say your product portfolio includes headphones. Avoid prioritizing messaging that focuses on your headphones sounding louder, being lighter, and cheaper than, say, Apple Beats. There is no space for simple "ers" anymore.

Rather, consider this example. Domino's Pizza introduced the "delivered in 30 minutes or less, or it's free" standard to the pizza category. For a long time, that difference alone pushed them to the top in terms of sales. Compare Domino's to Papa Johns' with their "Better Pizza, Better Ingredients" promise, with a focus on quality (and taste), over the speed of delivery. Both of these brands are all selling functional benefits in the same pizza category. But today, especially for the small local or single-location pizzerias, customers expect a *personal connection* with their pizzeria, infusing it with its own unique set of associations and emotional appeal. Or they can stay home and order from Seamless in close to the same time, without having to be involved with any brand directly.

Soleness is *Not* a Product Feature.

This chapter focuses on developing that point of differentiation, which we call the Soleness of your brand, and how this Soleness, unlike product features, can inspire irrational loyalty.

The process of Soleness is finding and claiming a market position that you can own and retain. When you design your product in a unique and compelling manner, based on the competitive approaches we'll discuss, you don't need to compete on price. In fact, you don't need to compete much at all, except for attention. And price? Your customers will *want* to pay a premium to justify their preferences and opinions!

In most customers' minds, there's only *one* Amazon, *one* Warby Parker, *one* Dollar Shave Club, *one* Everlane, *one* Barkbox, *one* MeUndies, and *one* Allbirds. We are innate category makers, it's how we stay on top of information, and as categories themselves have proliferated, there is literally only space in any mind for one representative of each category. That position in the mind of the consumer is taken up by specific brands.

These companies and their products stand alone because they've successfully infused their brand with some form of Soleness that cannot be replicated: either through their positioning relative to the competition, their ability to disrupt, or their capacity to create a new category. One way or another, they've achieved a state of Soleness, and their brand *is* the category for their brand followers.

Now, let's look at how *you* can build Soleness for your brand.

How to Build Your Sole Point of Uniqueness

The Option Planning Quadrant Matrix

We created the 2x2 Competitive Entry Strategy Matrix to help you understand the primary options available for your competitive positioning work.

Let's say you are entering a market with highly competitive saturation, and your capital accessibility is low, relative to competitors. The best strategic choice for you would be to position your brand based on "Intangibles," found in the lower right corner of the matrix.

COMPETITIVE ENTRY STRATEGY OPTION-PLANNING QUADRANT MATRIX

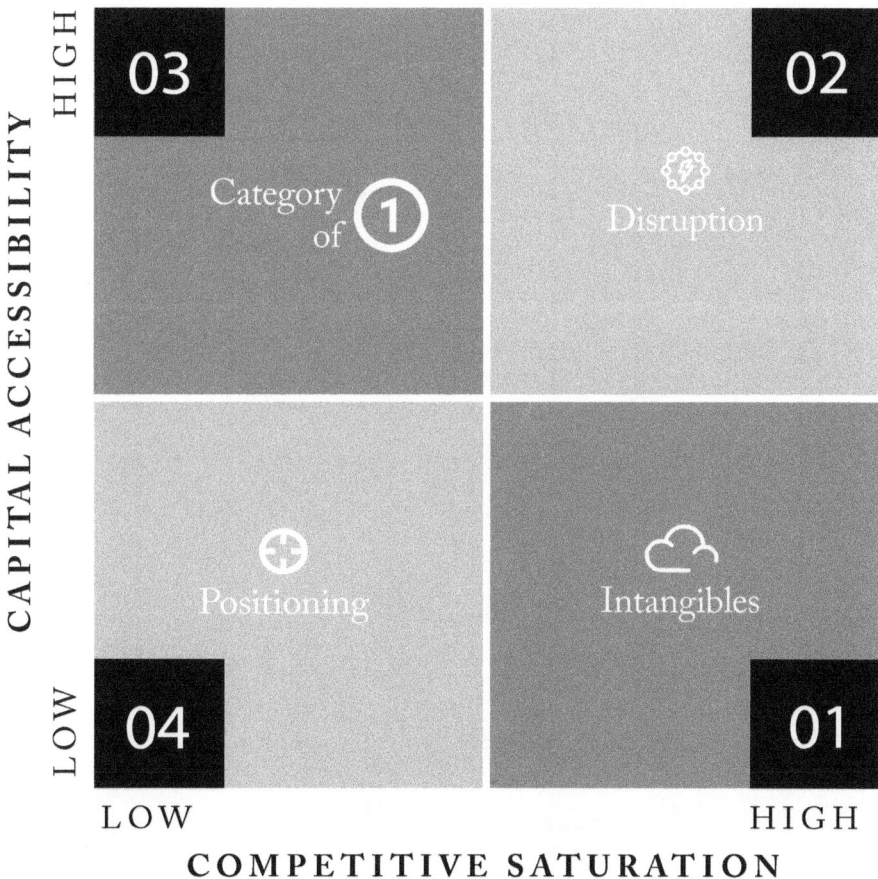

CAPITAL ACCESSIBILITY

HIGH

03

Category of ①

02

Disruption

Positioning

Intangibles

04

LOW

01

LOW   HIGH

COMPETITIVE SATURATION

On the other hand, if you are in a competitively saturated space, but you have significant financial resources, then the best option is likely the upper right-hand quadrant, "Disruption."

In a category with low competitive saturation and low capital, figuring out the relative position your brand will occupy in the mind of the customer versus competitors is likely the best use of your limited funds.

Lastly, in a low competition, self-created space, but with greater access to capital, creating a category of one is the best approach.

We'll help you decide with the help of real-world eCommerce examples.

Using Intangibles

Think of Warby Parker or Dollar Shave Club: well-designed eyeglasses and razors, no doubt, but neither are pioneering unique product designs. Yet, somehow, both brands have not only scaled as quickly as any successful software startup, but they've also accumulated a trail of rabid brand fanatics.

The "somehow," which accounts for their remarkable success is their use of brand intangibles.

Consider how these brands launched: both Warby Parker and Dollar Shave Club announced their arrival with highly emotional (and empathetic) stories. These stories were powerfully rooted in their brand purpose, and these simple but emotional appeals gave new audiences principles they could invest themselves in. These brands understood that product features and benefits don't build aspirational brands: inspiration does.

THE CASPER OF X

New DTC eCom startups are selling aspirations on top of products. All with a higher purpose or the key to a better life; or both.

Warby Parker
The original scale DTC eyeglasses co., vintage-inspired designs at "street" prices, social: donate specs to those in need.

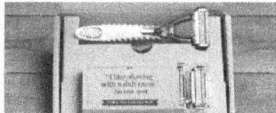

DOLLAR SHAVE CLUB
The original subscription based DTC razor company, on a "mission to build a bathroom."

BKR
Looks like a simple water bottle, but claims: "change the way you hydrate forever."

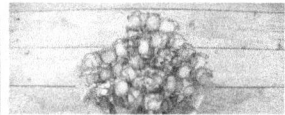

BOUQS
Flower-upstart aims to "create genuine moments of emotional connection."

RITUAL
Supplement startup describes itself as a "new kind of health brand," by skeptics for skeptics.

AWAY
Luggage startup that values "access over aspiration, and exploration over escape." Doesn't sound like another Samsonite!

These DTC brands seldom ever mention the products they sell, like razors, shaving cream, and prescription lenses. One reason is that, well, these items have been around for decades. What *is* new is their emphasis on "why" they're in business and their vision for how they aim to make a change in the world, or at the very least, a positive change in their customers' lives.

Let's look at the various directions you can take with your brand's intangibles to develop your own "Soleness":

- Story Driven Intangible
- Purpose Driven Intangible
- Giveback Driven Intangible
- Surprise Driven Intangible
- Personalization Driven Intangible
- Simplification Driven Intangible
- Sustainability Driven Intangible
- Optimism/Hope Driven Intangible
- Curation Driven Intangible

Story Driven Intangible

Pressed Juicery

Pressed Juicery's story begins with Hayden Slater, an unlikely proponent of a healthy lifestyle as a self-proclaimed "fast food junkie." However, things changed when, during his first year in NYU's theater program, he was enrolled, by default, to an introductory 8 am yoga class as part of the curriculum. His initial reluctance was quickly replaced, however, with sheer admiration for his yoga teacher's energy and beauty. He also took notice of her constant companion: a thermos of green juice. Drawing inspiration from her, Slater started including cold-pressed juice into his morning routine.

This healthy routine went by the wayside once he graduated and started working full-time at HBO. After the conclusion of an assignment, Slater purchased a one-way ticket to South Asia intending to spend a few months exploring before returning to his job. It was here in August of 2008 that his life took an unexpected turn. On an island in Koh Samu in the Gulf of Thailand, he tried a juice cleanse. What was initially supposed to be a 5-day routine, extended to 30 days as he noticed a dramatic increase in his energy, contentment, and peace of mind.

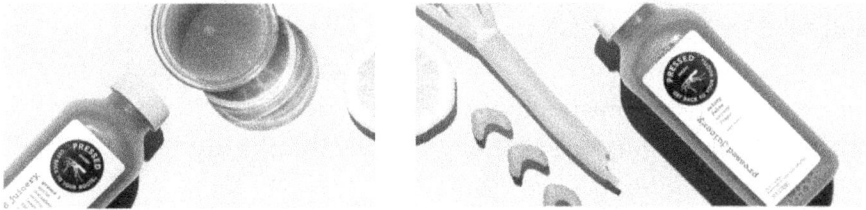

Upon returning to Los Angeles, Slater found himself at complete odds with the work culture prevalent at HBO. Sensing that it was no longer where he belonged, Slater decided to focus on the single thing that had the biggest impact on his life: cold-pressed juice. Although everyone around him thought this was a crazy idea, Slater considered that being fairly young with no major responsibilities was a unique opportunity, and he stuck to his convictions. In April 2010, he brought in two childhood friends, each contributing $30,000, and Pressed Juicery was born.

Their target market is not the elitist crowd, so they priced their juices at an affordable and accessible $5. Of course, the business was not immune to the trials and tribulations that challenge every new company. For Pressed Juicery, it came in the form of a surprise visit from the health department that led to a location being shut down. They subsequently sent a proactive invitation to the FDA, but their visit concluded with another closure. This led to a total revamp of the company's manufacturing process, enabling them to formally reopen in 2014. Today, the chain has 70 stores nationwide and has plans to expand into international markets, namely Japan and South Korea. Beyond juice, the company now offers coffee, smoothies and plant-based soft-serve. The brand now enjoys projected revenues above $75M for 2019.

One can certainly induce the power of Pressed Juicery's origin story in crafting its Soleness. There will certainly be other cold-pressed juices and similar product extensions, there will certainly also be copycats that try to emulate their business model: but none would be able to copy the Pressed Juicery story and how it drives all facets of the company's operations.

Purpose Driven Intangible

TOMS Shoes

As discussed in the brand purpose section, human beings are deeply motivated by a sense of purpose. Consciously and unconsciously, we seek meaning in our lives, and we feel the need to actively make a difference. The startup shoe company TOMS can be credited as being one of the pioneers of wearing its purpose on its sleeve, thereby imprinting meaning into their very DNA. The origin of this purpose started in Argentina, where Californian-native Blake Mycoskie was vacationing and saw children too impoverished to own shoes. He also witnessed the effect this had on their future development.

Upon returning to the US, Mycoskie started TOMS in his apartment, building the brand around a 'One for One' mission to donate one pair of shoes for every pair purchased. The brilliance of TOMS lay in how they effectively integrate profit and social impact. The "One for One" mission isn't just a business model; they have also focused nearly all of their marketing efforts on this social purpose.

Another key component of the purpose-driven brand is the One Day Without Shoes (ODWS) initiative. TOMS asks its digital community, the TOMS tribe, to post a picture of their bare feet on Instagram with the hashtag #WithoutShoes, and for every post, the brand donates a pair of shoes to a child in need.

To date, 86 million pairs of shoes have been donated, but this hasn't slowed down their growth: the company was most recently valued at $625 million.[20] The brand also collaborates with more than 100 'giving partners,' non-profit, humanitarian organizations with expertise in poverty alleviation and international development, such as Save the Children and UNICEF.

In the case of TOMS, it's their brand purpose based on the one-for-one model that has allowed TOMS to build its differentiation in the crowded shoe market.

Giveback Driven Intangible

STATE Bags

In 2009, the husband and wife team of Scot and Jacq Tatelman started a summer camp for kids from all five boroughs of NYC. After watching countless children bring their school supplies and belongings to the classroom and camp in trash bags or ripped shopping bags, the Tatelmans founded STATE Bags.

STATE's business model is strongly influenced by TOMS and its one-for-one concept. Like TOMS, STATE provides a backpack to a local child in need for every STATE bag purchased. This model inspired the name of their most popular bag: "The GIVE. BACK. PACK."

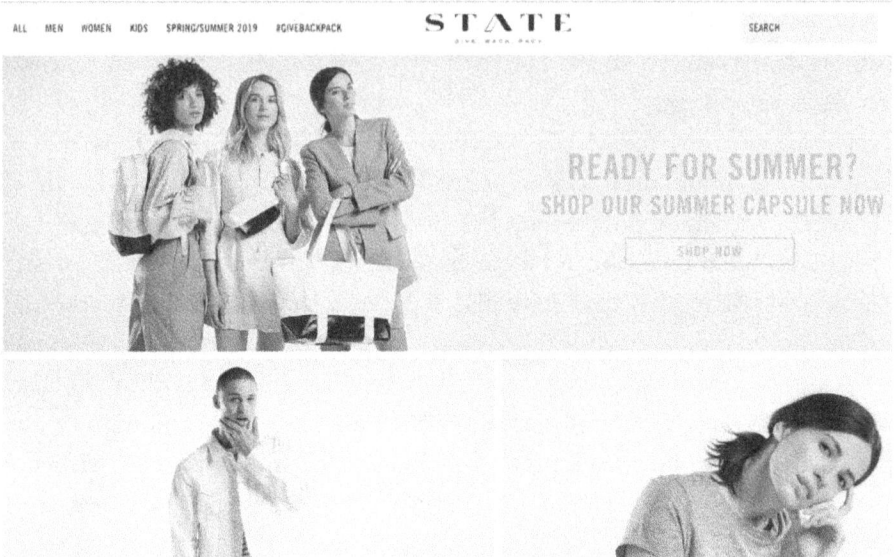

STATE donates bags to children at events called Bag Drops, where their teams of "PackMen" and "PackWomen" lead motivational rallies for participating kids. They hope to instill a spirit of belief in each child, along with, of course, a brand-new STATE backpack filled with school supplies.

But their Soleness lies in the melding of fashion and purpose. The company is credited with creating inexpensive, high quality, stylish backpacks whose appeal crosses genders and all ages, all while still making a major difference for underprivileged youth all across the United States.

Today STATE Bags is proud to be a Benefit Corporation, accompanied by fellow businesses creating public good by having a material, positive impact on society. The company hit the six-digit mark of donated bags in 2018 and is on track to double its overall business.

Surprise Driven Intangible

Greetabl

Merging their respective backgrounds in business and design, Greetabl was founded by Joe Fischer and Zoë Scharf in 2012. It all started with a creative wedding gift idea made from single-serving cereal boxes, which led the founders to recognize the existence of The Gifting Gap™ - which arises "when a card isn't enough, and $50 flowers are too much."

Greetabl offers an affordable option, ranging from $9 - $28, of sending sweet, personalized gifts to friends and family. Despite their accessibility, each gift is designed to delight both the recipient and the customer with their fun, easy gift creation process. As Greetabl proudly states on its website: "The only thing better than being surprised with a personalized Greetabl, is creating & sending one." Users have the power to completely personalize each element of the gift, from selecting a box print, to uploading personal photos, selecting a curated small gift, and writing their messages. The results are personal, thoughtful surprises for family and friends.

What is truly remarkable about Greetabl is that its offerings are commodity products, with no design innovations being attempted. The sole reason for their success is a delightful visual and verbal delivery – their Soleness. It's still an ordinary product just with added personalization and custom packaging: ordinary products that are elevated to delightful status.

This venture-backed eCommerce brand now serves 1000's of repeat customers across the United States and Canada.

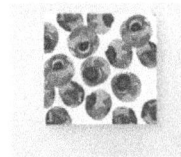

Personalization Driven Intangible

Anomalie

Inspired by her dilemma, Harvard Business School grad Leslie Voorhees launched Anomalie after struggling to find "the one" wedding dress that fit both the style she envisioned and her budget.

Leslie eventually leveraged her years of experience managing factories for Nike and Apple and reached out to a dress manufacturer in the Suzhou region of China. This manufacturer is credited with making 80% of the world's wedding dresses and made a natural partner to create a custom wedding dress for her. Following this successful partnership, she realized the same dress would retail for thousands of dollars in the U.S., while her dress only cost a few hundred. By November of 2016, just five months after designing her dress, Vorhees and her husband Calley Means had both quit their corporate tech jobs and dedicated themselves full-time to Anomalie, a company that would help other brides make the dress of their dreams on a budget.

The process is simpler than it sounds, too. The customer experience, according to Anomalie's website, "starts with the bride/designer completing a 15-question survey. This is followed by a personalized dashboard interface, where the bride then uploads "inspiration" photos to a "Pinterest-like" mood board. During this process, the bride is assisted by one out of a team of eight designated stylists to help guide a bride through the design steps. The stylist also liaises with the production team, which "aligns" the design with up to 130 dress variables on the back-end. The client then receives a proposed dress sketch, along with fabric swatches, for confirmation. Once the custom design hits the production phase in one of the factories in either Suzhou or Guangzhou, China, progress reports and photos of the dress are regularly sent to the client, and the manufacturing and delivery take about three months. Anomalie's direct-to-consumer model helps a typical bride stay within a dress budget typically ranging from $1,000 to $1,500."

Here, Anamolie's Soleness is built on the degree of customization they're able to offer at much lower price points in the wedding dress category, which has traditionally been fraught with monopolized, high prices.

Simplification Driven Intangible

Barn & Willow

If you've ever tried shopping for drapes and shades, you'll know it's a cumbersome process even at a neighborhood store being assisted by a specialist. But digitally native brand Barn & Willow is looking to change the way you shop for custom-made window treatments.

Not unlike Anomalie's founding being inspired by Leslie Voorhees's struggle to find the right wedding dress, Barn & Willow's Trisha Roy was dealing with her own pain point when she began the process of finding custom-made curtains for her new home. Her firsthand experience of how involved (and expensive!) the process was led her to realize there was an opportunity to make drapery shopping pain-free.

Barn & Willow addresses the problem two-fold: first, they operate as a virtually integrated brand by working directly with the finest mills in Belgium and skilled craftsmen in India to sew drapes. Second, they use

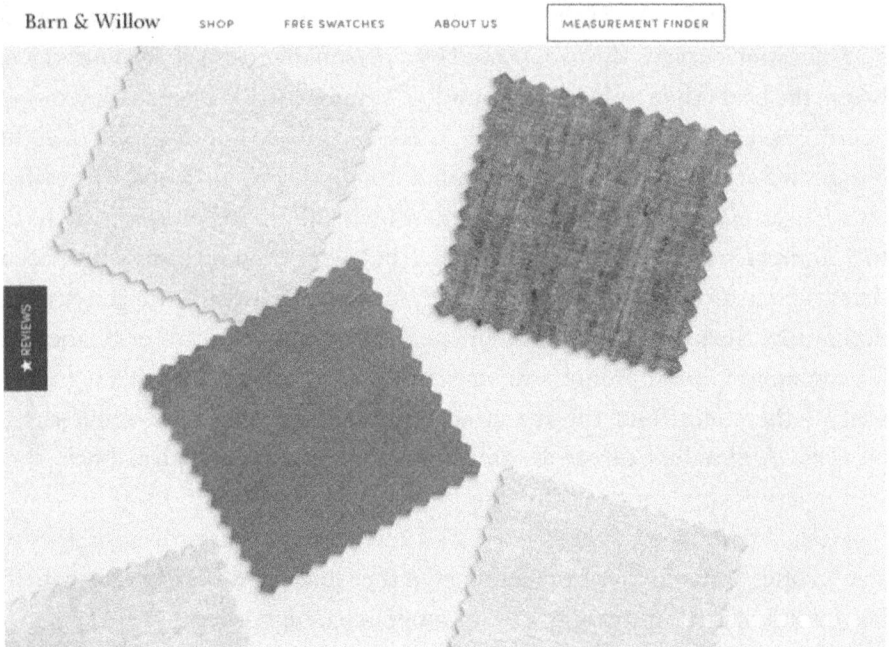

technology to create a simple experience for the customer to design, visualize and buy premium quality window treatments through a web-based "measurement finder" tool. All culminating in offering the best in class window treatments at a fraction of the industry-standard cost, delivered within 10 days, thereby deriving their Soleness.

Sustainability Driven Intangible

Rothy's

Rothy's sells shoes online: the twist? Rothy's sells washable, woven flats & shoes made from recycled plastic. Since its inception, this San Francisco based startup has cornered the market in combining comfort, style, and sustainability while at the same time replacing stilettos in the Bay Area and NYC. Not to mention, the Duchess of Sussex, Meghan Markle, recently showed off her eco-friendly affinity by wearing a pair.

On a mission to never rest on their laurels or a single style, the tenderfoot company has diversified to introduce The Flat, The Point, The Loafer, and recently announced The Sneaker. They've also expanded to offer a kid's line.

Surprisingly, when Roth Martin and Stephen Hawthornthwaite founded the company six years ago, they were clueless about how to make shoes, so eco-friendly shoes were certainly a stretch. After an involved manufacturing process, they finally determined how to turn the plastic from water bottles to yarn, how to dye that yarn such that the stretch and shape is maintained, and finally how to knit the yarn into shoes that people could actually wear. All leading to manufacturing their Soleness, again in the overly competitive women's shoe market.

The Impact? As Erin Lowenberg, creative director at Rothy's, disclosed in a recent article with Huffington Post,[21] Rothy's has already used almost 20 million bottles in the production of its shoes, which is impressive considering the brand has only been selling them for about two years.

Optimism/Hope Driven Intangible

BestSelf Co. (BSC)

BSC has taken the age-old tradition of journals, diaries, and calendars, and combined them with classic self-help strategies to renew optimism and hope.

BSC started as a project between two entrepreneurs, Cathryn Lavery and Allen Brouwer, who left their jobs to pursue their passion. They realized they were caught up in the typical work routine of long hours with nothing to show for it. Sensing that a change was needed, their inspiration led to BSC and the Self Journal to "create everyday tools for people to lead a life they can be proud of."

Leveraging the power of crowdfunding, they launched their concept on Kickstarter. The 2015 campaign far surpassed the $15,000 goal and raised a total of $322,695. With that money, they were able to develop The Self Journal - a powerful yet simple daily planner to help structure your day, enjoy life, and reach your goals quicker than you thought possible.

Their Soleness lay in transforming the use of journals and diaries, from merely time-management to melding it with the rising trend of self-help documenting.

≡ **Best Self** ▓ ⌄ ⚇ Q 🛍

#1 Tools for Personal Development

Your Best Life Starts Here

Find work-life harmony, think bigger, achieve more, and spark deeper connections.

SHOP NOW

Today they have added an assortment of products that all contribute to their mission to "connect and inspire humanity to think bigger and achieve more while enjoying today."

Curation Driven Intangible

As I introduce the next brand in the curation-driven realm, here is a bit of a personal revelation. I have a strong affinity to shop, online of course, for clothing. I would describe my clothing personality to be preppy, and I typically reach for pressed khakis, fitted jackets, and edgy T-shirts. But here is where the dilemma comes in: I am color blind, so it's hard for me to distinguish between colors, especially between grays and pinks, blues and purples, and greens and browns. This is why I have become such a big fan of Stitch Fix, as they have made personal stylists accessible to mainstream shoppers.

Stitch Fix

Stitch Fix is an online personal shopping service for women, men and kids. The curation process starts with 51 questions that take about 20

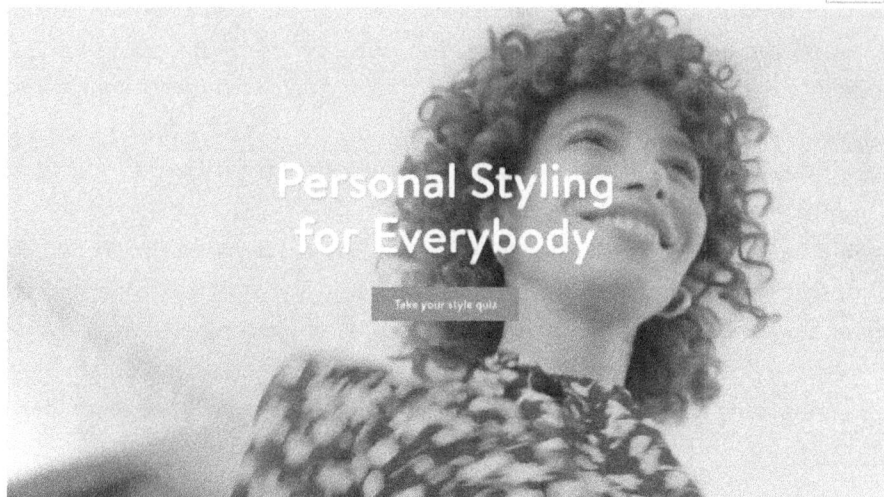

STITCH FIX   Women   Men   Kids   Style Guide   FAQ   Gift Cards   Sign In

Personal Styling for Everybody

Take your style quiz

minutes to complete. After this, Stitch Fix sends you a box of clothes customized to your style, size, and budget.

At the end of the day, Stitch Fix is still selling clothing, but the difference maker is curating hundreds of brands and using data science to build a recommendation process. Since 2011, they've received customer feedback on more than 100 million apparel recommendations allowing them to offer personalized pieces that fit the individual clothing profile of their customers.

Stitch Fix is run by the youngest female founder ever to take a company public, Katrina Lake, and has built a $2.5 billion business by revolutionizing the traditional shopping experience.

As evident in these examples, it's the intangibles of a brand, be it the Story, Purpose, Giveback, Surprise, Personalization, Simplification, Sustainability, Optimization, or Curation that have made these companies bigger than the actual commodity they represent and sell.

Using Disruption

The concept of disruption is best understood through the Blue Ocean Strategy, a marketing theory from a book written by W. Chan Kim and Renee Mauborgne (also titled <u>Blue Ocean Strategy</u>).

When every brand is battling for the same market position and to capture the attention of the same consumers, it creates "cutthroat competition [which] results in nothing but a bloody red ocean of rivals fighting over a shrinking profit pool." To deal with this, companies should instead look for "uncontested market space" and ways to reinvent the industry. This way, your brand captures a larger market share of untapped customers. These new spaces are described as "Blue Oceans," where brands can avoid this margin-eroding, vicious competition. By choosing to pioneer a Blue Ocean and focus beyond existing market demands, you can identify unmet needs (for example, needs beyond a lower price or incremental product improvements) and create new solutions that are far more profitable. In short, avoid head-to-head competition and focus on innovation.

To discover an elusive Blue Ocean, the strategy recommends that brands consider the "Four Actions Framework" to reconstruct customer value parameters in crafting a new value proposition. The framework poses four key questions:

1. *What* can I eliminate?
2. *What* can I reduce?
3. *What* can I raise the bar on?
4. *What* can I create that is new?

Blue Oceans (Should) Matter Even More to eCommerce Entrepreneurs

Blue Oceans matter because these markets are potentially large, and with the ever-increasing competition online, it's never been more important to find opportunities in the market to ensure your brand has space to grow. By continuing to innovate, your brand may even become a category of one.

Let's take a look at the components of the Blue Ocean Strategy using Casper, a DTC mattress company, as an example.

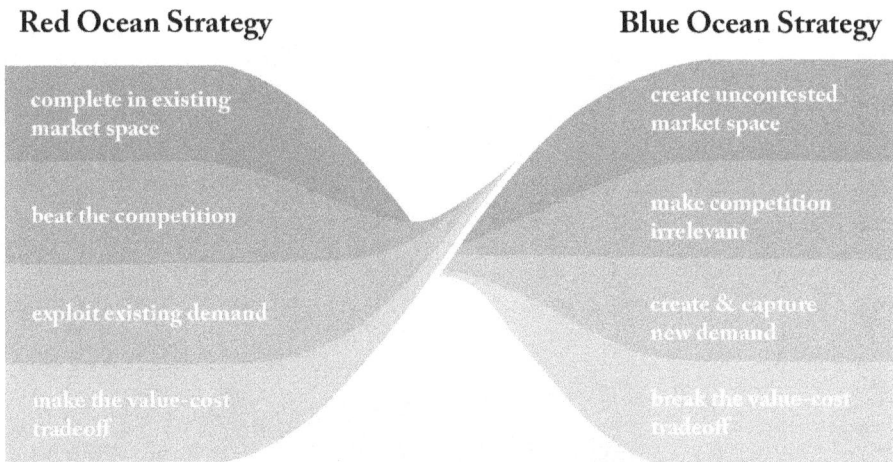

Red Ocean Strategy   Blue Ocean Strategy

Red Ocean Strategy	Blue Ocean Strategy
complete in existing market space	create uncontested market space
beat the competition	make competition irrelevant
exploit existing demand	create & capture new demand
make the value-cost tradeoff	break the value-cost tradeoff

Source: Kim, W. Chan and Renée Mauborgne (2015). Blue Ocean Strategy. Harvard Business Review Press.

Eliminate

Which of the factors that the industry takes for granted should be eliminated?

Before Casper, as a mattress buyer you had to choose a type of mattress (open spring, pocket spring, etc.), had to test its firmness depending on your preferred sleeping position, height, and weight, THEN had to choose an appropriate size (single, double, king size, etc.).

Finally, after making a decision, you had to negotiate with a pushy salesperson trying to upsell you. Casper eliminates all of these unnecessary steps by reducing the number of options and simplifying the buying process.

Reduce

Which factors should be reduced well below the industry's standard?

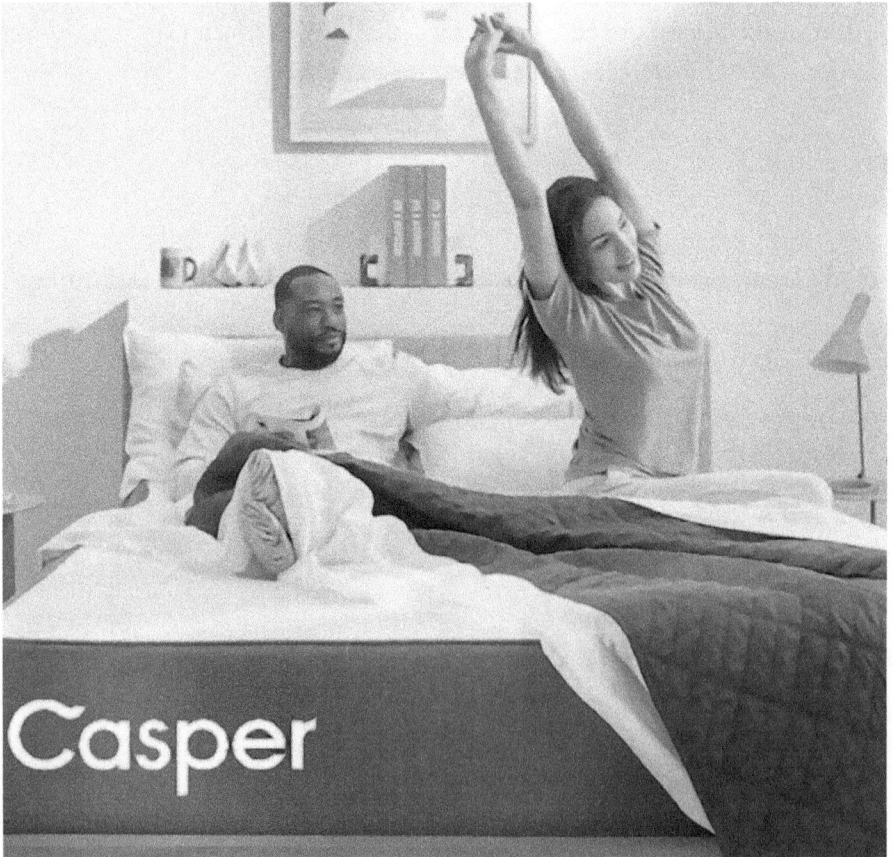

Gone are the days of awkwardly lying on a mattress in front of a salesman and then waiting around all day for delivery. Today, with a few clicks of a mouse, you can order a mattress from the comfort of your home and have it delivered for free within a 60-minute window of your choice.

Raise

Which factors should be raised well above the industry's standard?
Casper has totally reinvented the buying process and experience itself.

Create

Which factors should be created that the industry has never offered?
Casper offers: *"An Unbeatable Guarantee. Risk-free 100-night free trial."*
If you decide Casper's mattress isn't for you, they'll send a courier over to remove it from your home and either donate it to a local charity or have it recycled. Best of all, you don't even need to have the box.

Using Positioning

In their now classic book, Positioning, Al Ries and Jack Rout define positioning as how your brand optimally expresses its products and identity, to differentiate it from competitors and drive preferential purchase or use. According to the authors, what truly matters is the perception of your brand that's held by customers, and *their* interpretation is your brand's reality, not yours.

The power of positioning is captured when you can claim the first spot in a gap in the market. Not only does this ensure you get twice the market share than the next brand, it doubles again relative to the third brand. Consumers are comfortable placing you on different rungs of their mental ladder. The essential ingredient in securing the leadership position is being the first brand to capture consumer attention.

For the sake of clarity, we'll use a positioning map to analyze several DTC men's shoe brands across four parameters: handcrafted/leather shoes (high-end) versus sneakers (casual) and high-priced shoes versus sustainable/charitable driven brands. The map dictates the various positions that consumers are using to define these brands in their minds.

The Upper Right Quadrant: these brands offer formal shoes priced at a premium. As you can see, this quadrant is packed with five major players. Paul Evans is found at the far right, on top, with shoes priced at $450 a pair, made with the highest quality Italian, calfskin leather. Below that, you find Wolf & Shepherd, who does manage to stand out in the crowded category as "The Most Comfortable Shoes." In fact, a recent graduate won a half marathon while wearing the Wolf & Shepherd dress shoes. Under Wolf & Shepherd, we find the unisex, Boston based shoe brand M.Gemi, which still offers hand-crafted shoes in Italian workshops but with a slightly different twist. M.Gemi releases new, limited edition designs every Monday morning. Sitting below M.Gemi at a slightly lower price tier is Scarosso who also pride themselves on their Italian workmanship with the added benefit of customization through their online configurator. Finally, rounding off the top 5 is Jack Erwin, who started with the goal of creating well-made, well-priced men's shoes, with most of their offerings falling within the $200 price range. Jack Erwin is making more of a volume play with this strategy.

The Upper Left Quadrant: this section represents casual shoes (sneakers) at a premium price. This quadrant is only occupied by Greats, who were inspired to offer high-quality sneakers at a more reasonable price. The company has seen notable success with collaborations featuring the NY based designer Jason Wu and the NFL's Marshawn Lynch.

The Lower Left Quadrant: this segment of brands is on the casual end but is driven by sustainability. This quadrant is represented by the heavyweights, including the purpose-driven TOMS and sustainability-led Allbirds. TOMS, of course, is known for its "One for One" donation model, which has since been emulated by numerous eCommerce upstarts. Allbirds is recognized for its practice of sustainability by making shoes with natural materials like merino wool, eucalyptus tree fiber, and sugar. Also occupying a place here is the lesser-known Oliver Cabell, who employs ethical factories.

The Lower Right Quadrant: here we find sustainably made shoes on the formal end. The only brand in this section is Nisolo, whose vision is "to push the fashion industry in a more sustainable direction where success is based on more than just offering the lowest price. A direction that not only values exceptional design but the producer and the planet just as

POSITIONING MAP
MAJOR ECOM MEN'S SHOE BRANDS

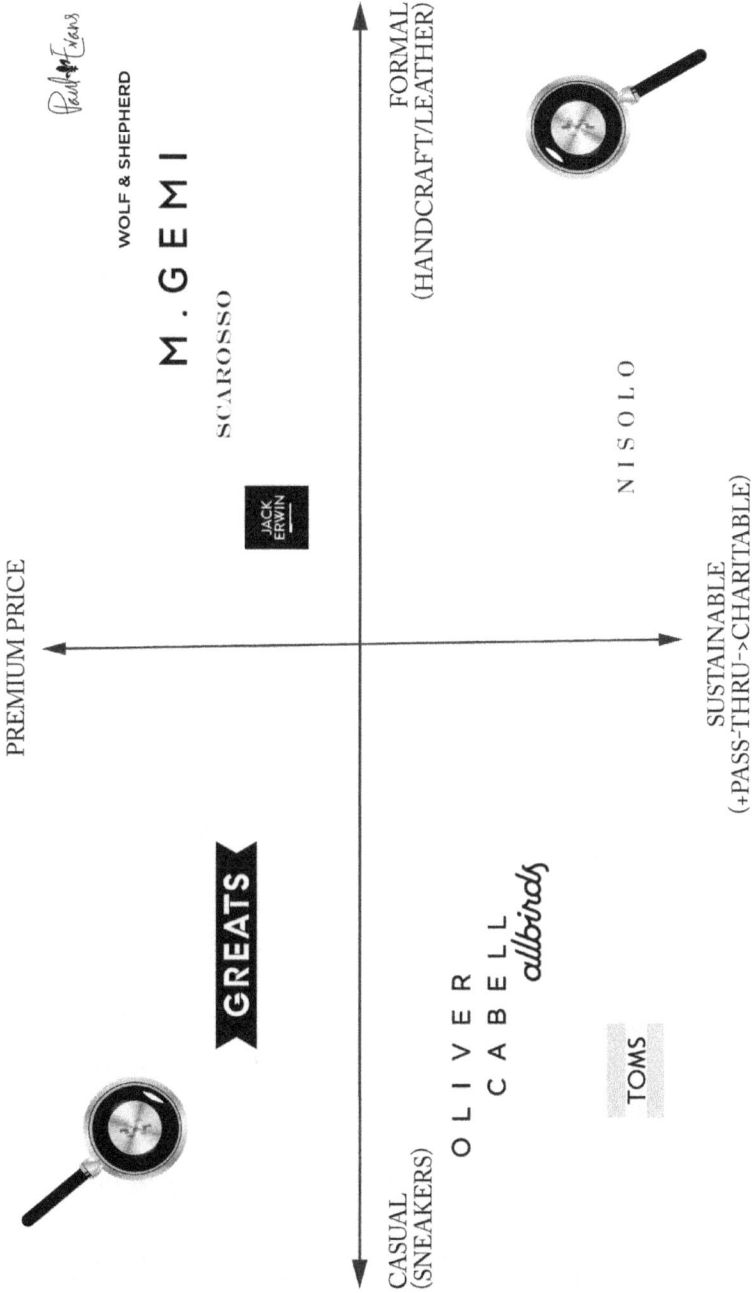

PREMIUM PRICE

FORMAL
(HANDCRAFT/LEATHER)

WOLF & SHEPHERD

M . G E M I

SCAROSSO

JACK ERWIN

NISOLO

SUSTAINABLE
(+PASS-THRU->CHARITABLE)

GREATS

OLIVER
CABELL
allbirds

TOMS

CASUAL
(SNEAKERS)

much as the end consumer." Nisolo producers, usually small, independent artisans, receive fair wages, and the brand practices ethical production in its factories.

The significant empty space on this positioning map signals untapped markets, which may be opportunities. We've marked these gaps with a magnifying glass icon.

The first spot is the lower right quadrant with a potential play in high-end, handcrafted shoes, with the likes of a Paul Evans but with a sustainability play in full force, appealing to the likes of the Bolvants and Berlutis.

The second opportunity is diagonally opposite the first, in the upper left section. Here, the opportunity is for both low-priced and high-priced sneaker brands. Greats is positioned in the middle, and there is an opportunity to come in and occupy either side of the pricing spectrum.

Category of One

Becoming a "category of one" brand is the holy grail of branding.

What does it mean to become a "category of one?" It means that no other brand is even in the same category as your brand. Your brand has created a new category that's deeply important to a (previously) under-served segment of consumers. While this certainly sounds attractive to any brand, it does require significant innovation. However, the work is worth it, as the buzz created by a new business model or approach will generate a huge amount of free publicity. Truly new ideas also create new demand, and the consumers targeted by the brand will be eager for a chance to try it. In turn, this excitement, as long as the experience lives up to the hype, will translate to significant "word-of-mouth" marketing. This is one of the major benefits enjoyed by category of one brands.

By reinventing or creating your own category, you quickly capture and own the new space. Being a first-mover brings significant growth opportunities, coupled with being able to scale quickly can create a competitive moat to new entrants. Of course, particularly if your category is profitable, the competition will come, but category of one brands tend to retain financial and mindshare advantages. Having been the first brand to define a category forges a robust link in the minds of consumers to your brand, and regardless of the quality of brands that come after you, you'll

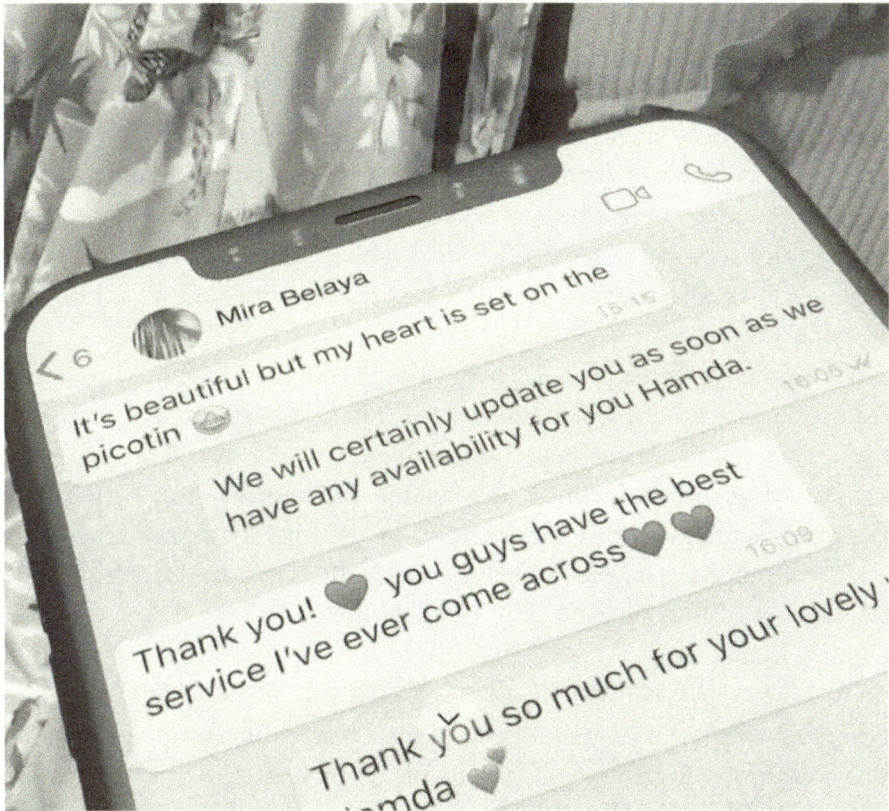

always remain top of mind. For instance, while there are many modern takes on the traditional circus, but there's only one Cirque du Soleil.

Because it requires significant innovation in terms of products and often systems and business models as well, a hallmark of category of one brands is disruption. Consider the initial mayhem caused by the entry of Amazon and eBay. Uber is a more recent example of a brand that has upended a traditional business. In the eCommerce world, Threads provides an excellent example of an emerging category of one.

Threads labels itself as the "Pioneers of Luxury Chat Commerce." As their CEO Sophie Hill explained in a recent interview with South China Morning Post, "Our mission is 'inspire, acquire, deliver.' So if you see something on Instagram, you would then swipe up through a Story, start chatting to one of our sales team and then all payment and invoicing would happen within that conversation."[22]

Traditionally, fashion is sold through standard eCommerce portals. However, Threads leverages chat platforms giving it the ability to offer a new type of retail. Rather than interacting with customers through websites, Threads engages consumers through WhatsApp & WeChat. Through conversations, Threads directly connects to customers and can offer a brand experience regardless of where the customer is in the world. This conversational model also offers a more highly personalized and interactive experience, similar to walking into a department store and speaking with an associate.

Additionally, Threads is very clear on who their audience is. They define these consumers as "a global audience of High Net Worth's" with whom they interact with amazing editorial, through this chat-based media.

Analyzing the competition and finding the best way to position your eCommerce brand is both a science and an art. Luckily, more science than art, but if you feel you need more guidance finding the best possible position for your business, don't hesitate to reach out to us.

———————————

Before moving on, it's our sincere hope that everything we're presenting in this book is synthesizing and that the bigger picture of branding is taking shape. But, if you feel at all like you need more guidance or clarification, you can always reach us via our Facebook group at facebook.com/groups/ecommercebrandbuilders where we'll be glad to help.

———————————

Approach for Meniml

After choosing one of the approaches to determine your Soleness, you'll find it's much easier to craft your brand's Soleness statement. In thinking of your own Soleness statement, consider these questions:

- *Who* is your *target* customer (segment)?
- *Which* of your customer's aspirations will your brand propel?
- *What* can you offer to fulfill your target's needs and wants that competitors can't or haven't put a stake in the ground for? (Remember, this should be *emotional,* not functional)
- *Who* is your *main* competitor?
- *What* makes you different from this competitor?
- *What* will make your target customer be most compelled to buy from you?

Writing Your Soleness (Positioning) Statement

This worksheet follows a very simple but effective format for creating a positioning statement, which we'll share with you here:

For (your target customer)

Who (state the main customer need or unique opportunity for them and your brand)

The (brand name) is a (type of product in what category)

That (your brand's key benefit or compelling reason to buy)

Unlike (your primary competitive alternative)

Our product (state your primary functional point of SOLENESS)

Our brand (state your primary emotional point of SOLENESS)

Here's how we completed the Soleness statement for Meniml and this is how we wrote it out in long-form (for the 7C Canvas):

Soleness Positioning Statement

Important, Unique, Believeable, Actionable, Sustainable

For today's adult Man* (*which we help define)
<u>Target customer</u>

Who wants a one-stop, complete but simple grooming solution
that goes beyond soap and shampoo, but below mascara
<u>Statement of want or unique opportunity</u>

The <u>Meniml brand</u> **is a** total men's grooming portfolio
<u>Name</u>   <u>Category</u>

That organizes, simplifies, and displays sequential
skin, hair, and body maintenance products
<u>Key benefit/compelling reason to buy</u>

Unlike women's beauty products that create more
problems than necessary
<u>Primary competitive alternative</u>

Our product simplifies while adding pride &
eliminates «shame» in beauty for Men
<u>Primary differentation</u>

Our brand guides its users in a new, integrated
but complete model of being a Man
<u>Primary emotional payoff</u>

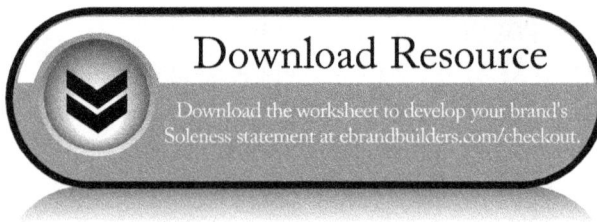

Download Resource

Download the worksheet to develop your brand's
Soleness statement at ebrandbuilders.com/checkout.

Now it's your turn to complete your Soleness statement, and then place it into your 7C Canvas.

Finally, don't forget to return to your C1 work and incorporate any new insights your customer and competitive analyses have uncovered into your brand core.

MENIML 7C CANVAS

◈ CORE

WHY DO YOU EXIST? PURPOSE.

To offer a new, complete model for today's man. Meniml seeks to bring together thousands of factionalized "men," providing examples and models that their own fathers, social peers, and role models could not.

essence
DASHING

WHAT DO YOU STAND FOR? VALUES.

- Independence
- Style – Cleanliness
- Self–Respect

▣ CUSTOMER

WHO'S YOUR AUDIENCE?

Jack is an 80's baby yet born with a timeless cool. Raised in Connecticut, always independent and curious, he engaged deeply with anything that interested him, from a stint one summer with a local circus, to bussing and traveling his way across Europe each summer in between his English studies at Brown University. Since college, he's blogged, chefed, worked as a journalist, boxing trainer, and even tried his hand at motorcycle racing after dropping in at a local contest and winning its $1,000 prize.

HOW DOES YOUR PRODUCT ELEVATE?

I am confident, stylish, self–reliant, handsome (or well–groomed). I care about having quality tools for all of my daily needs, including grooming, and like them to be well–organized and essential.

◉✕ COMPETITION

HOW ARE YOU UNIQUE?

Meniml is the brand for today's adult Man who wants a one-stop, complete but simple grooming solution that goes beyond soap and shampoo (but below mascara and lipstick). It organizes, simplifies, and displays sequential skin, hair, and body maintenance products, stocking only the necessities for maximum male grooming. UNLIKE women's beauty products that have excess SKUs to sell more to the same customers, our product simplifies while adding pride & eliminating "shame" in complete grooming for Men. Our brand guides its user's in a new, integrated but complete model of being a Man in itself.

⚒ COMMUNITY

WHAT CULTURAL GROUP DO WE IDENTIFY WITH?

Our community of men see our brand as a cultural rallying point. Unsatisfied with the contavailable tribes of 'umbersexuals, metrosexuals, or aggro–jock warriors, but knowing they're more than sterilized stallions in corporate suits and ties, they look for relationships with other "modern classic" men, who are self–reliant, tough but fun, curious but principled, confident but vulnerable. In other words, "whole men." They don't want to sit around a sweat lodge hugging other men and crying, but they do want to feel a connection to others.

◉ CREATIVES

NAMING   **LOGO**

COLORS

TYPOGRAPHY   **PACKAGING**

▤ CONTENT

STORY OF THE BRAND

BRAND STORIES

◲ CHANNEL

YOUR BRAND TOUCHPOINTS
OWNED CHANNELS

SHARED CHANNELS

PAID CHANNELS

5.0

CREATIVES

5.0 CREATIVES

When it Comes to Brand Creatives, Lead with Brand Values

When designing the creative elements of your brand, it's critical to go beyond the surface level details of colors, logo, taglines, and brand name. Your brand's creative assets are the ambassadors of your brand's identity in the world, but they will only resonate with consumers if they reflect the deeper character and values of your organization. At their best, creative assets are symbols of your brand's core identity, and they are not only visually appealing but borrow from your values a deep emotional appeal that speaks to what your brand stands for. When brand and design choices are aligned, creative assets communicate more effectively and create the foundation of loyal relationships with consumers.

Many companies make design decisions that are primarily descriptive. But the process by which a company decides what they create is often tied up in their purpose, values, and the contributions of all the people that sustain your brand. What you offer symbolizes what your brand cares about, and *who* you serve. When brand is at its best, this more human element is what dictates the tangible, functional products and benefits your company offers. The point of creatives is to translate these guiding principles into shape and color. When brands do this successfully, consumers don't just understand what you do when they encounter your name, logo, tagline, and so on, they know who you are. Of course, you want your creatives to spark interest in your brand, but unless creatives are aligned with your brand's purpose and identity, you risk eroding trust as customers may feel you're two-faced.

Assets built on the foundation of your brand's identity have more complex, layered meanings. When you focus exclusively on colors, logos, and slogans, you are in danger of designs that feel meaningless and empty. Without this connection to your identity, your creatives may be visually appealing, but they won't be memorable since they won't be reinforcing the brand. Thus, creative design should come later in the branding process, once your fundamental identity, values, and essence are thoroughly known and committed to. Until you do this deeper work, your brand will never fully connect, because brand isn't just what a product looks like on a shelf. This is notoriously difficult: it can take a fair amount of time and effort to come up with creative designs that communicate what you do at a basic level while also being visually appealing, offering a cohesive design, and effectively representing your brand's identity. And it should be a challenge. If it's not hard, it means you are still dealing with the symptoms instead of the disease, and that you are avoiding the deeper work that will produce results that pulse with meaning and powerfully attract your core audience.

Based on the approach mentioned above, creatives will focus on naming, logo, color, typography, and packaging.

Naming

Your choice of brand name has a profound effect on your brand's overall success in the marketplace. Your name isn't just the key "first impression" in the broader market world: a great name defines a brand's direction and guides its success. Great brand names also help consumers understand where and how a brand fits into their daily life.

Starbucks, for example, may not immediately suggest a coffee shop, but the name evokes energy and spontaneity, associations we make with coffee itself.

Google, to most, has become a verb, though it is based on "Googol," or 10100 to reflect the massive amount of information in the world, and help the company lay claim to being "the Category" of search engine.

Red Bull, meanwhile, evokes energy, passion, courage, and determination, which matches their brand's ethos.

Metaphors, in particular, make powerful brand names because the implied comparison between their literal meaning and the brand's identity invites consumers into the brand's story as they contemplate the meaning of the name. Amazon, for example, perfectly suggests their unparalleled volume of product offerings, like a jungle ready to be explored. In addition, these kinds of brand names give companies the room to grow and evolve. It's hard to believe that Amazon would be the retail behemoth they are today with their remarkable reach in so many sectors if they had called themselves "Books Online."

The best brand names need no explanation for consumers to understand the brand's identity and what they represent. It's important to remember that your brand's creative assets are a vehicle of meaning, and your name is a particularly powerful ambassador of your brand. We may be familiar with a company's logo and messaging, but we use the brand name when we talk about it and recommend it to our friends and family. Of all the creative elements, be sure you are deeply involved in the naming process: it's too important to delegate.

Effective creatives echo your brand's core values and hint at the emotional experience created by your brand. And in turn, when creatives are built on the foundation of your brand's identity, they'll resonate more deeply with consumers. This will also result in visual assets and a brand name that stands out because they'll stand for something more than design for its own sake.

To inspire ideas for your brand name and set your wheels in motion, here are six types of brand names that are prevalent within eCommerce.

The Six Brand Name Types

1. Founder Names:

These are brands with the founder(s) as their namesake:

M.Gemi: the luxury shoe brand is named after one of its founding members, Maria Gangemi, a longtime fan of Italian craftsmanship and artistry.

Tom Bihn: the business traveler hipster brand. When Tom was 10 years old, he asked his parents for help to purchase hiking and camping equipment. They suggested two options: get an after-school job and earn money to buy it, or "just figure out how to make it yourself." Tom chose the second option, and the rest is history: Tom has spent the last 40 years designing and making backpacks, travel bags, and briefcases.

Madsen Cycles: the eCom bicycle brand. The company's founder, Jared Madsen, has been riding bikes nearly all his life, and at 15, he started building bikes for a local biking company. All of this experience and passion has been invaluable in the founding of Madsen Cycles.

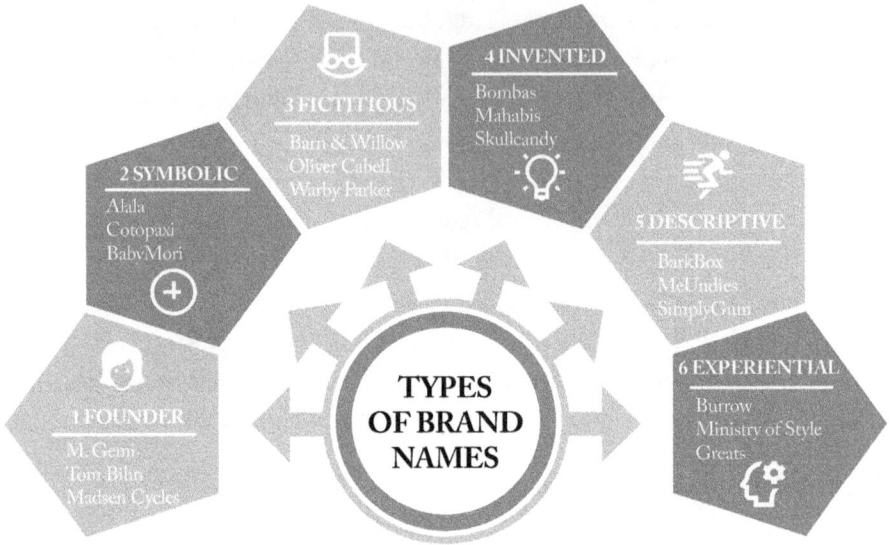

Types of Brand Names

4 INVENTED
Bombas
Mahabis
Skullcandy

3 FICTITIOUS
Barn & Willow
Oliver Cabell
Warby Parker

2 SYMBOLIC
Alala
Cotopaxi
BabyMori

5 DESCRIPTIVE
BarkBox
MeUndies
SimplyGum

6 EXPERIENTIAL
Burrow
Ministry of Style
Greats

1 FOUNDER
M. Gemi
Tom Bihn
Madsen Cycles

TYPES OF BRAND NAMES

2. Symbolic Names:

Names that symbolize a brand's purpose or identity:

Alala: the stylish sportswear eCommerce brand. From their website: "ALALA is a Greek goddess whose name signifies a battle cry, a call to arms. ALALA represents all that we aspire to be as modern women."

Cotopaxi: the innovative outdoor eCommerce brand. Their namesake is an active stratovolcano in the Ecuadorian region of the Andes and an important part of the local culture.

BabyMori: the organic-cotton baby clothing brand. The word "mori" means "forest" in Japanese, and the brand uses it as a nod to the purity of nature and its natural products.

3. Fictitious Names:

Like founder names, but the namesake is fictional or made-up:

Barn and Willow: the custom draped eCom brand, which we referred to previously under Intangibles in the Competition chapter.

Oliver Cabell: the custom designer footwear brand, which prides itself on building footwear on the "converging disciplines of art, craft, and technology."

Warby Parker: the original prescription eyewear eCommerce store. Their journey to choosing a brand name began in the New York Public Library when Warby Parker's founder Dave stumbled on a Jack Kerouac exhibition. In one of the displayed journals, Dave found the names Warby Pepper and Zagg Parker. As all four of the company's founders were strongly influenced by Kerouac, they decided to combine the two names, and Warby Parker was born.

4. Invented Names:

This name type uses made-up words:

Bombas: the cult-favorite sock startup that has donated 8 million pairs to homeless shelters since launching in 2013.

Mahabis: the London based label brand with its core product being the award-winning reinvention of the slipper.

Skullcandy: the company that designs and markets audio and gaming headphones, earphones, speakers, and more.

5. Descriptive Names:

Indicates what the company, product, or service is or does:

BarkBox: the subscription box filled with toys and treats for dogs.

MeUndies: the comfortable underwear store for men and women.

SimplyGum: the natural gum eCommerce brand.

6. Experiential Names:

These names build on the feeling or experience the brand delivers:

Burrow: the "couch in a box" brand. Their name mimics the comfort and security of nesting in one of their couches.

Ministry of Supply: the function-fashion eCom clothing brand. Ministry's apparel creates performance clothing for work and life so you can move freely, keep cool, and stay sharp.

Greats: the eCom footwear brand. They are passionate about building the best footwear in the game at the best price and passionate about building GREATS, a brand that they will be proud of and that you'll be proud to wear.

Five Characteristics to Test Your Brand Name

Do a quick assessment of your brand name by considering each of these characteristics:

1. Distinctive: How does the name stand out amongst the competition?
2. Sound: Say the name out loud. How does it sound? Is it easy to say? Is it poetic?
3. Stickiness: Is the name easy to remember? How many times do you have to hear it before you remember it?
4. Expression: Does the name demonstrate what your brand is all about? Does it fit your brand's personality?
5. Appearance: What does the word look like in print? Does it look as good as it sounds?

A brilliant brand name will excel in all five characteristics.

Naming Meniml

The name strikes a chord on several fronts.

Meniml is distinctive from other men's grooming brands, while also having a 3 beat alliterative sound.

The name leverages the hook of "minimal for men." It appeals to the functional aspects of what men desire from their skincare regimen – no fuss, no mess, and no excess.

The "ml" is also the abbreviation of milliliters, the unit of measurement used in most self-care products. But it also references that we package our products by measuring average monthly use - so at the end of the month, everything needs to be replenished at once, which is ideal for a subscription model.

A big bonus was the fact that the domain meniml.com was available for a whopping $7.99, certainly not the norm, but the extra creativity helped in securing the domain.

Overall, Meniml is both expressive and sticky and looks solid and streamlined in print.

The next step is to make the simple entry of Meniml in the 7C Canvas.

Now, it's time for you to choose your own brand's name.

MENIML 7C CANVAS

CORE

WHY DO YOU EXIST? PURPOSE.

To offer a new, complete model for today's man. Meniml seeks to bring together thousands of factionalized "men," providing examples and models that their own fathers, social peers, and role models could not.

WHAT DO YOU STAND FOR? VALUES.

- Independence
- Style – Cleanliness
- Self - Respect

essence DASHING

CUSTOMER

WHO'S YOUR AUDIENCE?

Jack is an 80's baby yet born with a timeless cool. Raised in Connecticut, always independent and curious, he engaged deeply with anything that interested him, from a stint one summer with a local circus, to busting and traveling his way across Europe each summer in between his English studies at Brown University. Since college, he's blogged, cheffed, worked as a journalist, boxing trainer, and even tried his hand at motorcycle racing after dropping in at a local contest and winning its $1,000 prize.

HOW DOES YOUR PRODUCT ELEVATE?

I am confident, stylish, self-reliant, handsome for well-groomed. I care about having quality tools for all of my daily needs, including grooming, and like them to be well-organized and essential.

COMMUNITY

WHAT CULTURAL GROUP DO WE IDENTIFY WITH?

Our community of men see our brand as a cultural rallying point. Unsatisfied with the comparative tribes of 'lumbersexuals,' metrosexuals, or aggro-'jock warriors,' but knowing they're more than sterilized stallions in corporate suits and ties, they look for relationships with other "modern classic" men, who are self-reliant, tough but fun, curious but principled, confident but vulnerable. In other words: "whole men." They don't want to sit around a crying, but they do want to feel a connection to others.

COMPETITION

HOW ARE YOU UNIQUE?

Meniml is the brand for today's adult Man who wants a one-stop, complete but simple grooming solution that goes beyond soap and shampoo (but below mascara and lipstick). It organizes, simplifies, and displays sequential skin, hair, and body maintenance products, stocking only the necessities for maximum male grooming. UNLIKE women's beauty products that have excess SKUs to sell more to the same customers, our product simplifies while adding pride & eliminating "shame" in complete grooming for Men. Our brand guides its user's in a new, integrated but complete model of being a Man in itself.

CREATIVES

NAMING

Meniml
www.meniml.com

LOGO

COLORS

TYPOGRAPHY

PACKAGING

CONTENT

STORY OF THE BRAND

BRAND STORIES

CHANNEL

YOUR BRAND TOUCHPOINTS

OWNED CHANNELS

SHARED CHANNELS

PAID CHANNELS

Logo

Part of your visual and verbal identity system, your logo is a key component that works in gestalt with a handful of other critical elements to form a coherent and compelling identity.

But what is a logo? Is it a name, or a name with unique colors, or a symbol, like the Twitter bluebird? Well, it's both and more.

Have you ever heard someone talking about a logo to a designer or brand geek about a logo and hear the response "what kind of logo?" and think "duh, it's a logo you dolt."

They're not being difficult: there are a dozen different types of logos.

One of our goals in this book is to break down branding to its most important and practical components and then remove anything irrelevant. But sometimes some useful options need to be discussed.

Here is a range of logotypes ranging from the literal to the abstract.

In eCommerce, based on our client work and certainly having a good sense of what is prevalent, 95% of the logos are Wordmarks.

THE SPECTRUM OF TYPES OF LOGOS

LITERAL

ABSTRACT

WORDMARK

Google

This style uses the brand name in type alone. Wordmarks have become trendy in recent years, a la tech startups - both for minimalism, and lower cost to produce.

LETTERFORM

NASA

Where individuals letters are custom designed.

COMBO MARK

THIRDLOVE

This style pairs a wordmark with a symbol or shape. Becoming so recognizable for your brand over time that it can eventually stand alone as your identity design.

EMBLEM

ASSEMBLY
·36·

Using a more traditional emblematic style: best for traditional or legacy-based brand names and marks.

MASCOT LOGO

Just like it sounds, and analogous to a sports team, where a human or near-human (animal) represents the entity.

PICTORIAL MARK

Purely symbolic, but with a literal reference (e.g. a bird).

ABSTRACT MARK

Purely symbolic, but without a literal reference.

Meniml Logo

By taking the first step of naming the skincare line Meniml, the next step of choosing a logotype made the process much easier. Meniml's association with "minimal" suggested opting for a simple wordmark with the relevant type treatment, which we will discuss in the Typography section.

We went through the following variations, all with the intent of striking the minimal aspect:

MENIML

BurfordRusticLine

meniml

Helvetica Neue LT W1G Thin

meniml

Futura

meniml

Libre Franklin

meniml

PF DinDisplay Pro

Ultimately, we chose the middle variation as our logo. You'll find an in-depth discussion on why we went with the Futura logo in the typography section. For now, we'll add the logo to the 7C Canvas.

MENIML 7C CANVAS

◈ CORE

WHY DO YOU EXIST? PURPOSE.

To offer a new, complete model for today's man. Meniml seeks to bring together thousands of factionalized "men," providing examples and models that their own fathers, social peers, and role models could not.

essence
DASHING

WHAT DO YOU STAND FOR? VALUES.

- Independence
- Style – Cleanliness
- Self-Respect

✿ CUSTOMER

WHO'S YOUR AUDIENCE?

Jack is an 80's baby yet born with a timeless cool. Raised in Connecticut, always independent and curious, he engaged deeply with anything that interested him, from a stint one summer with a local circus, to busting and traveling his way across Europe each summer in between his English studies at Brown University. Since college, he's bagged, crafted, worked as a journalist, boxing trainer, and even tried his hand at motorcycle racing after dropping in at a local contest and winning its $1,000 prize.

HOW DOES YOUR PRODUCT ELEVATE?

I am confident, stylish, self-reliant, handsome (or well-groomed). I care about having quality tools for all of my daily needs, including grooming, and like them to be well-organized and essential.

⚔ COMMUNITY

WHAT CULTURAL GROUP DO WE IDENTIFY WITH?

Our community of men see our brand as a cultural rallying point. Unsatisfied with the comparative tribes of lumbersexuals, metrosexuals, or jagoff–jock warriors, but knowing they're more than sterilized stallions in corporate suits and ties, they look for relationships with other "modern classic" men, who are self–reliant, tough but fun, curious but principled, confident but vulnerable. In other words, "whole men." They don't want to sit around a sweat lodge hugging other men and crying, but they do want to feel a connection to others.

◉ COMPETITION

HOW ARE YOU UNIQUE?

Meniml is the brand for today's adult Man who wants a one-stop, complete but simple grooming solution that goes beyond soap and shampoo (but below mascara and lipstick). It organizes, simplifies, and displays sequential skin, hair, and body maintenance products, stocking only the necessities for maximum male grooming. UNLIKE women's beauty products that have access SKUs to sell more to the same customers, our product simplifies while adding pride & demanding "shame" in complete grooming for Men. Our brand guides its use's in a new, integrated but complete model of being a Man in itself.

◎ CREATIVES

NAMING

Meniml
www.meniml.com

LOGO

meniml

COLORS

PACKAGING

TYPOGRAPHY

☰ CONTENT

STORY OF THE BRAND

BRAND STORIES

◳ CHANNEL

YOUR BRAND TOUCHPOINTS

OWNED CHANNELS

SHARED CHANNELS

PAID CHANNELS

Color

Color is an important part of visual perception, and it is also a key consideration for reflecting your brand's core essence and personality in your brand's identity design.

Color influences an audience emotionally and is often the first thing people notice when they interact with a brand. If used correctly, it has the power to create positive associations and improve recognition with an audience. If misused, it can confuse or drive an audience away.

This is often a good starting point for considering your brand's expanded color scheme. It is common for brands to have a primary color and one or two accent colors, but accent colors will open up a world of opportunity for integrating dynamic designs and functionality within your branding. We encourage all new brands to define a full-color palette with their design firm before creating branded materials. Defining this palette will ensure consistency and help you achieve a unified look and feel across all brand atmosphere touchpoints.

Keep in mind, the meanings of color shift between cultures and subcultures, so it's important to carefully consider the emotions and meaning each color and hue communicate, and whether this meaning shifts in various markets. Red—the color of blood—is often associated with vitality, heat and anger; blue—because of its connection to clear sky and calm water—regularly plays soothing roles within designs and works of art. But not all color associations are universal: for instance, in India, red's primary association is purity and spirituality, hence why it's the traditional color of wedding dresses. This role is associated with white in much of the West, but in many Asian countries, white is associated with death, mourning, and is worn at funerals. These are general associations, and we'll share a detailed list of common associations for 9 key colors to provide directional guidance for choosing your brand colors. But if your brand has international reach, do keep the different, culture-specific color associations of your brand color in mind.

THE PSYCHOLOGY OF COLOR

WHITE: relates purity, simplicity, cleanliness

GRAY: points to balance, neutrality

BLACK: signals power, sophistication, mystery

BROWN: conveys ruggedness, reliability, endurance

RED: suggests strength, love, danger, excitement

ORANGE: symbolizes creativity, determination, and success

YELLOW: represents freshness, happiness, and optimism

GREEN: signifies nature and sustainability

BLUE: communicates trust, security, competence

PURPLE: hints at glamor, elegance, style

PINK: associated with caregiving, femininity, and beauty

Three Primary Color Processes (Based on Specific Media Uses)

It is important to get quickly acquainted with the three primary color processes, as it will provide you with background information when you work with a designer.

RGB **Digital & Web**
(What you see on screen)

CMYK **Standard Print**

PMS **Production Print**
(e.g. Packaging)

CMYK (Cyan, Magenta, Yellow, Black): Best option for digitally printed media. This process contains four percentage values for cyan, magenta, yellow, and black. For example, a pure yellow is represented as C0 M0 Y100 K0.

PMS (Pantone Matching System): Universal color system for printing standards to maintain high quality on traditional printing presses. This is used for print jobs that require precise color matching, and because all of your brand's communications should look consistent, we recommend choosing Pantone colors to match CMYK jobs. It's as simple as telling the digital print vendor that the orange should be matched as closely as possible to Pantone 165C. Knowledge of the PMS color process is also critical for any *brand packaging production*.

RGB (Red, Green, Blue): Used for digital display because each color combination is projected in the form of light rays. This model contains three color values from 0 to 255 for red, green, and blue. Yellow, for example, would read R225 G255 B0.

COLOR AND BRANDING

Color helps boost brand perception
Research shows that color increases brand recognition by over 80%, so selecting a consistent color scheme can help create a sense of attachment with consumers. Choosing the right colors can also create positive associations in the minds of consumers.

Color attracts attention
It's proven that color images hold attention far more than double the time of black-and-white images. However, you must pick the right colors; the wrong decision can be a catastrophic failure as it was for Pepsi with their blue "Crystal Pepsi." Or Heinz's green ketchup (once initial interest subsided).

Colors help emphasize or conceal information
Fine print, for example, is often shown in grey scale to avoid catching the attention of viewers. Likewise highlighting conversion points and the right information can drive sales.

Color helps you appeal to the right audience
Different colors appeal to different demographics. The attention of children is caught by a different color code than what attracts women or men. Choose colors in your design scheme that target your ideal audience.

Use color to shape perception
See graphic on the preceding page for the psychology of color.

Color helps an audience process information better
Color-coding information can boost memory. Research has found that color can improve readership by 40%, learning from 55-78% and comprehension by 73%.

Meniml Color Choice

With Meniml, we selected *two* primary brand colors based on how they worked together to communicate the appropriate meaning of "Meniml."

Part of Meniml's underlying product and brand value is "simplicity," or minimalism and essentialism, to help our customers carry this over into other areas of their life.

When segmenting the market, we discovered a need to define a simplified, integrated, and new model of masculinity which borrows from various subcultures but creates a unique, compelling whole. This "minimalism as *ethos*" needs to carry through to everything about the brand and its products, so for our color choice, we started by looking at a "blank canvas" color for packaging, web, etc. In the broader beauty category, white is a common background color choice, but this is predictable and overused. Apple was one of the first modern brands (in the U.S., as it was more common in Japan) to use a white canvas for packaging. As a new men's brand, which we hope will define its own category, our canvas color is black. Black is luxurious, but also mysterious, just like the Meniml customer who is multidimensional. Tough, but fun and tender, decisive, but smart and thoughtful. Black is on-brand.

The secondary color needed to be, understandably, strong to stand out against the black. A blue hue would be predictable as a secondary color, and it's used heavily in multiple markets, including the beauty category. Red, in general, is overused in male-centric categories, but it does depend on the particular hue. Fire-engine red tends to communicate aggression, anger, and excitement. Or moving down towards pink (nurturing, caring), the passionate/love warmer red. Crimson, however, is a deeper red, the color of royalty AND rebellion. It's more controlled and sophisticated, like a Meniml man.

Next, we will add the Meniml colors, of black and crimson, to the 7C Canvas.

MENIML 7C CANVAS

◈ CORE

WHY DO YOU EXIST? PURPOSE.

To offer a new, complete model for today's man, Meniml seeks to bring together thousands of factionalized "men," providing examples and models that their own fathers, social peers, and role models could not.

essence
DASHING

WHAT DO YOU STAND FOR? VALUES.

- Independence
- Style – Cleanliness
- Self–Respect

💬 CUSTOMER

WHO'S YOUR AUDIENCE?

Jack is an 80's baby yet born with a timeless cool. Raised in Connecticut, always independent and curious, he engaged deeply with anything that interested him, from a stint one summer with a local circus, to busting and traveling his way across Europe each summer in between his English studies at Brown University. Since college, he's blogged, crafted, worked as a journalist, boxing frames, and even tried his hand at motorcycle racing after dropping in at a local contest and winning its $1,000 prize.

HOW DOES YOUR PRODUCT ELEVATE?

I am confident, stylish, self–reliant, handsome (or well–groomed). I care about having quality tools for all of my daily needs, including grooming, and like them to be well–organized and essential.

⚙️ COMMUNITY

WHAT CULTURAL GROUP DO WE IDENTIFY WITH?

Our community of men see our brand as a cultural rallying point. Unsatisfied with the combative tribes of lumbersexuals, metrosexuals, or aggro–jock warriors, but knowing they're more than sterilized stallions in corporate suits and ties, they look for relationships with other "modern classic" men, who are self–reliant, tough but fun, curious but principled, confident but vulnerable. In other words: "whole men." They don't want to sit around a sweat lodge hugging other men and crying, but they do want to feel a connection to others.

◎ COMPETITION

HOW ARE YOU UNIQUE?

Meniml is the brand for today's adult Man who wants a one–stop, complete but simple grooming solution that goes beyond soap and shampoo (but below mascara and lipstick). It organizes, simplifies, and displays sequential skin, hair, and body maintenance products, stocking only the necessities for maximum male grooming. UNLIKE women's beauty products that have access SKUs to sell more to the same customers, our product simplifies while adding pride & eliminating "shame" in complete grooming for Men. Our brand guides its user's in a new, integrated but complete model of being a Man in itself.

◉ CREATIVES

NAMING
Meniml
www.meniml.com

LOGO
meniml

COLORS

TYPOGRAPHY

PACKAGING

▤ CONTENT
STORY OF THE BRAND

BRAND STORIES

◪ CHANNEL
YOUR BRAND TOUCHPOINTS
OWNED CHANNELS

SHARED CHANNELS

PAID CHANNELS

Typography

"Typography is visualized language" - eBB's Ren

Typefaces are an essential resource employed by graphic designers to convey brand meaning, just as architects employ glass, stone, steel, and other materials. The first typefaces were modeled on calligraphy, but we are so exposed to fonts today, that we often just see them as "letters." But typography translates words into designs that express meaning and emotion, which makes typography deeply relevant to brand work.

Typography is another layer of meaning behind the words you use when your brand speaks; it is the visual crossover of your verbal design. Be sure you're paying attention! Typography is one of the most important design elements in your branded materials. When you consider typography options with your design team, keep readability and brand cohesion at the forefront of your mind.

You want your chosen fonts to have attributes that support your brand identity without competing with your logotype font.

Is your brand modern and casual? If so, you may want to see sans-serif font options. Is it built on tradition, or does it speak to an older demographic? A serif font might be better suited.

You will also want to consider how your fonts communicate in different media (e.g., print, web). In addition, not all fonts are available with both web and print licenses, so be sure to verify these details before making your final decision.

Finally, don't neglect to consider how fonts transform at different sizes, weights, and colors.

Many times, it will make sense to have more than one typeface in your branding materials—for example, a highly stylized font for headers and a simpler font for larger blocks of text. But ideally, you want to select a single font family for your brand. That is, one distinctive font to display on all branded materials. As a baseline, aim for the same brand font in your web and print (e.g. packaging) materials for consistency. Worst-case scenario, find a similar font for "correspondence" like email, letters, etc. We use Century Gothic for this purpose as it's standard with most PC and iOS systems, so there is no issue with reformatting when emailing clients or people we correspond with.

It used to be that when our agency clients were migrating online, we'd use the "offline" brand fonts to drive the primary font selection for the web. Today with eCommerce being our exclusive focus, we maintain most communication via web, so now we prioritize "web fonts" that work offline as well. And while we, like many, are biased towards san serif fonts, it's *not* right for all brands.

Also, to clarify, if you use your name in your logo, all bets are off. You could very well be designing custom lettering for your logo, but even if you use a separate font family in the logo or wordmark, as long as you find similar, supporting brand fonts for everything else, you will still retain consistency.

What are the best "crossover" typefaces that work in print and web? For legibility, the cleanest and simplest, even when bolded, are the safest bet, but there is only a handful of "common" or widely used fonts that fit this description.

Here are some "common" but clean and elegant fonts that work well in most places, and while our personal preference is towards the hyper-modern san-serif, such as Futura, all of these fit the criteria of readability, elegance, versatility, and strength.

Futura
Aa Qq Rr
Aa Qq Rr

Minion
Aa Rr Qq
Aa Rr Qq

Sabon
Aa Ee Rr
Aa Ee Rr

Georgia
Aa Qq Rr
Aa Qq Rr

Franklin Gothic
Aa Ee Rr
Aa Ee Rr

Helvetica
Aa Ee Rr
Aa Ee Rr

Keep in mind: you should also look at the range of fonts in your chosen typeface's family. They can look very different in italics or bold formatting. And often, there are several styles within each set of typeface beyond bold and italics. This is a positive as it gives you flexibility without losing consistency. There is no more obvious case of a "brand amateur" than using multiple typefaces in core areas. Even if the average consumer doesn't consciously notice the inconsistent use of typography, they will at least "feel" something is off. But if you can find a broad typeface family, you can get away with using multiple variations within that family, which helps you maintain consistency without constraining your creativity. Here, for example, is a "modern classic" font in all of its family's variations (Adobe Garamond Pro), aka 20 years old, but still very versatile:

ANATOMY OF A TYPE FAMILY · ADOBE GARAMOND PRO, *designed by Robert Slimbach, 1988*

The roman form is the core or spine from which a family of typefaces derives.

ADOBE GARAMOND PRO REGULAR

The roman form, also called plain or regular, is the standard, upright version of a typeface. It is typically conceived as the parent of a larger family.

Italic letters, which are based on cursive writing, have forms distinct from roman.

ADOBE GARAMOND PRO ITALIC

The italic form is used to create emphasis. Especially among serif faces, it often employs shapes and strokes distinct from its roman counterpart. Note the differences between the roman and italic a.

SMALL CAPS HAVE A HEIGHT THAT IS SIMILAR TO the lowercase X-HEIGHT.

ADOBE GARAMOND PRO REGULAR (ALL SMALL CAPS)

Small caps (capitals) are designed to integrate with a line of text, where full-size capitals would stand out awkwardly. Small capitals are slightly taller than the x-height of lowercase letters.

Bold (and semibold) typefaces are used for emphasis within a hierarchy.

ADOBE GARAMOND PRO BOLD AND SEMIBOLD

Bold versions of traditional text fonts were added in the twentieth century to meet the need for emphatic forms. Sans-serif families often include a broad range of weights (thin, bold, black, etc.).

Bold (and semibold) typefaces each need to include an italic version, too.

ADOBE GARAMOND PRO BOLD AND SEMIBOLD ITALIC

The typeface designer tries to make the two bold versions feel similar in comparison to the roman, without making the overall form too heavy. The counters need to stay clear and open at small sizes. Many designers prefer not to use bold and semi-bold versions of traditional typefaces such as Garamond, because these weights are alien to the historic families.

Italics are not *slanted* letters.

TRUE ITALIC

TYPE CRIME:
PSEUDO ITALICS
The wide, unguinly forms of these mechanically skewed letters look forced and unnatural.

Some italics aren't slanted at all. In the type family Quadraat, the italic form is upright.

QUADRAAT, *designed by Fred Smeijers, 1992.*

Meniml's Chosen Font Family

This was an interesting one, because typically "men's brands" use many of the same motifs and design elements, including thick and blocky typeface. As mentioned in the discussion of Meniml's colors, our model for Man 2.0, Meniml men are still strong but don't exhibit the type of strength that needs to puff its chest out. It stands up for itself, or perseveres, but is confident and thus does not need to yell. At the same time, we couldn't use a consistently ultra-thin font as it would likely transform our packaging from "minimal" to illegible! We used a "secret style" font, used by a handful of designers and creators, including Nabokov and Stanley Kubrick, which is very recognizable, but simply not trendy since it's not well known. We included an example of this earlier: Futura.

Futura

Aa Qq Rr

Aa Qq Rr

Zuführung

a b c d e f g h i j k l m
n o p q r s t u v w x y z
0123456789

Futura is elegant, strong, understated, but still has personality. It is Meniml's "ginger" to Helvetica's "tofu." It's bold yet elegant and stands out on packaging, and its regular weight is clean enough that we don't have to go above 14 points to make a statement.

Most importantly, Futura matches Meniml's ethos of minimalism and simple aesthetics. The typeface's designer, Paul Renner, didn't want to rely on past designs and instead used near-perfect circles, triangles, and squares to shape the letters. He also gave them near-perfect weight. Balance and simplicity are exactly what Meniml attempts to bring to its self-care line, and its approach to masculinity.

As we usually do, I will now place the chosen font family in the 7C Canvas.

Switching over to you, and if you are working with a designer, choose a font family that would be apt for you based on the core development work that you have already done.

MENIML 7C CANVAS

CORE

WHY DO YOU EXIST? PURPOSE.

To offer a new, complete model for today's man. Meniml seeks to bring together thousands of factionalized "men," providing examples and models that their own fathers, social peers, and role models could not.

essence
DASHING

WHAT DO YOU STAND FOR? VALUES.

- Independence
- Style – Cleanliness
- Self-Respect

CUSTOMER

WHO'S YOUR AUDIENCE?

Jack is an 80's baby yet born with a timeless cool. Raised in Connecticut, always independent and curious, he engaged deeply with anything that interested him, from a stint one summer with a local circus, to busing and traveling his way across Europe each summer in between like English studies at Brown University. Since college, he's blogged, crafted, worked as a journalist, boxing trainer, and even tried his hand at motorcycle racing after dropping in all at a local contest and winning its $1,000 prize.

HOW DOES YOUR PRODUCT ELEVATE?

I am confident, stylish, self-reliant, handsome (or well-groomed). I care about having quality tools for all of my daily needs, including grooming, and like them to be well-organized and essential.

COMPETITION

HOW ARE YOU UNIQUE?

Meniml is the brand for today's adult Men who wants a one-stop, complete but simple grooming solution that goes beyond soap and shampoo (but below mascara and lipstick). It organizes, simplifies, and displays sequential skin, hair, and body maintenance products, stocking only the necessities for maximum male grooming. UNLIKE women's beauty products that have excess SKUs to sell more to the same customers, our product simplifies while adding pride & eliminating "shame" in complete grooming for Men. Our brand guides its user's in a new, integrated but complete model of being a Man in itself.

COMMUNITY

WHAT CULTURAL GROUP DO WE IDENTIFY WITH?

Our community of men see our brand as a cultural rallying point. Unsatisfied with the contrative tribes of lumbersexuals, metrosexuals, or aggro-jock warriors, but knowing they're more than sterilized stallions in corporate suits and ties, they look for relationships with other "modern classic" men, who are self-reliant, tough but fun, curious but principled, confident but vulnerable. In other words, "whole men." They don't want to sit around a sweat lodge hugging other men and crying, but they do want to feel a connection to others.

CREATIVES

NAMING

Meniml
www.meniml.com

LOGO

meniml

COLORS

TYPOGRAPHY

Futura

PACKAGING

CONTENT

STORY OF THE BRAND

BRAND STORIES

CHANNEL

YOUR BRAND TOUCHPOINTS

OWNED CHANNELS

SHARED CHANNELS

PAID CHANNELS

Packaging

The Importance of Packaging

- A third of purchase decisions are based on packaging.[23] In fact, for many products, when we think about or visualize products, we don't picture the product itself but its packaging. When you think of Coke, for example, do you imagine the liquid or the bright red can? Emotional connections are often formed around packaging rather than products, and a unique look can also serve as visual differentiation from your direct competitors.

- Businesses with strong packaging report a 30% increase in consumer interest.[24] Aside from giving your products physical protection, great packaging addresses 3 core questions consumers have about any product: Do I need this? Will it improve my life or make it easier? Is it a good value? Of course, these questions have emotional as well as rational answers, and packaging can help you strongly position your products in the minds of consumers, influencing purchase decisions and increasing interest in your brand.

- 52% of consumers say they'd return to a business for another purchase if their order arrives in premium packaging. Not only do roughly 90% of consumers re-use packaging (such as tissue paper and boxes),[25] but premium packaging sends the message that you believe in the quality of your products and stand behind them. Premium packaging thus powerfully contributes to consumer trust (so long as the products keep your brand promise, of course).

- Packaging can boost social media presence: 40% of consumers share photos of packaging when it's interesting or of gift-like quality,[26] pop-media even has a new description for great packaging design, "Instagram Worthy Packaging Design."

- 74% of young adults post pictures of packaging online.[27] Great packaging delights customers, but these kinds of photos of your packaging can help build your brand awareness if it's photogenic enough to share.

- Packaging should express a brand's persona and have readable text to encourage customers to spend more time looking at it. Choose key benefits of your products to highlight on your packaging. You can effectively target your ideal customers if you identify the benefits most important to them. By displaying your brand's personality in the visual design and the copy, you ensure consistent brand identity and help your products make their way into the hands of the right customers. It also creates a coherent brand experience.

- Customers also appreciate simple packaging if it's made with sustainable materials. Sustainable packaging is a particularly smart approach if it's in line with your brand's values. However, it can benefit most brands as customers are increasingly looking to do business with companies that consider their wider impact on their community and the environment.

- With unboxing becoming more meaningful, packaging is an important element of a brand's story and the customer experience. Your product packaging is often one of the first physical touchpoints consumers have with your brand. Having great packaging can effectively set-up expectations, create excitement, and build trust.

Example of recent packaging design completed by the eBB team for new Swiss Wearable-Tech Athleticwear.

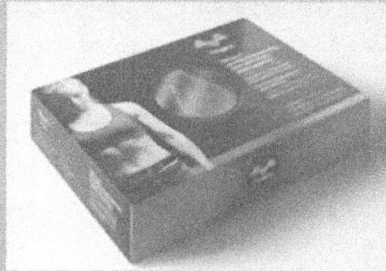

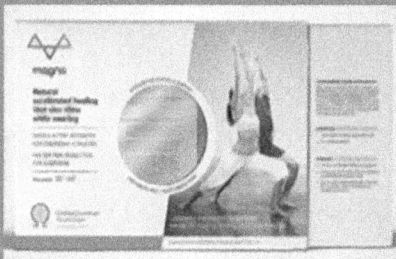

Separate package design for 2 different channels with Persona reflective models for photoshoot.

Above: eCom & Specialty
Left: Mass & Drug

- Unboxing and "haul" videos are both in the top 10 most popular video types on YouTube. In our visually intense, "sharing" culture, having aesthetically pleasing packaging is becoming a marketing method in its own right.

- Make sure packaging has visual continuity with your brand colors, logo, and style. As you can see, your product packaging is an integral part of your brand's identity, so it needs to be consistent with the look and feel of your brand. Part of fulfilling your brand promise is ensuring your identity and communications are consistent and reliable, so you want your packaging to align with every element of your brand.

- Packaging sends the message that you care about the product and the customer experience. Remember, the bottom-line practical function of packaging is to protect the product. The quality and care that goes into your product, therefore, reflect the quality and care given to your products and the customer experience. Premium, gift-like quality packaging also sends the message that your brand is proud of what you offer customers.

Meniml's Creative Strategy for Packaging

The men's grooming sub-category, up until the 2000s, has been relatively undefined and limited to development in a handful of product segments: with shaving being the predominant focus. However, since the 1970s, a high concentration of gay men have fueled growth in the women's skin and hair care categories, despite not being directly marketed to.

More recently, leading female-focused brands have experimented with repackaging products for men, specifically in "anti-aging" areas such as in-home hair coloring. However, there are two trending segment "definers" in the millennial generation that have pushed new developments to cater to the cultural split between the new "metrosexual" and the new "mountain/barbarian man."

Established fashion brands extended into fragrances, specifically to target the rise of the metrosexual man, like Calvin Klein's flagship "androgynous" product, "CK One" with moderate success. Likewise, the millennial "beard tribe" social trend has been capitalized upon by beard-centric hair care and grooming niche brands, most notably, Beard Brands.

COLOR DISPLAY

Should be attractive to the target market, set the right tone, and send a message of what your product is. Brighter colors pop and are fun, but less serious. White denotes innocence, cleanliness, and simplicity. Black power, control and luxury. Red is exciting. Green denotes harmony; often associated with eco-friendly products.

BRAND SPILLOVER

About 52% of online consumers say they would likely return to a business for another purchase, if they receive products in premium packaging. 90% reuse product packaging boxes and bags after purchase.

GREAT PASS-ALONG

A study shows that young adults (18-25) are 74% more likely to share a photo of product packaging through social media when the product has been ordered online. 40% would share packaging on social media if it was interesting.

TYPOGRAPHY DISPLAY

Fonts have personalities that may be elegant, cool, austere, delicate and straightforward.

PACKAGING INFLUENCE IS SUBCONSCIOUS

First impressions take about 7 seconds, making subsequent judgements based on quick info. Your packaging represents your brand's promise to deliver a quality experience. Your brand is represented by your product packaging, the same as your landing page, funnel, website, lead magnet etc.

CONS

Packaging that includes brand icons taps into the hearts and minds of consumers and reminds consumers of the quality and personal experience associated with the product.

CONVENIENCE

Effective product packaging helps the consumer quickly find the brand and specific product variant.

AESTHETICS

Draw consumer attention. Research suggests a third of product decision making is based on packaging, along with personal preferences.

Meniml's Differentiation

We'll look at this from a combined product and brand perspective:

The category itself is not unique, but the target segment and men as a group in HBC is a newer development.

Our ingredients are organic – and each formulation aims for as few ingredients as possible while maintaining higher than average quality standards.

Most beauty and self-care products, particularly those targeted to women, are sized to maximize margins for the company. This leads to a lot of frustration as your face wash might need to be replenished long before (or after) your moisturizer, making these products a constant rotating presence on your shopping list. Meniml, by contrast, sizes by average monthly usage, so used consistently, each product will last a full month before needing to be replaced. This not only makes re-ordering easier (you make 1 purchase a month, not 1 every week), it's also ideal to offer a subscription model, further simplifying the process.

These are indisputable facts, not empty marketing claims. They also sync up with the aims of Meniml's customers and could be touted as product benefits.

Effective packaging combines all your brand's creative elements as well as expresses your brand's core values. This can be a tricky balancing act, but if you've done the deeper brand work and have designed your visual identity around these values, synthesizing these elements will be more straightforward.

Again, our packaging links back to our customer persona, the Rebel Royal. As we mentioned in their respective sections, name, logo/typography, colors, were all selected to express the Rebel Royal's approach to self-care and Meniml's vision of a more inclusive model for men today. By synthesizing all your brand elements into packaging, you ensure your products speak directly to the tribe of people who matter most.

MEN: GROOMING INTO BEAUTY AND
THE FACTIOUS MODELS OF "MAN" TODAY

Product Selection into Specific Package Formats

Because we know the behavioral associations and values of our target audience, it's fairly easy to figure out an initial product line.

Starting with a shower routine, Meniml's first product is a liquid body wash in a convenient pump-bottle, it's lightly scented with sandalwood-meets-vanilla and orange (a scent we keep consistent across all products and long-term could be developed into a branded cologne).

Next is a shampoo combined with conditioner, again with the same scent. Moving to skincare, Meniml offers soothing shaving gel, followed by a male pH balanced facial cream with healing oils and moisturizer.

Finally, there's a blended holding creme/gel for hairstyling that's light-holding and adds sheen - placed last as not all men use a hair styling product, so it's easy to omit without leaving a gap in the numbering system.

The Rebel Royal has quiet confidence: he knows he's awesome, and people can see it for themselves in his actions, so he doesn't have to boast. His scent is thus attractive, manly (sandalwood vs musk), but subtle and consistent.

To sum up, the product portfolio for the initial brand would include 5 different SKUs:

1. Body Wash
2. Conditioning Shampoo (2-in-1)
3. Shaving Gel
4. Face cream (heal & moisturize)
5. Blended Holding Crème/Gel

The category and product differentiators are simple and bold to simplify finding and application.

(We'll let the Dollar Shave guys handle the razors.)

The direction of the packaging speaks to authenticity with its ultra-minimalism. This is seconded by the fact that while the formulations for the products are both unique and specific for men's needs, customers can get more information easily from the Meniml site. Here they'll discover that each product is simply and exactly what the label says.

Based on the Packaging that we have chosen to proceed with, I will place the main SKU in the 7C Canvas.

Now it's your turn to think about your own brand's expression through brand packaging.

no fuss
no mess
no excess

body wash

menim|

BODY

MENIML 7C CANVAS

⬡ CORE

WHY DO YOU EXIST? PURPOSE.

To offer a new, complete model for today's man. Meniml seeks to bring together thousands of factionalized "men," providing examples and models that their own fathers, social peers, and role models could not.

essence **DASHING**

WHAT DO YOU STAND FOR? VALUES.

- Independence
- Style – Cleanliness
- Self-Respect

🎧 CUSTOMER

WHO'S YOUR AUDIENCE?

Jack is an 80's baby yet born with a timeless cool. Raised in Connecticut, always independent and curious, he engaged deeply with anything that interested him, from a stint one summer with a local circus, to busting and traveling his way across Europe each summer in between his English studies at Brown University. Since college, he's blogged, crafted, worked as a journalist, boxing trainer, and even tried his hand at motorcycle racing after dropping in at a local contest and winning its $1,000 prize.

HOW DOES YOUR PRODUCT ELEVATE?

I am confident, stylish, self-reliant, handsome (or well-groomed). I care about having quality tools for all of my daily needs, including grooming, and like them to be well-organized and essential.

⚒️ COMPETITION

HOW ARE YOU UNIQUE?

Meniml is the brand for today's adult Man who wants a one-stop, complete but simple grooming solution that goes beyond soap and shampoo (but below mascara and lipstick). It organizes, simplifies, and displays sequential skin, hair, and body maintenance products, stocking only the necessities for maximum male grooming. UNLIKE women's beauty products that have excess SKUs to sell more to the same customers, our product simplifies while adding pride & eliminating "shame" in complete grooming for Men. Our brand guides its user's in a new, integrated but complete model of being a Man in itself.

◎ CREATIVES

NAMING
Meniml
www.meniml.com

LOGO
meniml

PACKAGING

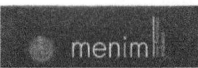
menim|

COLORS

TYPOGRAPHY
Futura

🤝 COMMUNITY

WHAT CULTURAL GROUP DO WE IDENTIFY WITH?

Our community of men see our brand as a cultural rallying point. Unsatisfied with the combative tribes of lumbersexuals, metrosexuals, or jagoff-jock warriors, but knowing they're more than sterilized stallions in corporate suits and ties, they look for relationships with other "modern classic" men, who are self-reliant, tough but fun, curious but principled, confident but vulnerable. In other words, "whole men." They don't want to sit around a sweat lodge hugging other men and crying, but they do want to feel a connection to others.

▤ CONTENT

STORY OF THE BRAND

BRAND STORIES

🖼️ CHANNEL

YOUR BRAND TOUCHPOINTS
OWNED CHANNELS

SHARED CHANNELS

PAID CHANNELS

eCommerce Examples

Jeni's is an eCommerce ice cream company. While it's hard to show their packaging in its full glory, they use a mix of vibrant colors and whimsical but detailed font and descriptions. Wait... did we mention Jeni's is an eCommerce ice cream brand? And a successful one. In this case, given all of its distribution is via express shipping and not on-premise, it was the brand communications and packaging that convinced its initial prospects to give them a shot, sight unseen and "flavor untasted," to be precise. And those initial tasters became a very vocal promotional committee from there, pushing the brand's last year calendar sales above the 7-figure mark.

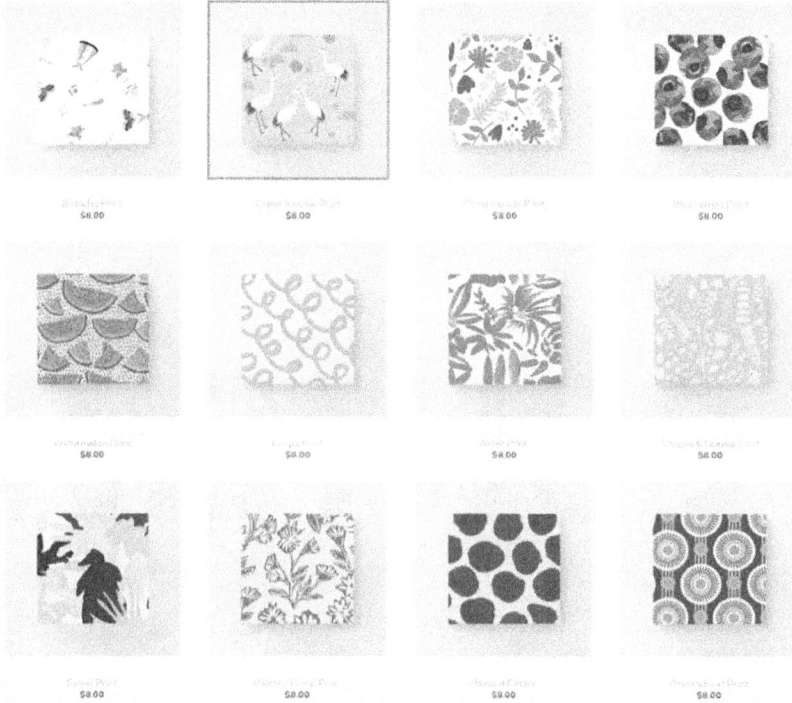

Greetabl, yet another successful eCommerce brand that we discussed earlier under Intangibles in the Competition section, is a custom-design greeting card company. Their package design, apart from being stellar, is interesting for 2 reasons. First, as a printed product, the designs shown on their site are, with a little trust, exactly what their customers will get. But second, this is also a case where the "Packaging *is* the Product!"

6.0
CONTENT

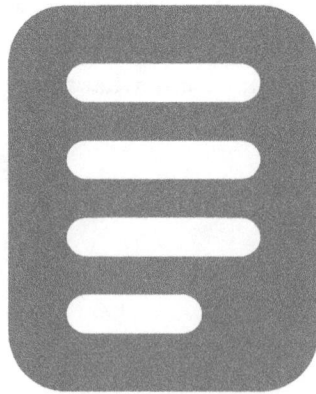

6.0 CONTENT

Introduction & Framework

Information is abundant out there from content-marketing experts who recommend different formats and stylistic directions, but don't really tell you how to create great content. And you have probably heard too many times that "marketing is about publishing great content," but there's rarely any guidance on how you should go about it.

Content marketing has been around for decades, but the reason it's become so popular over the last decade is that content is no longer controlled by media outlets, content specialists, and traditional publishers. This is why it is such a major opportunity for business owners and young brands. As David Scott, author of The New Rules of Marketing, has said:

"Prior to the Web, organizations had only two significant choices to attract attention: buy expensive advertising or get third-party ink from the media. But the Web has changed the rules."[28]

Many clients have hired great designers to "create content," but after weeks have elapsed, they see beautiful layouts come back with blank text. Others have hired copywriters, and then receive a big document which often sounds good, but has no perspective, and doesn't sound as if it came from their brand. This is ultimately a case of "doing things right," but not knowing what the right things to do are. The good news is, you can create better, more interesting, and high-quality content yourself, eliminating the need to train and hire a small team of outside specialists for your key pieces. This is what we'll teach you.

First of all, to create great content, the key is to *tell authentic and great stories*. Without realizing it, you're already creating content every day in your discussions with other people. Relating short stories about events, opinions, and people in your life is a natural human activity. If you can do it in your day-to-day life, you can certainly do it for your brand.

The essential difference is who your audience is. For content to be interesting, compelling, valuable, and entertaining, it has to be directed at your target customer. This is one of the major benefits of developing your brand's persona, as it helps you craft your voice and content to appeal directly to this ideal consumer. Anyone can be a great content marketer, as long as they can speak directly to a specific audience.

Wait... *a story?* Like: I grew up in a small town in the Midwest, where we'd all get together as a community for fairs, school events, and group sports. It was a happy and peaceful, idyllic place. Then, developers moved in and started buying people out of their own homes. Since I studied law, I gathered the community leaders and together, we fought a 5-year court case to eventually get back our land rights and homes. Today, the community has doubled in size, reinvigorated by this challenge. Our celebrations are even bigger, and the brain drain from the prior generation who'd moved away came back with their young families and have created new businesses and services. The town is stronger and more relevant than ever before.

Sure, this is a story: It has initial harmony, a challenge, a hero (or heroes) who come forward, conflict, then peace is restored.

But your brand stories don't have to be as complicated! This familiar pattern, "boy meets girl, boy loses girl, boy gets girl back, and they live happily ever after" is a simpler story, but it is just as exciting as the first one. It's also deeply compelling because it is an essential story. Because storytelling is a natural aspect of human communication, all you really need to do is find the right stories for your audience, infuse those stories with your brand voice and perspective, add authentic details and people will come to you to listen and then share. Content marketing is simply the core of sharing human stories and connecting. From a business and brand perspective, creating great content can and will:

- Attract customers.
- Educate your buyers about a purchase they are considering.
- Overcome resistance or address objections.
- Establish your credibility, trust, and authority in your industry.
- Tell your brand story.
- Build buzz via social networks.
- Build a base of fans and inspire customers to love you.
- Inspire impulse buys.

But you may ask, are we talking about blog posts and books? Not necessarily: stories can be embedded in dozens of formats; in fact, many consumers prefer smaller, visually oriented bite-sized content compared to longer formats like articles.

Technically, "content" is anything *created* and uploaded to a website: the words, images, tools, or other assets that reside there. All of the pages of your website, then, are content: the Home page, the About Us page, the Frequently Asked Questions (FAQ) page, the product/landing pages, and so on. All of the things you create as part of those pages or as part of your marketing — your videos, blogs, photographs, webinars, white papers, eBooks, podcasts, and so on — are content, too. And finally, all of the things you publish at outposts that are off your own site — your Facebook page, your Twitter stream, and your LinkedIn group page, for example —are *forms* of content. This does not mean you have to publish content through all of those channels and micro-channels to have an impact on your brand tribe. You only need to use the formats that your specific audience likes to consume the most, that best fit your brand and business goals, and that fit your talent and budget directives. We'll discuss these details at length in this chapter.

But the content you create will position your company and brand not just as a seller of products or services, but as a reliable source of information, which is a unique "product" in and of itself. Even for your most budget-conscious, left-brain customers, if you are providing entertaining or informative content, they will, consciously or subconsciously, apply the value of that information to the literal "total" value of your product. This economic framework, combined with the law of reciprocity, is what compels your content consumers to buy more of your products more often, and they'll be less sensitive to price comparisons with competitors.

The Changing Face of Content

Beckon, a lead marketing performance platform, recently found that "a small fraction of branded content, just 5% of it, accounts for 90% of engagement. The other 95% of a brand's content typically has single-digit views and likes."[29] And this 95% of wasted content is still being produced in old, run-down content factories.

Indeed, marketers are still:

- Creating content that serves no purpose, other than to pacify internal departments that are engaged in content marketing.
- Engaging in defunct methods of building links.
- Posting 500-word list posts thinking they are consumable.
- Pushing content through social organically.
- Repurposing topics that have already written about, with the same insights and perspective.
- Aggressively promoting products in blog posts.

Meanwhile, the brands producing the 5% of content that is sticky and viral are reaping all the benefits.

These savvy marketers have realized that to use content to build brand awareness, differentiate from competitors, secure customer loyalty, drive more traffic to product pages, and increase sales for their eCommerce stores, content must be approached differently than it has been over the past few years. These organizations are producing content that has a creative bend, that fits with the company's purpose and values aligns with their customer's expectations, and has an allocated budget for distribution. As a result of these efforts, they are generously rewarded by their readers/buyers. According to a study conducted by kapost.com, a SaaS content platform provider, the average conversion rate of sites with content marketing is 2.9%, compared to the average of sites without a content strategy at 0.5%.[30] This translates to almost 6 times more conversion, which in turn brings in more marketing dollars to outspend the competition, build a value-based relationship with customers, educate and guide customers towards a buying decision, and create positive brand appeal.

How do you create content that resonates with your audience? To answer this, we need to revisit the age-old tradition of storytelling. When you look at the current branded content landscape, very little of it uses story, whether it's to share your brand values or to give your customers a window into your brand's personality, which is the starting place for content that truly resonates and attracts customers.

Storytelling Drives Successful Content Marketing

In days of old, when we were still hunters and gatherers, our social lives took place around the glow of a campfire: women prepared the evening meal while their menfolk swapped stories of the day's hunt. It was here, too, that the tribe's elders handed down the myths and legends surrounding their gods and ancestors. Knowledge and experience were passed down through generations through these stories, and they helped shape the identity of the tribe, gave it values and boundaries, and helped establish its reputation among rivaling tribes.

It was storytelling in its purest form.

More recently, research in cognitive science has reaffirmed just how central storytelling is to our identities. Our brains are hardwired to recognize and process our worlds through a story. In fact, when we hear a great story - the neurons of the brain fire at five times the capacity, they bring us in and engross our attention.

Research using fMRI scans showed that when listening to a story, the areas of our brain that consistently light up are those associated with "theory of mind." This part of our brain imagines the motivations, intentions, beliefs, and feelings of others. In other words, our empathy is strongly triggered. And because we are so deeply engaged with the perspective of the protagonist of the story, be it a brand or individual person, the information is more easily encoded in our minds, and we remember it more readily. In addition, because we remember stories well, we're able to share them.

Essentially, stories are emotional delivery vehicles that appeal to the subconscious parts of the brain and the decision-making areas that assist in the buying process. Research reveals that these deeper realms of the mind have a far greater impact on our decisions (and purchase decisions) than do the conscious, logical areas. Stories reach into these depths and influence us to make subconscious, emotional, and sometimes "irrational" decisions (which is not necessarily anti-rational). And we justify those decisions logically and rationally later. All logic, data, and facts are trumped by the stories we encode and believe, and this resides in the part of the brain where we make decisions. Ultimately, stories trump facts.[31]

With the massive information overload in the digital space and an overabundance of choice and me-too products, unique brands and stories are becoming dominant differentiators. Storytelling sets the tone for your brand and brings your brand purpose and values to life. Because story connects so deeply to customers, guiding and shaping what they are thinking and feeling, focus on "how" you're communicating, not just "what."

Great stories change minds. They allow your customers to see your products in a different light and allow you to take them on an emotional journey. At their best, they can add meaning and context to our lives. This is, ultimately, the purpose of all this content that we are creating.

Stories not only help you connect with the right audience, but they can also create an audience.

As we'll demonstrate next, these Five C's also serve as relevant sources for stories.

The Two Types of Stories in Branding

eCommerce brands need to engage in two forms of storytelling: the brand story (or story of the brand), and brand storytelling.

Brand Story

This is the origin story of your brand. It delves into how your company came to be, including who started it, when, where, and why it was started, and the challenges you overcame to grow your business into what it is today. Your origin story provides the pillars of who you are and why you do what you do for consumers and the community. The story of the brand then serves as the foundation upon which all future stories (i.e., your brand storytelling) is based. As you can see, your brand story is thus tightly connected and interwoven with your brand's core work: your purpose, values, and essence. This foundational ethos should be present in any telling of your brand story and form its central emotional appeal.

Brand Storytelling

The storytelling type is led and guided by the brand story, the same way the themes and emotions of a superhero's origin story resonate and ripple through all of their subsequent adventures and challenges. Brand storytelling also reflects your brand strategy and will incorporate the insights you gained from the questions you answered in the Customer, Community, Competition

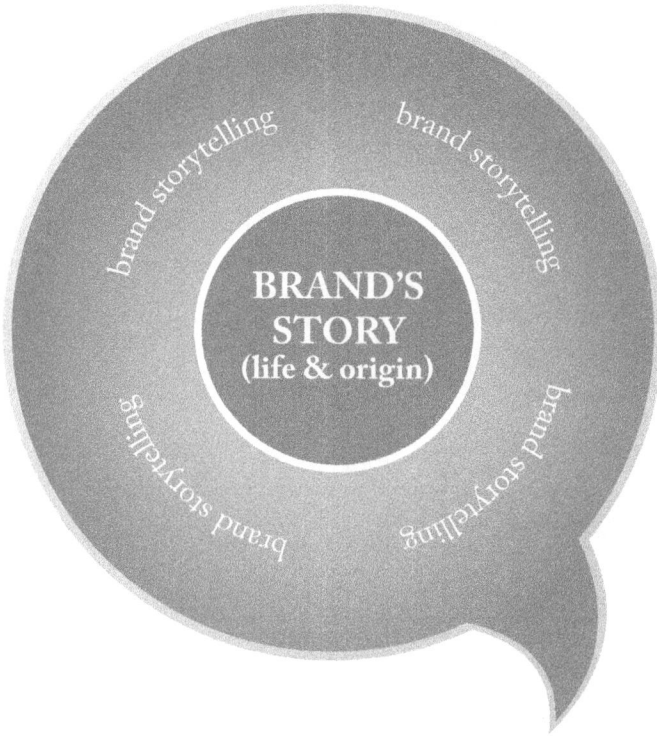

and Creatives sections. Brand storytelling translates your internally developed brand strategy into stories that customers connect to and love. Brand storytelling is how you communicate with and relate to customers in their world.

The difference between brand story and brand storytelling can seem slight, but there are important distinctions to get straight. That's why it's helpful to think of a superhero franchise. The origin of your brand, like that of a superhero, is fixed and mostly unchanging. It sets up all the themes, concerns, and the overall emotional tone of subsequent stories. It's in these later stories, in brand storytelling, where your brand, like a superhero, evolves, learns, and grows, all while staying in touch with your roots. To tailor this specifically to branding, brand story and brand storying differ across 4 dimensions: their definition, volume, objective, and form and delivery.

BRAND STORY VS. BRAND STORYTELLING

	BRAND STORY	BRAND STORYTELLING
DEFINITION	Your brand's story is the origin story of your brand and tells how your company came to be. It includes who started it, when/where/why it was started, and the challenges of birthing agonizing, and growing it, and how you overcome them to become what it is today. Your origin story provides the pillars of who you are and why and what you do for others. The story of the brand then guides all future stories i.e., it's what your brand storytelling is based upon.	Brand storytelling is led and guided by the story of the brand. It's a by-product of your core brand strategy and results from the responses to the individual questions that you've answered for your Company, Customer, Community, Competition & Creatives. Brand storytelling bridges the gap between your internally developed brand strategy and how that is conveyed & relayed to your customers.
VOLUME	As a singular origin story, the story of your brand is set, and continues to act as a central reference point for your day-to-day storytelling. The story of your brand can evolve over time, as time has passed, but its essentials never change.	Brand storytelling supports that Core. The story of the brand can be seen as the daily proof or behavior in the real-world of the brand.
OBJECTIVE	The role of the story of the brand is strategic and more broadly guiding.	Brand storytelling is tactical, how your brand expresses itself though social, paid media, & PR. It's the daily execution of content that shares the perceptions of buyers towards your brand.
FORM+ DELIVERY	The story of the brand primarily resides on the "About" page of your website, and secondarily, at times, in the purpose/promise intro on a homepage.	Brand storytelling encompasses your Facebook Ads and posts, blog posts, videos, Tweets, Pins etc.

Definition:

As discussed.

Volume:

As a singular origin story, the brand story is set, and continues to act as a central reference point for your day-to-day storytelling. The story of your brand can evolve, but its essentials never change.

Brand storytelling supports this core, the story of the brand, and if anything, it can be seen as the daily proof of how the brand behaves in the real world.

Objective:

The role of the brand story is strategic and acts as a broad guide for all of a brand's content and storytelling. Whereas brand storytelling is tactical: it's how your brand expresses itself through social, paid media, and PR. It's the daily execution of content that helps to shape the perceptions of buyers towards your brand.

Form + Delivery:

The brand story primarily resides on the "About" page of your website, and secondarily at times in the introductory purpose/promise intro on the homepage.

Brand storytelling encompasses your Facebook Ads and updates, blog posts, videos, Tweets, Pins, etc.

Finding Your Brand Stories

You may have noticed that brand story has a lot in common with our first C, Core, especially your brand purpose. In fact, the other C's, Customer, Community, Competition, and Creatives, are all effective sources and germination points for all the content your brand will produce. Creating content that's inspired by the first 5 C's will also ensure that your content is fully aligned with your brand. This contributes to making your brand "sticky," as with every brand interaction, you'll be reinforcing your brand's core identity and essence. This makes customers more likely to choose your brand when they're ready to buy.

Let's see how you can use the first 5 C's to create compelling, aligned content with the eBrandBuilders' Content Creation Framework.

Here, you can clearly see how the "Story of the Brand" correlates with your Core, while brand storytelling lines up with Customer, Community, Competition and Creatives.

Meniml's Content

Taking the example of Meniml, let's look at how the framework allows you to create content that is in total alignment with your overall brand strategy.

Meniml's Brand Story

This story is, of course, tightly aligned with the brand's core.

Core Based Stories: These stories are aligned with your purpose, essence and values. For Meniml, we identified some of our values to be independence and self-respect. As such, our origin story is aligned with this set of values, as you will see on page 206.

Meniml's Brand Storytelling

Now, Meniml's storytelling can be crafted using the next 4 C's.

Customer Based Stories: These stories keep the customer at the forefront of all communication. In the case of Meniml, we would demonstrate results from the usage of our products through case studies, testimonials, and so on. We could also create customer profiles that highlight how our customers are living by the "Rebel Royal" ethos.

Community Based Stories: These stories would keep community events at the forefront. As Meniml community events are based around "urban scavenger hunts on mountain bikes," our stories would share event information, interviews, images, and highlight experiences.

Competitive Based Stories: For Meniml, we would feature some of our key differentiators versus our competition. These would be the selection of ingredients, the process of choosing our contract manufacturers, certifications, and our clear, numbered system for application.

Creatives Based Stories: This would encompass stories on how we came up with our logo, the origin of the name Meniml, why we opted for our

eBrandBuilders' CONTENT CREATION FRAMEWORK

CORE	CUSTOMER	COMMUNITY	COMPETITION	CREATIVES
• Why (Purpose)	• Who is your audience?	What is the larger group that they belong to?	What do you do uniquely better than most?	• Naming
• Company	• What are their needs, wants, and desires?			• Logo
• Stand				• Colors
• Essence	• What is the higher good?			• Typography
				• Packaging

BRAND STORY — BRAND STORYTELLING

CORE BASED STORIES	CUSTOMER BASED STORIES	COMMUNITY BASED STORIES	COMPETITIVE BASED STORIES	CREATIVES BASED STORIES
• Create "value" based stories.	• Create content mapping to sales funnel stage	• Encourage user-generated content	• Frame what differentiates you from competitors through comparison tables, visuals, etc.	• How did you come up with your company name?
• Share your "once upon a time"	• Produce content on customer interests vs. product	• Share images, videos on community activities and events		• What is the story behind your logo?
• Why did you select this niche?			• Conduct deep dive product reviews	• Why did you choose the colors that you chose?
• On topical topics, state your brand's position	• Through case studies, show client results			
• How did you choose your factories?	• Share customer service stories of your team going the extra mile			• How does packaging further extend your brand?
• How do you follow ethical practices?	• Share customer's compelling stories			
• What are the results of causes you support?	• Feature the latest research by experts in your category			
• How do you deliver on your promises?				

particular color palette, how and why we style our photos and videos the way we do, and so on.

As evident, working through such a framework allows you to build your content via storytelling in a structured fashion, covering all the bases. Additionally, it allows you to work through each section individually and then time your stories as you schedule your editorial calendar (which we explore later).

How to Shape Your Brand Stories

Don't be intimidated if you're not a writer. The good news is, you don't have to be to create compelling, effective brand content. With all the work you've done exploring and developing the first 5 C's in relation to your brand, content is easy. You now have a ready-made and exhaustless source for stories going forward. But now, the question is how to make sure these story *ideas* are delivered in a compelling and emotionally satisfying way, ensuring you're grabbing and holding the attention of your target audience. If this sounds impossible, don't worry, there are reliable, repeatable frameworks you can use to ensure every story you tell has a discernible, effective shape.

The Hero

First, remember this core principle: *the customer needs to be the main protagonist, the hero of the story.* Of course, the word "hero" conjures many dramatic images of defusing nuclear weapons, thrilling car chases, and epic battles. While these may be staples of storytelling in Hollywood blockbusters, heroism comes in many forms. From offering support to a friend in need to preparing for an event that brings everyone together to making a stranger feel welcome: all of these simple acts can rise to the level of heroism when they help us reconnect to each other. Heroes don't need to save the world to feel effective, competent, and empowered. In terms of brand storytelling, heroism can be found in any act that helps us feel whole. The solutions and guidance of brands can, therefore, transform the everyday into the heroic.

Frameworks for Brand Stories: the 6 Master Stories

Your eCommerce business has characters (a hero, a mentor, a villain) that all exist in a particular landscape (the setting). The hero (your buying customer) has a personal goal that she is trying to achieve. She also struggles with a villain or two (those pesky things that keep getting in the way). You are there to help her (to be their mentor or guide). Both of you have special powers and abilities: characteristics that make it possible for you to work together and succeed.

And all of this comes together in a plot: a particular framework that guides how the story unfolds. It begins with your brand purpose —your "Big Why"— and the impetus for how your business got started, the very start of our 7C framework.

Your business' "why" is the foundation for your brand story. This origin story will help you select certain metaphors, archetypes, symbols, and language for all your communications. For example, going back to our superhero analogy, consider Spiderman, who resolves to use his new-found powers for good after the tragic death of his uncle, who told him, "With great power, comes great responsibility." This is a lesson that ripples throughout Spiderman's decades of stories and adventures, as Peter Parker constantly finds a way to do the right thing, even when it's painful or inconvenient, to honor his uncle's legacy. Defining the themes and metaphors you'll carry forward from your brand story is thus critical to creating an emotional through-line in all of your brand storytelling that will engage customers and keep them interested.

When it's done well, your story unfolds in a way that's both familiar and engaging to your Hero/Buying Customer. Remember: everything you do to market your online store becomes a piece of that same story.

According to the experts, 99% of all stories ever told can be categorized at their most basic level into one of these seven plots, as outlined in Christopher Booker's book, The Seven Basic Plots: Why We Tell Stories, a 700+ page epic that took 34 years of research and writing to complete.

Likewise, every great brand aligns itself with one of these seven plots. To help you craft your brand story, I suggest that you take a look at the six most commonly employed plots (in terms of branding), and think about which one of these stories you want to tell:

OVERCOMING THE MONSTER

There is an evil force threatening our hero/world/humankind. The hero must fight and defeat the monster, which will be tough, but in the end, they taste victory, and receive the reward.

Pop Culture: Star Wars, James Bond, Independence Day

Brand examples: Many DTC brands fighting against the old traditional model of middlemen are bringing high-quality products at 30-60% off savings.

Prerequisite: The presence of an antagonist. What are you up against?

RAGS TO RICHES

Our protagonists starts out from humble beginnings, often outcast or poverty. But the tide changes, which results in the hero acquiring influence, riches, and a partner.

Pop Culture: The Wolf of Wall Street, Cinderella, The Memoirs of a Geisha.

Brand Example: Alibaba. 54-year-old Ma had applied for work at several places rejected by all, before being hired as a teacher at a local university, earning just $12 a month. Ma co-founded Alibaba with 17 others — some students —out of his apartment in 1999, starting as an online marketplace for businesses, fledgling for 4 years. Ma, is now Asia's second-richest man with a net worth of $44 billion.

Prerequisite: Reaching rock bottom with nothing on the anvil, and out of the blue comes the magic wand.

THE QUEST

With quest, the hero sets off in search of a specific price, overcomes hardships and temptations, till they are victorious. They may have weaknesses which have held them back in the past that they need to overcome to succeed.

Pop Culture: Raiders of the Lost Ark, The Princess Bride, Finding Nemo

Brands: Here brands place values at the forefront to battle obstacles. You see a lot of DTC brands battling against pollutants, chemicals, high prices, complexity, excesses. Soylent uses plant-based protein making it require less water and produces less CO_2 than livestock. Soylent drinks reduce food waste with a year-long shelf life and don't require refrigeration until opened, unlike fruits and vegetables that get tossed after a few days or weeks in the fridge.

Prerequisite: Your core Brand Purpose and Values, that serve as burning motivation to continue your path.

VOYAGE AND RETURN

While still based on a path, the Voyage and Return is markedly different from The Quest. On this journey, the hero goes to an unusual place, meets new characters, conquers the hazards and returns with wisdom.

Popular examples: The Odyssey, Gulliver's Travels

Brand examples: Cotopaxi and its gear-for-good. This plot is dependent on learning something—a better way—as a result of a journey. Starbucks' Howard Schultz learned from backpacking across Europe that coffee shops in America could be more than just donut transport vehicles.

Prerequisite: What "travels" that brought you wisdom you could bring back and share with the world.

COMEDY

A light-hearted story that involves confusion, miscommunication, and frustration, which results in chaos, and finally, a happy ending.

Pop Culture: Some Like It Hot, The Man Who Knew Too Little, The Jerk.

Brand Example: PooPourri is an example that uses a hilarious concept to illustrate an unfortunate situation in which their buyer might be faced with if they are not using their product. Comedy (& Tragedy-sidebar below) are tough to pull off as brand story plots/rallying points. Even Geico uses a solution-story ad to match every one of its viral comedic ads.

Prerequisite: Topics that can only be addressed with humor and are offensive otherwise.

REBIRTH

Rebirth is similar to Tragedy, except the protagonist rises from the dead better than before. The hero redeems themselves through reinvention and renewal, after facing a life-changing event.

Pop examples: Deadpool, How the Grinch Stole Christmas.

Brand examples: Shopify, Apple 2.0 - the return of Jobs. Shopify's founders didn't pivot by coming up with a new idea, but rather selling an idea they'd already had for a different company. They didn't like any eCommerce products on the market, so instead, they built their own. The shop wasn't successful, but they loved the storefront they built, so they decided to sell it to other businesses. The rest is history.

Prerequisite: Did your brand have to pivot? Did you as a founder restart your career through your new company?

Technically, there is another Master Story: Tragedy. The inverse of Comedy, here the story does not have a happy ending. Unlike other archetypes where they achieve victory, here the hero is generally a good character with some flaws and frustrations. Along their journey, they succumb to temptations and break societal rules, leading to their undoing and fall. To a storyteller, an audience uses Tragedy as a "purgative," that is they sympathize with, but do not identify with the protagonist. This is why there are plenty of pop-cultural references (think King Lear to Deer Hunter), but seldom do businesses and brands use this framework.

Master Stories at Work: Meniml's Origin Story

Part of the unique value Meniml provides is a "new," integrated role model for "what is a man." This model unifies several other factious segments into a more productive and stronger image of man. The story template that best brings this ethos to life is that of the Prodigal Son, or Voyage and Return.

The Origin of Meniml

(The following names are not fictitious, as you may have noticed, they are the same names on the cover of this book.)

Neil and Ren were discussing some recent branding work late one night, when the topic of men's beauty brands came up. Neil had been studying the space after purchasing a starter kit from Brickell, a men's skincare brand online. Offering a mini-review, he explained to Ren, "The products work, and they are reviewed well, but something feels like it's missing. I'm not even sure I need this SPF cream, a morning moisturizer, *and* a night moisturizer... but they work. There are just so many options that I ended up buying a starter kit. And it has me thinking; I really believe there's a place for another men's beauty brand."

Neil has founded –and sold– a portfolio of natural beauty related eCommerce businesses, so he has a solid background in natural formulations and materials for health. In addition, Ren just came off a 3-month development project for L'Oréal, working on the beauty upstart Gaia, and he also has experience with other men's brands: Haggar and Porsche. Ren shared an observation he had recently reached while working with Gaia: "A week ago, I might have been a bit more skeptical about launching another men's beauty brand. But while we were looking at opportunities for Gaia, I realized they have product innovation, but they're over-SKU'ed in an over-branded space. And comparing the segments to target men today, compared to a decade ago, I realized branders are overlooking something critical, something that might be a huge opportunity." Now, Neil was intrigued.

Ren explained, "Everyone focuses on women as a buying group and logically so since they either make or influence the majority of purchase decisions. But when marketers targeted men a decade ago, the only segments they focused on were defined by demographics: age and income. But over the last few weeks, looking at today's male segments, I noticed something *culturally* very different.

"What I've noticed is that culturally, we're in an interesting place for men. There are now multiple subcultural segments and different models for "what is masculinity." And these segments aren't defined by age, they're cross-generational, especially with Millennials and Gen Xers, who'd likely be our age demo.

"Of course, there have always been male subcultures, like punks in the '80s, but these segments have always been minorities, somewhere between 1-5% of the population. But now, there's no longer a major model for men. Instead, there are four "dominant" models, each of which represents just above 10% of the population. But from all the conversations we had with men in these groups, there's still a "missing" model that integrates all of the positive associations from each into a modern man.

"For example, the neo-warrior subculture is almost cultish, but it prioritizes physical strength so much that it neglects qualities like intellectual strength and creativity. These attributes and values are important today to any man or woman.

"I think there's a real identity gap for men... and the right brand identity could serve as a guide for thousands of men, almost like a role model as to 'what is a real man today.'"

This made sense to Neil, and things clicked into place, "I get it. Something that cuts through the noise and offers a simple but inclusive model of masculinity. I was thinking we can call it 'Meniml.'"

"Hell yeah! Minimal for men?"

"Exactly," Neil explained, "men are buying more beauty care products today than ever before...look at the numbers."

"I did, but it isn't clear how any of those brands define a "man." It doesn't seem like Brickell and the others really have a focused target. Like the model for women in the '50s, "men" is just spiritual tofu."

Neil agreed but suggested there were practical concerns with modern men's beauty brands as well, "Well, the biggest customer complaint is still that no one provides a clear regimen."

Ren was inspired, "Holy $h##! What if we simplified packaging and only sold a specific set that met the baseline needs for a complete regimen. We could even number it, so it's self-organizing for the user, which will save time in application and use. You know, when we were creating packaging mocks at

Gaia, none of the sizings for packaging was based on user needs, it's all based on dollars per ounce to be competitive. We could size everything so that all the products have an average 30-day usage cycle, and Neil suggested we can spell Meniml with "ml" to symbolize that each product is precisely measured. That way, we could make it easy for customers to simply reorder automatically at the end of every month. Gone is the rush orders on one small product one day, then another the next week, or half-empty bottles, or waste...that is "simplifying" too.

"Ren, we got to do this."

...

And they did. As they say, "stay true to your origins," and this truly was the origin story of Meniml.

And I will now proceed to document an abridged version of the Brand Story in the 7C Canvas.

MENIML 7C CANVAS

◈ CORE

WHY DO YOU EXIST? PURPOSE.

To offer a new, complete model for today's man. Meniml seeks to bring together thousands of factionalized "men," providing examples and models that their own fathers, social peers, and role models could not.

essence — DASHING

WHAT DO YOU STAND FOR? VALUES.

- Independence
- Style – Cleanliness
- Self–Respect

💬 CUSTOMER

WHO'S YOUR AUDIENCE?

Jack is an 80's baby yet born with a timeless cool. Raised in Connecticut, always independent and curious, he engaged deeply with anything that interested him, from a stint one summer with a local circus, to bustling and traveling his way across Europe each summer in between his English studies at Brown University. Since college, he's blogged, chefed, worked as a journalist, boxing trainer, and even after dropping in at a local contest and winning its $1,000 prize.

HOW DOES YOUR PRODUCT ELEVATE?

I am confident, stylish, self–reliant, handsome (or well–groomed). I care about having quality tools for all of my daily needs, including grooming, and like them to be well–organized and essential.

⊗ COMMUNITY

WHAT CULTURAL GROUP DO WE IDENTIFY WITH?

Our community of men see our brand as a cultural rallying point. Unsatisfied with the combative tribes of humbersexuals, metrosexuals, or aggro–jock warriors, but knowing they're more than sterilized stallions in corporate suits and ties, they look for relationships with other "modern classic" men, who are self–reliant, tough but run, curious but principled, confident but vulnerable. In other words, "whole men." They don't want to sit around a sweat lodge hugging other men and crying, but they do want to feel a connection to others.

◎ COMPETITION

HOW ARE YOU UNIQUE?

Meniml is the brand for today's adult Man who wants a one–stop, complete but simple grooming solution that goes beyond soap and shampoo (but below mascara and lipstick). It organizes, simplifies, and displays sequential skin, hair, and body maintenance products, stocking only the necessities for maximum male grooming. UNLIKE women's beauty products that have excess SKUs to sell more to the same customers, our product simplifies while adding pride & eliminating "shame" in complete grooming for Men. Our brand guides its user's in a new, integrated but complete model of being a Man in itself.

◉ CREATIVES

NAMING
Meniml
www.meniml.com

LOGO
meniml

COLORS

PACKAGING
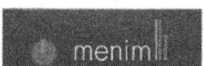
meniml

TYPOGRAPHY
Futura

☰ CONTENT

STORY OF THE BRAND

Neil and Ren were discussing men's beauty brands and Neil remarked, "I really believe there's a place for another brand." Men are buying more beauty care products than ever before but it does not seem that have a focussed target. Men are spiritual too. Ren observed today segments aren't defined by age, they're cross–generational. This made sense to Neil, and things clicked. "I got it. Something that offers a simple, but inclusive, model of masculinity and we can call it "Meniml."

BRAND STORIES

🖼 CHANNEL

YOUR BRAND TOUCHPOINTS
OWNED CHANNELS

SHARED CHANNELS

PAID CHANNELS

Formulas to Develop Brand Storytelling

Brand storytelling brings together your brand, your business strategies, and the life stories of your audience.

To get the brand storytelling right, it's critical to make sure each story has a defined beginning, middle and end. This may sound obvious, but many brands fail to fully develop the middle, which is where the key conflict resides. The middle is the source of all drama, and the depth of these conflicts drives the biggest payoff in your story's resolution or the solution in your customer's lives. A common, but useful, example of the importance of your story's "middle" is fully developing how another brand (or, an earlier version of your product if this is a redemption story) is failing to meet customer needs. Without the middle, when your solution is presented at the end of the story, it's not going to have the same impact or make as positive an impression on consumers. We shoot ourselves in the foot by skipping this piece.

The following are various storytelling formulas, each with fully developed beginnings, middles and ends. We've used Meniml as the example brand in each formula. These formulas can be applied to all the content that you produce from FB ads, social media updates, website copy, and more.

The "And - But - Therefore Approach"

Also referred to as the "ABT storytelling method," a simple formula that forms the DNA of all stories. It was first defined by Randy Olson, a USC film school graduate. Olson got the idea from the most unlikely of all places: South Park. When a script isn't working for Trey Parker, South Parker co-creator, he replaces "ands" with "buts" to find and develop conflict and tension in the story, the key ingredient to entertaining an audience. This buildup then requires a resolution, the story's "therefore" that concludes the narrative.

And: Present the problem and characters.

But: Build up tension with complications and twists, leading toward a solution.

Therefore: Resolve the problem.

Jeffrey is a 30-something who has recently moved out of a roommate-filled home to his own apartment. As an adult, he felt it was time to strike out on his own. *But* his self-care routine also needed a fresh start: he knew he couldn't get away with air-dried hair and soap and water alone, and after moving he'd also lose access to his metrosexual roommate's vast collection of beauty products, even though he never knew which products were right for him or how to use them. He knew it was time to figure out his own self-care regimen, *but* he didn't know where to start. He didn't want to surf vlogs trying to figure out exactly what he needed, and he was overwhelmed on his first "personal care" shopping trip at his local CVS. But as he stood in the CVS aisle, he remembered hearing about a new "total" care line for men, real men. Meniml: that was it. He remembered hearing their name on a podcast because it was easy, and he liked easy. And minimal. *Therefore,* he brought up the Meniml site on his mobile phone right in the middle of the CVS, where only moments before he'd been overwhelmed and under-prepared. Right on the homepage, he found a single set for "all-day" care that he'd have by the time he got back from work in the afternoon, just in time to get up to grade before his second date with Velma. She could be the one. But she was completely in control, self-sufficient, and cared for herself. Jeff knew he had a shot if he could just get his look together, too. It was up to Meniml.

He clicked "Buy Now" and headed home, waiting in anticipation.

The Before - After - Bridge Structure

This formula focuses on conversions, and it works by addressing the specific pain-points of your buyer. There are 3 stages:

Before: Describe the situation prior to your solution.

After: Show the situation, post employing your solution.

Bridge: Present your solution as a bridge between the Before and After.

Greg is a 35-year-old boy. That is, he's always relied on the products of girlfriends and roommates to take care of himself. But after a date where he really felt connected, he received a follow-up email the next day: "It was nice to meet you, but I only date men, not slobs. Buy a comb and call me when you figure out how to use it. Thanks for dinner, by the way, Jen." While he knew it was time to change, he didn't know where to start. He bought several Amazon recommendations, only to find everything was a different facial moisturizing cream. His skin went from sun-protected and baby soft to broken out and irritated the following week. His hair was still frizzy and flyaway, and he didn't know what he was missing, or even when to use what.

Then he found Meniml. It was like Garanimals for his clothing when he was a kid, with each product labeled in order of use. He started with the body wash in the shower, #1, then washed his hair with the combined shampoo and conditioner, #2, he then shaved with Meniml's shaving gel, #3, and soothed his skin with the healing and moisturizing face cream, #4, finally, he used the blended holding cream to put the finishing touches on his hair, #5, and was ready for the day.

In total, it took him 6 minutes to go from groggy to groomed and completely prepared. As he looked at the clock on the way out the door, he realized that not only did he have a product that led him through a regimen, the clear routine saved him his usual 20 minutes of meandering in the bathroom, saving him time even though he did nothing but take a shower before!

Dale Carnegie's Magic Formula

After years of interviewing and consulting with contemporary leaders and businessmen, Dale Carnegie wrote How to Win Friends and Influence People, one of the most popular non-fiction books of all time. Carnegie's three-step "Magic Formula" for capturing the attention of any audience is as follows:

Incident: Describe the buyer's experience.

Action: Demonstrate the specific action taken to alleviate the experience.

Benefit: The benefit the buyer will receive as a result of taking that action.

More and more men are delving into personal care and grooming than ever before, yet it's a confusing road for most. From a marketer's presentation perspective, there are dozens of "necessary" products for an individual man who wants to be properly groomed. It's even more confusing asking a male friend for advice, not knowing who will ridicule you with "what, you use more than soap?" and who will overwhelm you with "you really need to know your pH before you can even consider specific brands and products."

Meniml is designed to guide men through a complete but essential personal care regimen, with products labeled specifically to explain their use. Meniml also offers a single set for all men, so gone are the 4 different variations just for one man's type of skin. There's no reason why any man needs 4 separate products for day moisturizing, night moisturizing, sun protection, and razor burn, but rather one well-formulated men's skincare product that incorporates all these uses. A user simply buys one Meniml kit,

which is measured to last an average of 30 days, as the "ml" in Meniml suggests, and can expect a replenishment kit just before the end of that 30-days. No worries, no thinking. Well-groomed in less time than it takes to find the soap behind the toilet.

Pixar's Storytelling Rule

Pixar is an award-winning animation studio responsible for iconic films like Toy Story and The Incredibles. Their team of writers has many years of experience writing and rewriting scripts to perfection, culminating in a simple formula that ensures their story ideas are both complete and compelling. Here is their formula:

Once upon a time, there was ____.

Every day, ____.

One day ____.

Because of that, ____.

Because of *that*, ____.

Until finally, ____.

Once upon a time, there was a young man named Kenny, who never learned how to take care of himself. *Every day*, he'd brush his teeth and wash his hair and yet would sit in embarrassment at his group lunch table as his peers chatted without self-consciousness with their female counterparts. He, by comparison, felt like a slob.

One day, he heard about a new brand: "Meniml," whose products lead the user through a clear routine while promising superior personal care and grooming in half the time one typically takes to shower and brush your teeth. He went ahead and purchased from meniml.com. *Because of that,* Kenny immediately had a simple regimen without even thinking about it and got the attention of the fairer sex at work. He wasn't sure if it was because he looked better, or if it was simply because he felt more confident knowing how to care for himself easily.

Because of this momentum, he started systemizing other home and work tasks and found everything became easier and more joyful.

And *because of this attitude,* after a few months, he was noticed as the model of confident, cool, and control and was quickly promoted to manager. *Until finally,* he bought his own house, and the well-groomed manager Kenny opened its door on his first day with his fiancée, Jenny, the same woman known coolly to him as Jennifer at his work lunch table only a few months before.

Star – Chain – Hook Formula

This formula is the creation of Frank Dignan, a consultant from the University of Chicago Press, and it's highly effective at putting a refreshing spin on advertising messages.

Star: Open with an attention-grabbing, starry opening.

Chain: A string of convincing features/benefits, stats, and facts.

Hook: An urgency induced call-to-action.

Here's how we could use the Star - Chain - Hook formula with Meniml: Ditch clueless slob for old-school cool.

Meniml has a clearly labeled, ordered regimen that takes the guessing out of self-care that's refilled automatically every month.

Simple routine; Simply dashing. Order your kit today.

Let us wrap Brand Storytelling by taking our last example, of Star - Chain - Hook formula and make it part of the 7C Canvas.

MENIML 7C CANVAS

⬡ CORE

WHY DO YOU EXIST? PURPOSE.

To offer a new, complete model for today's man, Meniml seeks to bring together thousands of factionalized "men," providing examples and models that their own fathers, social peers, and role models could not.

essence
DASHING

WHAT DO YOU STAND FOR? VALUES.

- Independence
- Style – Cleanliness
- Self- Respect

👤 CUSTOMER

WHO'S YOUR AUDIENCE?

Jack is an 80's baby yet born with a timeless cool. Raised in Connecticut, always independent and curious, he engaged deeply with anything that interested him, from a stint one summer with a local circus, to busting and traveling his way across Europe each summer in-between his English studies at Brown University. Since college, he's blogged, chefed, worked as a journalist, boxing trainer, and even tried his hand at motorcycle racing after dropping in at a local contest and winning its $1,000 prize.

HOW DOES YOUR PRODUCT ELEVATE?

I am confident, stylish, self-reliant, handsome (or well-groomed). I care about having quality looks for all of my daily needs, including grooming, and like them to be well-organized and essential.

🗣 COMMUNITY

WHAT CULTURAL GROUP DO WE IDENTIFY WITH?

Our community of men see our brand as a cultural rallying point. Unsatisfied with the combative tribes of lumbersexuals, metrosexuals, or retgro–jock warriors but knowing they're more than sterilized stallions in corporate suits and ties, they look for relationships with other "modern classic" men, who are self- reliant, tough but vulnerable. In other words, "whole men." They don't want to sit around a sweat lodge hugging other men and crying, but they do want to feel a connection to others.

◉ COMPETITION

HOW ARE YOU UNIQUE?

Menim is the brand for today's adult Man who wants a one-stop, complete but simple grooming solution that goes beyond soap and shampoo (but below mascara and lipstick). It organizes, simplifies, and displays sequential skin, hair, and body maintenance products, stocking only the necessities for maximum male grooming. UNLIKE women's beauty products that have access SKUs to sell more to the same customers, our product simplifies while adding pride & eliminating "shame" in complete grooming for Men. Our brand guides its user's in a new, integrated but complete model of being a Man in itself.

👁 CREATIVES

NAMING

Menim
www.meniml.com

LOGO

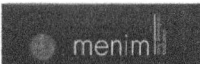

menim

PACKAGING

COLORS

TYPOGRAPHY

Futura

▤ CONTENT

STORY OF THE BRAND

Neil and Ren were discussing men's beauty brands and Neil remarked, " I really believe there's a place for another brand." Men are buying more beauty care products than ever before but it does not seem that have a focussed target. Men are spiritual tofu. Ren observed today segments aren't defined by age, they're cross–generational. This made sense to Neil, and things clicked, "I get it, inclusive, model of masculinity and we can call it "Menim."

BRAND STORIES

Star: Ditch clueless slob for old-school cool.

Chain: Menim? less a clearly labeled, ordered regiment that takes the guessing out of self–care that's refilled automatically every month.

Hook: A simple routine for simply dashing. Order your kit today.

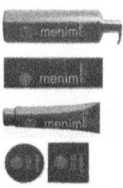

▣ CHANNEL

YOUR BRAND TOUCHPOINTS
OWNED CHANNELS

SHARED CHANNELS

PAID CHANNELS

The Editorial Calendar

How Does it Help?

Now that you've acquired a deeper understanding of the type of content you need to develop - your Brand's Signature Story, the Story of the Brand, and your brand's narrative through Brand Storytelling – this section will introduce the editorial calendar.

The editorial calendar is simply a schedule to keep track of all the brand storytelling your eCommerce store will engage in.

It's a tool that facilitates:

Listing any and all ideas you're generating day-to-day.

Direction for the posting schedule for the next quarter (which allows you to plan your content).

Project management among various staff that will be part of content generation.

Scheduling for various content pieces: text, audio, video, infographics and more.

How Does it Work?

There are slight variations in every editorial calendar, but the eBrandBuilders' editorial calendar is customized based on the Content Creation Framework. It includes:

- Date when the content is scheduled to be published.
- Who will author the content?
- The title/headline of the content.
- The brand storytelling type the content is addressing.
- The format of the content.
- The buying stage the content addresses.

Here is what the editorial calendar will look like for Meniml:

MENIML'S EDITORIAL CALENDAR

PUBLISH DATE	WRITER	HEADLINE	CONTENT TYPE	FORMAT	FUNNEL STATE
9/14/2020	Sinead	"The How-To guide for Men who want to follow a simple Skin Care routine – But can't get started"	Customer – How to Videos/ Guides	Text + Video	TOFU*
9/21/2020	Roger	"Skin Type Test: Discover yourSkin Type in 60 secs and get personal recommendations"	Customer – Quiz	Text	MOFU**
9/28/2020	Brianna	The "why" behind Menial. What was the reason for launching a skincare business	Core – Why (Purpose)	Text	TOFU
10/05/2020	Cecil	Discover how Harry, a self-described workaholic transformed his skin in 7 days	Customer – Experiences	Text + Video	BOFU***
10/12/2020	Ren	Seattle Skin Initiative	Core – Value 2 (Cause Based)	Text	TOFU
10/19/2020	Neil	"How do declutter your home in 10 days and lead a simpler, happier life"	Minimalism	Text	TOFU
10/26/2020	Jenna	"Five top Dermatologists reveal their best skincare regimen "	Customer – How to Videos/ Guides	Text + Video	TOFU
11/02/2020	Michael	"Spend 5 mins to respond to this survey and receive a $10 discount"	Customer – Contests and Giveaways	Survey	MOFU
11/09/2020	Suzie	"See how Meniml ranks against the Top 10 Men Skincare Brands"	Competition – Comparison	Infographics	BOFU

* Top of Funnel
** Middle of Funnel
*** Bottom of Funnel

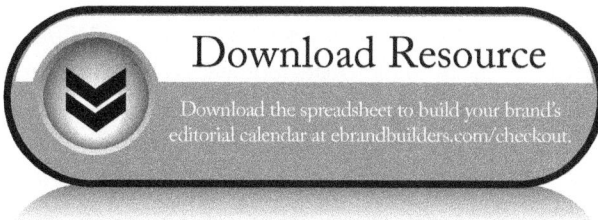

Download Resource

Download the spreadsheet to build your brand's editorial calendar at ebrandbuilders.com/checkout.

Content Amplification

So far, you've created compelling content that is on-brand, and aligned with the 5C's. Now your content is ready to be *amplified*!

The 1x1x1 Approach

This is a technique, as depicted on the right, we use at eBrandBuilders for eCommerce startups to help you plan and hone your content. It entails the following three considerations:

1.1 Type of Content

What kind of content are you publishing: a blog post, video, or podcast? The selection of this option is dependent on your comfort/skill set and at least to begin with, I would recommend that you choose one format and delve into others only when you have gained absolute mastery over the first.

1.2 Paid Media Platform

The platform on which you decide to publish is obviously reliant on the nature of the content you chose under "type of content."

1.3 Time of Week

This frequency relates to how often you publish content every week. Once a week is the standard but do what's best for your audience.

The goal of starting out this way allows you to measure what's resonating with your audience. Once you get an initial read on the nature, platform, and frequency, you can change one element at a time – similar to A/B testing – to see how you can improve on the various metrics. For example, you might discover that blog posts elicit higher engagement from your audience than podcasts, or that if your content is posted on a certain day of the week, it's seen and shared more often.

To carry on the tradition of demonstrating what this approach would look like from a practical standpoint, we will go back to our brand, Meniml. In order to select the type of content, we use the Editorial Calendar and focus on the first topic within the Customer cluster. One of the topics, we have listed there is:

The 30 Day Single Post Amplification Process

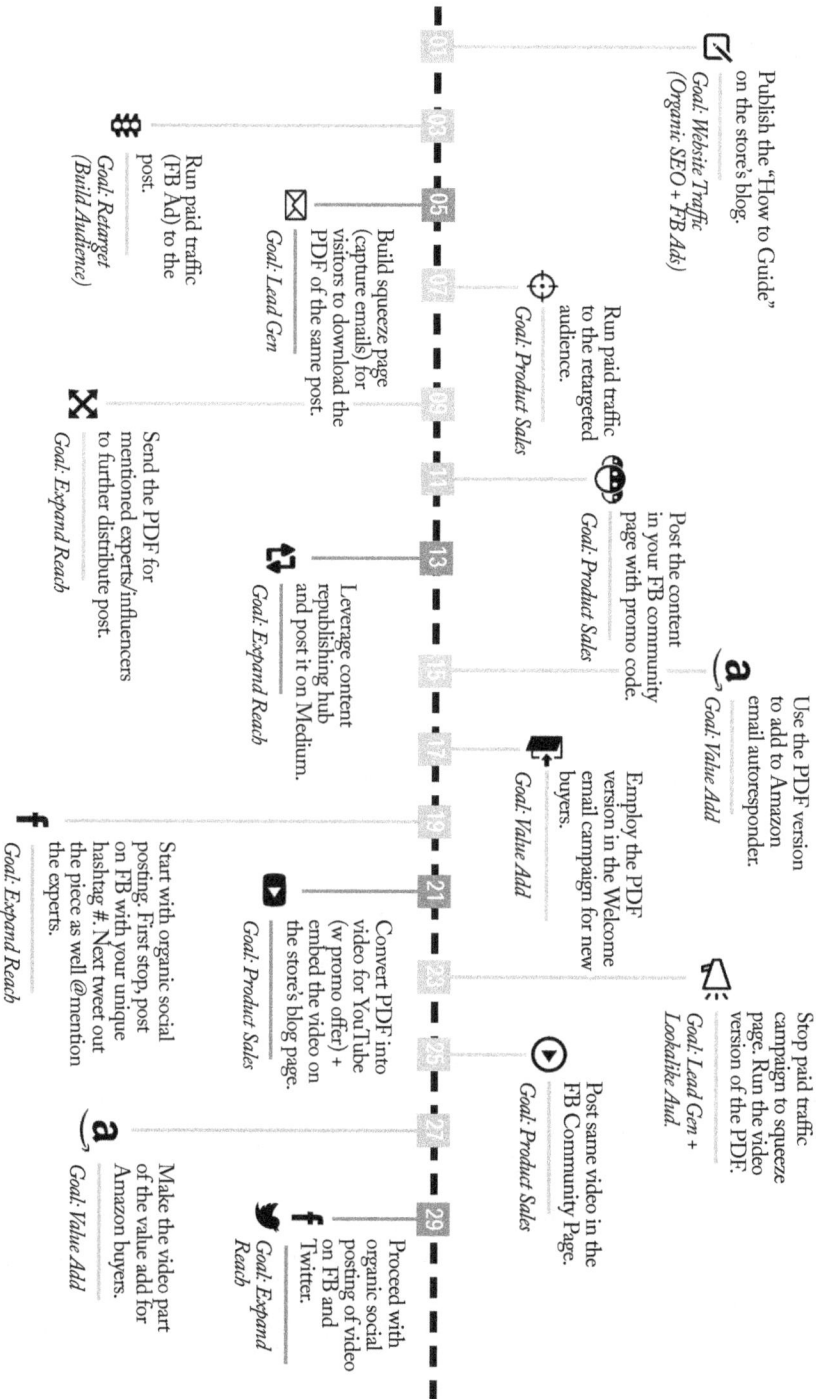

01 — Publish the "How to Guide" on the store's blog.
Goal: Website Traffic (Organic SEO + FB Ads)

03 — Run paid traffic (FB Ad) to the post.
Goal: Lead Gen

05 — Build squeeze page (capture emails) for visitors to download the PDF of the same post.
Goal: Lead Gen

07 — Run paid traffic to the retargeted audience.
Goal: Retarget (Build Audience)

09 — Run paid traffic to the retargeted audience.
Goal: Product Sales

11 — Post the content in your FB community page with promo code.
Goal: Product Sales

13 — Leverage content republishing hub and post it on Medium.
Goal: Expand Reach

Send the PDF for mentioned experts/influencers to further distribute post.
Goal: Expand Reach

a — Use the PDF version to add to Amazon email autoresponder.
Goal: Value Add

15 — Employ the PDF version in the Welcome email campaign for new buyers.
Goal: Value Add

17 —

19 —

21 — Convert PDF into video for YouTube (w promo offer) + embed the video on the store's blog page.
Goal: Product Sales

23 — Stop paid traffic campaign to squeeze page. Run the video version of the PDF.
Goal: Lead Gen + Lookalike Aud.

25 — Post same video in the FB Community Page.
Goal: Product Sales

27 — Proceed with organic social posting of video on FB and Twitter.
Goal: Expand Reach

29 — Start with organic social posting. First stop, post on FB with your unique hashtag #. Next tweet out the piece as well @mention the experts.
Goal: Expand Reach

a — Make the video part of the value add for Amazon buyers.
Goal: Value Add

"The How-To Guide for Men who Want to Follow a Simple Skincare Routine - But Can't Get Started."

We will start our content marketing efforts with this topic and proceed to write a long-form blog post of 2,500 words. In order to build awareness for the brand, this post will need to offer highly valuable content that beats anything else that comes up in search results for the same keywords. In this case, the keywords are "Men Skincare Regimen." Our initial competitive research will involve browsing the other results: what is the rest of the content lacking? How can we be different? How can we meet consumer expectations better?

Once you have written such a pillar post/cornerstone content, all efforts should now turn to amplifying this post and leveraging all available channels to maximize exposure.

The amplification method follows the 1:1:1 process to a T with the actual tactics mentioned in the graphic itself.

To Summarize:

In the first week, the single "How to Guide" post has been posted on the blog, used to retarget with FB Ads, employed as a PDF download, and then concludes with another round of retargeting.

In the second week, we start by leveraging influencers to accelerate the distribution of the guide, post it on our FB community page, share it on Medium, and add the PDF version for Amazon buyers.

In the third week, we include the post as a value add in our 'Welcome' email campaign, start posting on Facebook, and convert the PDF to a video for YouTube (as a series of slides).

Culminating with the last week, where we now run the video version in our paid traffic campaign, share the same video on our FB community page, provide the video as a value add for Amazon buyers, and proceed with the organic social posting by putting the video on FB and Twitter.

The entire approach can be easily replicated for your brand with substitutions made with your specific: content piece, preferred social platforms, and marketplace.

Wrapping Up

Since you're creating content geared towards a specific audience, you're attracting qualified traffic, which will result in qualified leads, i.e. a potential customer who is more likely to buy your products since they've already shown an interest in them.

Because the traffic you're receiving is laser-focused on your niche, you have a better chance of converting visitors into customers. By creating engaging content, you can communicate with your customers on an ongoing basis. You provide your customers with the information they need at each point in the buyer's journey. This differs from traditional marketing that usually only focuses on content that sells.

Content marketing encourages you to create all types of content that's helpful to your customer. If your company sells backpacks to travelers, find a niche that is relevant to your customers, for example, you could start a blog that centers around unique travel destinations you or your extended team have visited, featuring new information on those locations and special tips: from local customs to "local" finds tourists don't know about, to tactics for getting around at a lower cost.

This comes down to the master seller's insight: people don't like to be sold to, but they love to buy.

Hopefully, you're beginning to see how, in our 7C system, every element of your brand is closely sewn together, so everything your brand does is instantly recognizable and consistent. This ultimately makes your brand "sticky," making it more memorable to consumers. This is real brand power, and it's advertising you can't buy - though you can create it by following our 7C approach.

7.0
CHANNEL

7.0 CHANNEL

You've come this far.

You've made it to the last "C," which means you've covered a lot of territory:

You've determined the purpose of your brand, the core reason your brand exists, what your company stands for, and your essence.

You've learned how to dig deeper into your audience to learn who they are, beyond numbers and gender, and you know what higher good your product serves in their lives.

You've learned how to create a customer persona and use that to build and nurture a community of loyal brand fanatics.

You've figured out how to build a competitive edge and to hone your brand's unique attributes to set you apart from the competitive pack.

You've learned how to construct a meaningful visual identity, including your name, colors, logo, typography, and packaging, so everything aligns with your brand's core attributes.

You've discovered the core story of your brand as well as your day-to-day storytelling for conveying your message to your audience.

You should now be (almost) ready to introduce your new brand or rebrand to the marketplace.

This means it is now our responsibility to discuss the why, what and how of marketing channels so you can have the most cost-efficient, yet highest yielding launch.

But you'll have to be strategic.

Customer attention spans are at their lowest and combined with the fact that competition is at a fever pitch, eCommerce entrepreneurs will discover a tough marketplace without the right guidance. Assuming you are closer to the beginning of your journey, at least with this specific brand, it's likely you don't have a financial war chest of marketing dollars on hand to be able to afford wasting even one touchpoint or media vehicle in your launch.

As you work through this chapter, you'll discover the tools and vehicles you'll need to move the needle fastest with the lowest initial investment. Also included is a walk-through of what a strategic, sequential, and multi-channel marketing initiative looks like.

Unfortunately, we don't have the space here to lead you through every tactical piece of a full-blown, let's say, Facebook campaign, but we will show you all of the necessary points and options to consider to set up and successfully implement a successful, omnipresent plan.

In closing, Meniml will again serve as the guiding example to showcase overall business and marketing objectives for the first 12 months. Based on these metrics, a complete marketing plan will take shape, enlisting the various touchpoints and channels that we will need to focus on to reach our first-year goals.

The Multi-Channel Approach

The foundation of a modern eCommerce channel strategy is multi-channel marketing. Multi-channel marketing is connecting with your prospects and customers wherever they like to be online, whether that's marketplaces, social media, messaging apps, or online communities. The right presence will enable consumers to buy from you whenever they want to and on their terms.

One of the core benefits of multi-channel marketing is the ability to generate multiple exposure points for the brand to match the customer's buying journey.

On the social channel of an eCommerce store, for instance, this might take the shape of a buy now button within a tweet, a sponsored post on Instagram, a buyable Pin (on Pinterest), and/or, of course, the array of sales tools offered by Facebook.

Marketplaces under the heading of multi-channel marketing take the form of Amazon, Walmart/Jet, eBay, Etsy, Google Shopping and others.

Today your brand needs to be omnipresent to be heard, seen, and to stay above the noise. This push toward multi-channel online shopping is not the invention of eCommerce stores but has rather been initiated by consumers. With the evolution of eCommerce, online shoppers have become accustomed to their basic needs being met consistently, quite similar to the Maslow Hierarchy of Needs we discussed in Chapter 2, and so they are now demanding greater convenience with options to purchase from a brand through multiple channels.

According to a survey by the National Retail Federation (NRF) over the 2018 Thanksgiving weekend, more than half of US consumers (54%) reported shopping both online and offline, while 25% were online-only and 21% just shopped in-store.[32]

> **More than half of US consumers (54%) reported shopping both online and offline, while 25% were online-only, and 21% just shopped in-store.**
>
> **- National Retail Federation**

The importance of having a multi-channel presence also extends to both the initial product search and social channels.

Inception of Product Search

From the much-awaited Internet Trends Report 2018, Mary Meeker, its author, released some telling stats. According to the latest findings, 49% of consumers begin their product search on Amazon; 36% begin on a search engine (e.g. Google); the remaining 15% initiate a search on social and other marketplace channels.[33]

As Amazon functions as *the* product search portal, it's logical for eCommerce stores to have a presence on Amazon and related channels. This presence allows brands to provide their solutions to customers when and where they're actively looking for products related to their problems.

Product Finding =
Often Starts @ Search (Amazon + Google)

(Where do you begin your product search?)

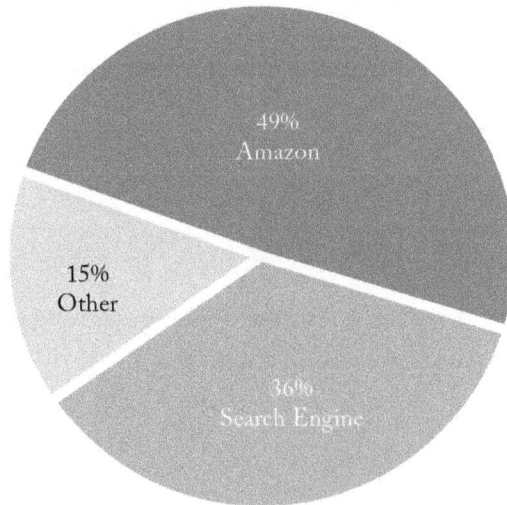

49%
Amazon

15%
Other

36%
Search Engine

Social Media Drives Product Discovery + Purchases

Returning to Meeker's study, the contribution of social channels toward the discovery and subsequent *purchase* of products is also significant:

- 78% of consumers aged 18-34 have discovered products through Facebook, Instagram and Pinterest,
- 34% on Twitter, and
- 22% through Snapchat.

Product Discovery on Platforms

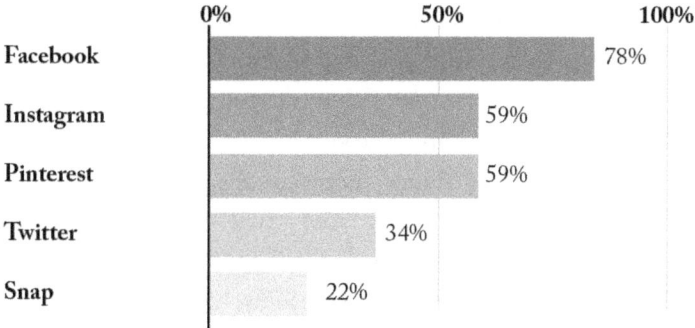

	0%	50%	100%
Facebook			78%
Instagram		59%	
Pinterest		59%	
Twitter	34%		
Snap	22%		

Source: US (18-34yrs old), Kleiner Perkins 2018 Internet Trends

Of those that discovered products through social, 55% ended up purchasing these products, with 11% of those buying immediately.[34]

Social Media = Driving Product Discovery + Purchases

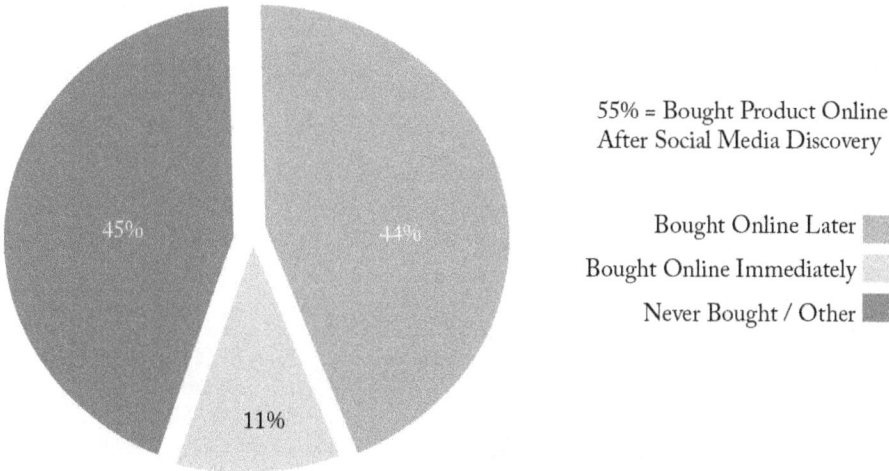

45%

44%

11%

55% = Bought Product Online
After Social Media Discovery

Bought Online Later
Bought Online Immediately
Never Bought / Other

Source: Kleiner Perkins 2018 Internet Trends

Benefits of a Multi-Channel Approach

Marketplaces Increase Your Trust Factor

Despite the widespread growth of eCommerce, securing consumer trust remains a core driver of sales both on- and off-line. An effective way for new or smaller eCommerce brands to quickly inspire trust is to piggyback off the established trust of larger marketplaces. By selling on these well-regarded platforms, your brand is linked in a customer's mind with the marketplace's brand equity, longevity, and reach.

A study conducted by UPS found that almost all U.S. online shoppers (97%), made purchases on online marketplaces.[35] However, even on the largest platforms, third-party sellers represent the majority of their actual inventory and thrive by "borrowing" the trust extended to the online marketplace itself. As an eCommerce store owner, you can also start building brand awareness by leveraging these exchanges.

Increase Spending

According to Stitch Labs, retailers who sell through a branded eCommerce site (like Shopify, Magento, WooCommerce, or BigCommerce) make

Revenue Growth: Branded Website + Marketplaces(s)

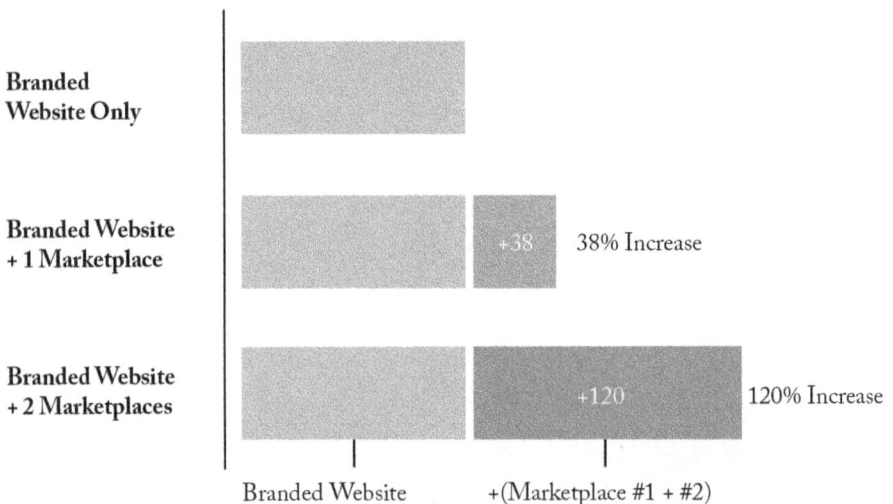

Branded Website Only

Branded Website + 1 Marketplace — +38 — 38% Increase

Branded Website + 2 Marketplaces — +120 — 120% Increase

Branded Website   +(Marketplace #1 + #2)

Source: Stitch Labs

38% more revenue by also having a presence on a single marketplace (like Amazon, eBay, or Etsy). And retailers who added a second marketplace showed an average revenue growth of *120%*.[36]

Even without utilizing branded eCommerce sites, retailers who sell on two marketplaces see 190% more in revenue than those who only sell on one.[37]

Revenue Increases from Multiple Marketplaces

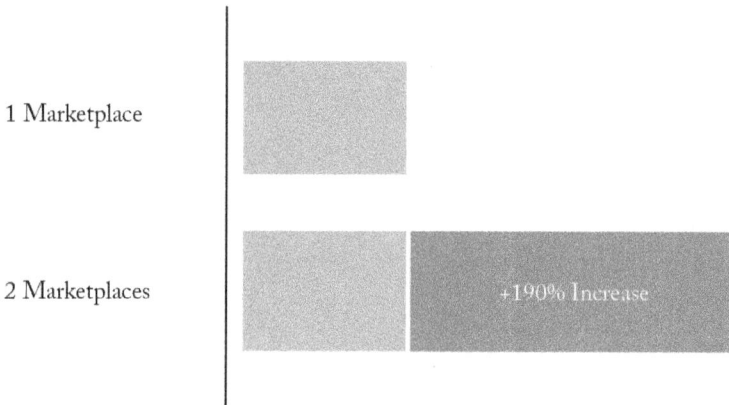

1 Marketplace

2 Marketplaces

+190% Increase

Source: Stitch Labs

These virtues of the multi-channel approach certainly paint a bright picture for eCommerce retailers. But each channel comes with its own set of screening filters, complexities, and infrastructure requirements that need to be factored into your strategy. This chapter focuses on presenting the high-level statistics, demographic data, pros and cons of each channel to help you craft the approach that's right for you. We'll also present some of the eCommerce-specific features that are relevant to your stores.

Over the next 24 months, "omnichannel" marketing will become the marketing way in eCommerce. We'll help you prepare to take advantage of it.

The Three Channels

The multi-channel strategy is best executed with three core channels in its mix: owned channels, shared channels, and paid channels.

Owned Channels

Owned channels are the in-house channels you create and control, including your store's website, blog, email lists, and retail product pages. Technically, retail presence is an overlapping of owned and shared as when a retailer stocks your products, sales aren't fully under your control, but we include it here for simplicity. As social is moving toward a pay-for-play model, these channels have been clustered under Paid.

The list of owned media includes:
- Website
- Mobile
- Customer Service
  ◦ Live Chat/Blog/Messenger
  ◦ Email
  ◦ Phone
- Email Marketing
- Retail

Shared Channels

Shared channels are those you share with other sellers, meaning they are channels over which you have limited control, and you must follow all stipulated rules and regulations. For example, a marketplace owner could terminate your presence without warning while retaining its customer base. This is a risk you take to have access to millions of buyers, regardless of whether sales come from your own brand and efforts.

The list of shared channels includes:
- Marketplaces
  ◦ Amazon
  ◦ Walmart
  ◦ Kickstarter/Indiegogo
- Partnerships
  ◦ Brand Collaborations
  ◦ Affiliates
  ◦ Blogger Outreach

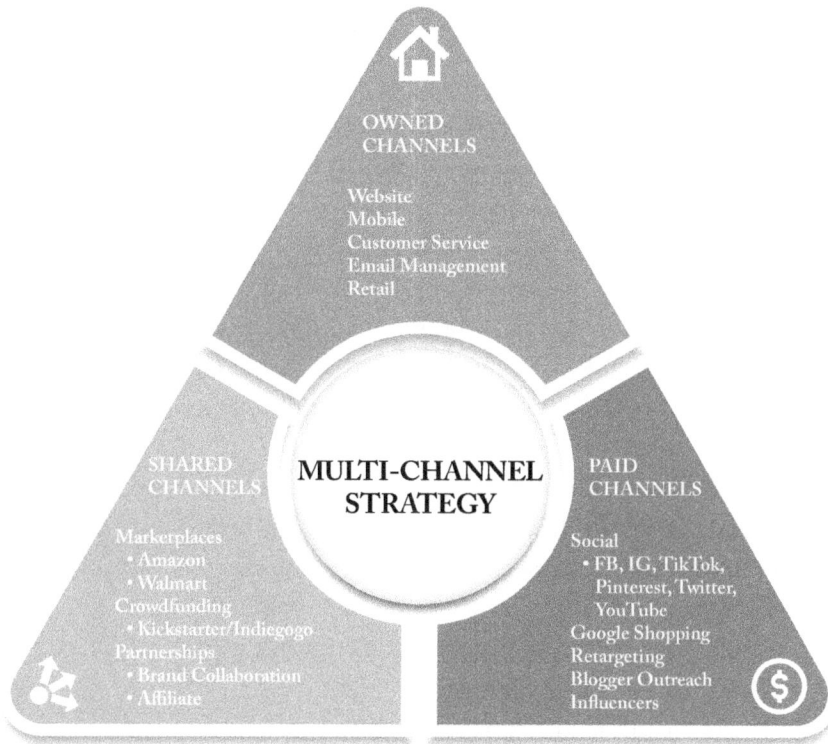

OWNED
CHANNELS

Website
Mobile
Customer Service
Email Management
Retail

MULTI-CHANNEL STRATEGY

SHARED
CHANNELS

Marketplaces
• Amazon
• Walmart
Crowdfunding
• Kickstarter/Indiegogo
Partnerships
• Brand Collaboration
• Affiliate

PAID
CHANNELS

Social
• FB, IG, TikTok,
  Pinterest, Twitter,
  YouTube
Google Shopping
Retargeting
Blogger Outreach
Influencers

Paid Channels

Paid channels refer to all the third-party sites where you pay for advertising. Therefore, any online marketing platform that the company pays for will fall into this category. Digitally, it includes all the social channels, display advertising, and affiliate marketing. Traditionally, this would also include TV ads, radio spots, and print advertising.

Paid media channels include:
- Social
  - Facebook
  - Instagram
  - TikTok
  - Pinterest
  - Twitter
  - YouTube
  - Google Shopping
- Retargeting
- Influencers

Owned Channels

Website

Although you want a multi-channel presence, everything starts with your own website. For eCommerce brands, site ownership means brand stewardship: it's where you communicate your brand story and engage in ongoing storytelling, build relationships with customers, and send a branded email to your repeat buyers to invite them to a wine tasting event. The website's role is to deliver a brand experience and meet the needs of consumers. To be there when the customer desires to take action, your site should offer quick solutions and reduce friction, thereby increasing the likelihood of a sale.

With the proliferation of digital media, customers encounter your brand through multiple channels, but the most significant and the majority of brand interactions happen through your website (or should!). Your eCommerce store needs to stay at the center of all the brand touchpoints that constellate around it. As the owned entry point to your brand, your site needs to look, act, and feel flawless.

We'll now look at the critical elements to your website's success, beginning with your site's load times.

Load Times

Pages that load slowly frustrate customers, often leading them to abandon your site for the competition. Quick loading pages, on the other hand, reduce bounce rates and keep visitors on your site longer. But the margin for error is slim: research shows that, on average, consumers expect pages to load in under 3 seconds before they lose interest. This may seem like a tight timer, but with the right approach, it's possible. MachMetrics found that among US retail sites, the average loading time on mobile is 9.8 seconds.[38] Beating this industry average can gain you a serious competitive advantage.

Load Time Statistics

The impact of load times on your customer experience cannot be understated. Skilled recently compiled the results of twelve studies and found 79% of consumers who are frustrated with a site's performance, including speed, are less likely to buy: even a one-second delay can lead to a 7% drop in conversion rates. This may not seem like a significant reduction, but if your site makes $100,000 a month, a one-second improvement in page speed can earn you an additional *$7,000* a month. Increasing page load times can also boost organic traffic by 20% and page views by 14%.[39]

> **A one second delay in page response can result in a 7% reduction in conversions.**
>
> If an e-commerce site is making $100,000 per day, a **1 second page delay could potentially cost you $2.5 million in lost sales every year.**

Optimizing Your Site for Speed

If you have a Google Analytics account, you can check your load times under the Behavior tab. Several tools can test your site's speed, including WebPageTest, Pingdom, and GTmetrix. You'll need this baseline to start making improvements.

Your site host is your foundation, and the memory and bandwidth made available to your site will impact loading times as well as your site's speed as traffic increases, especially during holidays and sales. The right hosting service will also guard against crashes, which shut your site down altogether. Another helpful option is using a content delivery network that will cache your site and make it available to visitors through local servers, no matter where they are in the world, rather than fetching your site from a single location. Cloudflare and Amazon CloudFront are good CDN options.

Kinsta suggests that, on average, images represent 54% of your site's weight,[40] so they are the most likely culprit slowing you down.

Images need to be high-quality but minimizing image size will speed-up loading. Crop out unnecessary white space and make sure your products take up 80% of your image's real estate while keeping margins consistent. Having a plain white background helps images load quicker, too.

The rule of thumb is to post images 1,000 pixels in width or height with a file size lower than 100kb in jpeg format. While PNG offers higher quality, it should only be used if you need transparency.

Use thumbnails in search results and category pages and only display the full image on individual product pages. If you want to post videos of your products as well, host them offsite on a service like YouTube or Vimeo.

Wrap-up with a Reload

While website loading times sound like the concern of the IT department, they have a profound effect on the customer experience. Making sure your website is totally optimized to limit loading times and improve performance will not only reduce bounce rates and keep visitors on your site longer, but it can also lead to significant upticks in conversion rates and revenue.

Product Photos

One of the major drawbacks of eCommerce is that consumers don't have the opportunity to see, touch, and interact with your products physically before deciding to buy. High-quality, clear product photos are the best way to bridge this gap. Attractive visual content not only grabs visitor attention and keeps them engaged longer, but they also boost conversion rates.

For most eCommerce buyers, these images are the first contact people have with your brand, making them brand ambassadors and part of your brand's voice. They can also be visual assets that boost brand awareness if they are viewed and shared across your channels.

Finally, when customers receive items, if the products meet the expectations set by your photography, you powerfully build trust, creating repeat customers.

The Benefits of Great Product Photos

Pages with photos result in 650% higher engagement than text-only, and it increases people's willingness to read your content by 80%.[41]

Consumers are also far more likely to remember your brand if you have photos. According to research, people remember 80% of what they see, but only 20% of what they read,[42] not to mention, our brains are much better at taking in visual information, as we process it 60,000 times faster than text.[43]

One photo isn't enough, however. Salsify found that 60% of online shoppers said they require at least three product images to consider clicking the buy button. And 13% percent said five or more images were necessary.[44]

Tips for the Best Photos

The single most important quality is authenticity: images must be an honest reflection of the product's likeness and quality. Photos should be high-resolution and have a consistent, coherent look across your channels.

More Images Mean More Sales

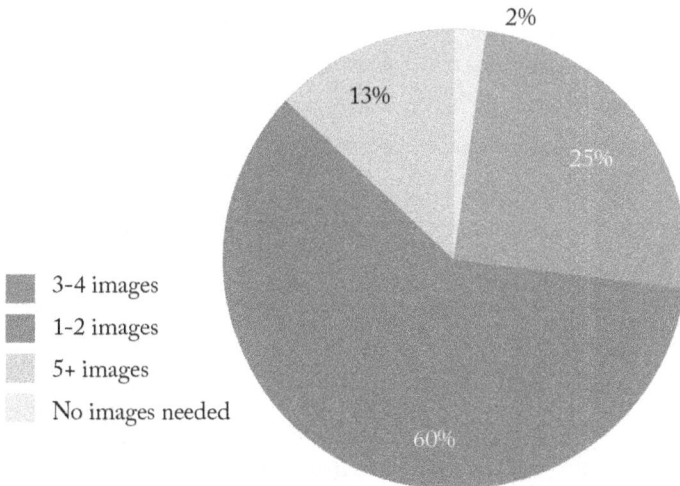

- 3-4 images
- 1-2 images
- 5+ images
- No images needed

Source: Salsify.com

Stylistically, there are two options: simple photos with your product against a plain white background; or lifestyle photography that features your product being worn or used, these images also reflect your brand's persona. In general, simple product photos are the best option for your product pages, as the plain background ensures the product is highlighted. Lifestyle photos are better for marketing material, Amazon, and in social media posts.

The most basic equipment you'll need is a camera: either a DSLR camera or a smartphone will do. You'll need a tripod to keep your camera steady, a background sweep, and adequate lighting. You may opt to purchase a lightbox if you mainly deal with smaller items like shoes and jewelry. Once your studio is set up and you're happy with the results, take notes on the placement and distance between all your elements so you can easily recreate the look in subsequent shoots.

Your priority is to get the main product photo, your "hero shot." This will be the default photo for each product. Because this image will have the biggest impact on conversions, take several test photos and adjust your camera settings to get the right look.

Next, focus on capturing secondary photos to fill in the story of your product and give consumers a true sense of the item. Showcase the item from various angles to highlight details and benefits. If you offer different colors or other options, be sure there's a photo of each variation.

Once you have all of your photos, process and edit them. In terms of the size, compression, backgrounds, etc. follow the same principles covered in the "Load Times" section. Additionally, the goal of this stage is to make them as visually pleasing as possible, while also retaining true-to-life colors and lighting. Use this step to ensure all your images have consistent margins, alignment, and shadowing.

Once you're happy with your images, create a style guide for both lifestyle and simple product photos. This guide will minimize mistakes, improve consistency, and save you time in subsequent photoshoots. Include the proper color palette, saturation, focal length, shadows, composition, context, and content required to "brand" your images.

Summary

Having appealing product photography is a simple but critical requirement for eCommerce success. Images help consumers make more informed decisions, but they also help build trust and can even promote broader brand awareness. Visual elements like photos are more memorable than copy alone and help consumers understand and retain more information about your brand and products, too.

Product Descriptions

Are Product Descriptions Still Important?

While product photos and videos drive engagement and conversions, they don't replace the necessity of solid product descriptions. Great descriptions can fill in the blanks about the features, specifications, and benefits of your products that can't be visually captured. An attractive photo may capture a visitor's attention, but your copy is the "in-store assistant" that can close the sale by addressing why the product is relevant to consumers and how it will fit into their lives.

Of course, product descriptions alone don't sell your product. Copy works *with* your images, videos, and reviews to paint a complete picture for the consumer, helping them imagine themselves using the product, and building confidence in your brand. By answering any questions a consumer may have, descriptions lower the barriers to making a purchase. As such, you ignore copy at your own peril. Not to mention, copy's importance is only growing with the popularization of voice-powered AI assistants like Amazon's Alexa. As more consumers shop via voice, product copy is becoming the primary messaging vehicle your customer encounters when searching for a product.

Product Descriptions by the Numbers

Salsify found that descriptions are considered by 76% of consumers to be the most important type of information on a product page, followed by reviews (71%), and then images (66%). Salsify also found that 94% of consumers will leave a website if they can't find the information they need.[45]

Features Ranking on Product Pages

Product Descriptions	76%
Reviews	71%
Images	66%

Source: Salsify.com

Tips for Better Product Descriptions

Product pages should entice consumers to buy, but also manage expectations of your product. If customers feel let down by the product's quality once it arrives, this kind of disappointment leaves a lasting negative impression of your brand. As such, prioritize accuracy in your description and resist the temptation to fluff up your copy with buzzwords like "innovative," and "premium quality." These types of phrases are used so often they lack meaning, and customers are more than likely to skim over them.

Write your copy for your ideal consumer and infuse it with your persona work: attempting to appeal to everyone leads to vague, irrelevant language. Knowing what your ideal customers are looking for will help target your language, making it more credible and relevant. Stick to facts, but don't offer a dry list of specifications. Instead, present specs and features in terms of how they benefit your core audience, this will infuse product benefits with life. For instance, Apple's description of their iPhone doesn't just list its optical image stabilization; they explain "optical image stabilization and fast lenses [give] outstanding photo quality and video even in low light."

Use your copy to paint a picture for customers by using words that evoke the senses. Send readers on a mini-experience. M&M's iconic "Melts in your

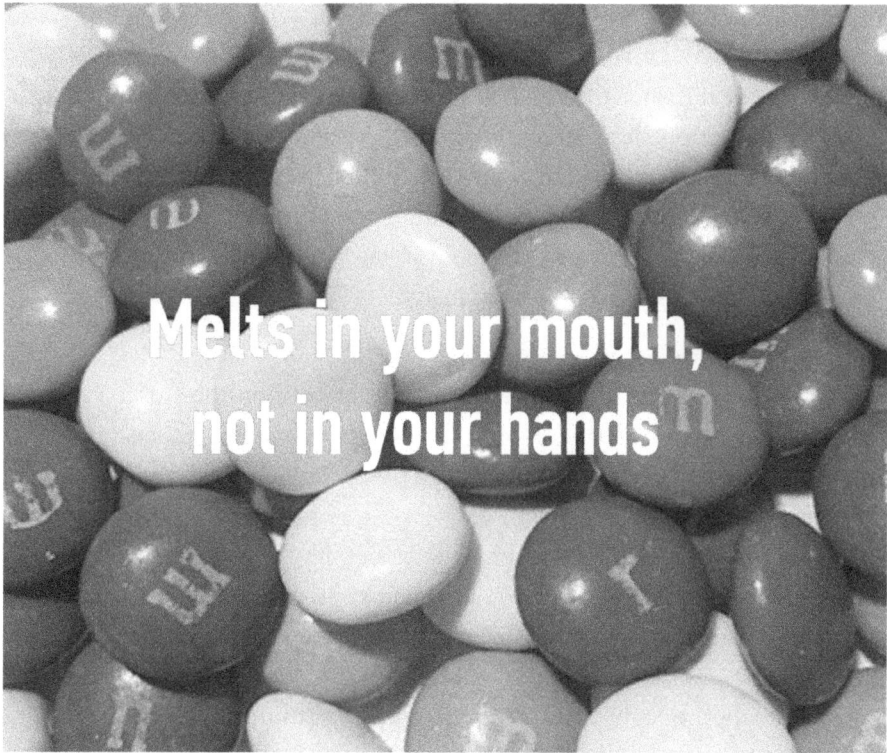

Melts in your mouth, not in your hands

mouth, not in your hands" generates a clear image in the mind and captures an important benefit of M&Ms. Also, stick to concrete language. Unless the picture you're painting with words is tied to the real world, consumers are going to have a hard time connecting to your product.

Consumers are less likely to read articles, but they do read headlines, so make your copy "scan-able" by breaking it up with bullet points, subheadings, and lists.

Make sure your language choice also reflects your brand's visual identity. If you have a formal, sleek look, bright and overly cheerful language is not going to feel right and will confuse consumers. As such, showcase your brand voice: when everything your brand says and does align, you powerfully anchor your brand in the minds of consumers. By using your brand voice effectively, you can transform your products into expressions of your brand's mission and values.

The Bottom-Line

A picture may be worth a thousand words, but any good eCommerce merchant will tell you it takes at least one thousand and *one* words to sell. Visual content alone isn't enough: product descriptions are a critical aspect of the product page ecosystem where every element supports the consumer's journey towards a purchase. Great product copy can help make it clear how relevant your products are to your target customer's life while reinforcing your brand's purpose and unique identity.

Payment Options

You've done all the hard work of setting up your online store. You have products and inventory, you've gone through the branding process, and you know your target customer. But you can't be profitable until you've set up a payment system.

The payment process is an important aspect of your site's overall customer experience. Payment is the moment when customers choose to trust you with their sensitive, personal information, and a seamless, trouble-free experience is the backbone of your credibility and can single-handedly determine whether consumers become repeat customers.

Most payment methods popular with eCommerce merchants are managed by a third party who acts as a gateway between your store and the bank account of your customers. This service may require transaction fees, and each provider will have different policies regarding fraud protection and chargebacks, so familiarize yourself with the various rules and policies of each payment option you pursue. *But the most important factor to consider is what particular options your target audience wants.* If your customers are not comfortable with your payment options, they're not going to buy.

One of the main drivers of preference for eCommerce shopping is the ability to shop and buy at any time, anywhere, and on any device, so convenience and ease of use must be prioritized in your selections. If your customers prefer mobile shopping, and your payment methods are clunky on mobile, you're going to lose a lot of revenue and frustrate your core audience.

Payment Methods by the Numbers

Research by Statista indicates that, in the Americas in 2019, Credit Cards are still the preferred online payment option by 82% of consumers, followed by PayPal at 66% and Gift Cards at 41%.[46]

Most popular payment methods of online shoppers
(in selected regions as of January 2019)

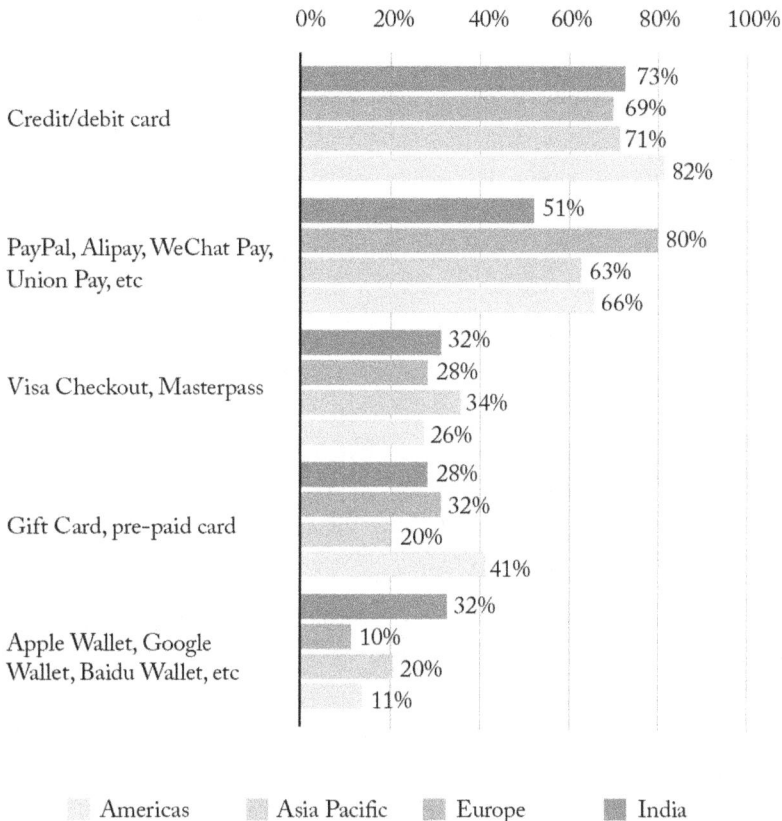

Chart x-axis: 0% 20% 40% 60% 80% 100%

Credit/debit card
- 73%
- 69%
- 71%
- 82%

PayPal, Alipay, WeChat Pay, Union Pay, etc
- 51%
- 80%
- 63%
- 66%

Visa Checkout, Masterpass
- 32%
- 28%
- 34%
- 26%

Gift Card, pre-paid card
- 28%
- 32%
- 20%
- 41%

Apple Wallet, Google Wallet, Baidu Wallet, etc
- 32%
- 10%
- 20%
- 11%

Legend: Americas — Asia Pacific — Europe — India

Source: Statista 2019

Choosing the Right Payment Options

First and foremost, the best option for your store is always the preferred option of your core audience. While cryptocurrency, for instance, is only preferred by 3% of US shoppers overall,[47] it might be the most popular method in your category and thus critical for *you* to accept. Having a consumer's preferred method supports comfort and trust.

Security concerns also remain a top priority for consumers. This explains much of the popularity of APMs like digital wallets, since customers pre-load their personal and credit card or bank information into their account, giving customers an extra layer of encryption while making payments. Customers are also spared having to re-enter their information on each purchase. PayPal and Square are leaders in this space, but many digital wallets require customers to complete their purchase off-site by redirecting them during the checkout process. This can be a confusing, startling step for some customers.

It's important to consider the fees associated with each potential option. Typically, there's either a usage or transaction fee, which may be required monthly or per transaction. Research the cost of each option thoroughly. If you are planning on serving international shoppers, make sure you support payment options that can deal with foreign currency as there will likely be an extra cost to handle exchanges.

Consider what payment structures you offer. If you offer a monthly subscription service, then you'll need a recurring billing function. Does your payment provider support your model?

How user-friendly are your payment methods? Consider how much of your sales will be made through mobile and whether the mobile payment experience is streamlined and easy to follow.

Finally, review the customer support each payment option provides in case customers have a problem. Most customers are not going to distinguish between your personal customer service and the service of various payment providers, so be sure your options have robust service that customers are satisfied with.

Wrapping Up with Payment Options

The role payment methods play in the customer experience is often overlooked. Customers must be comfortable completing a purchase and sharing their personal information with you to ensure long-term success. Research all of your payment processing options to find the best for your target customers' preferences and consider the checkout experience from their point of view.

Free Shipping

Why You Should Offer Free Shipping

In the battle for online consumers, it's no longer a question of who has the lowest prices. Increasingly, free shipping options heavily influence a customer's eCommerce brand choice.

Of course, there is a cost involved in providing free shipping, but research has shown it leads to an increase in sales, reduced cart abandonments, as well as an increase in your average revenue per user, making the expense a smart investment.

The Benefits of Free Shipping, by the Numbers

The 2019 Walker Sands report found that for the fifth year in a row, free shipping was the top online purchase driver. Consumers have grown to

What would make you more likely to shop online?

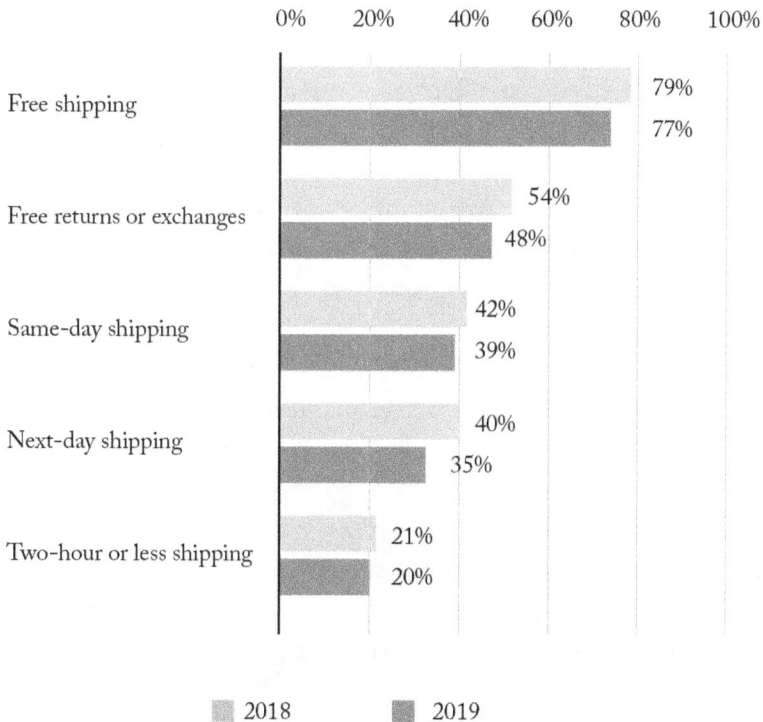

	0%	20%	40%	60%	80%	100%

Free shipping
- 79%
- 77%

Free returns or exchanges
- 54%
- 48%

Same-day shipping
- 42%
- 39%

Next-day shipping
- 40%
- 35%

Two-hour or less shipping
- 21%
- 20%

2018   2019

Source: Walker Sands Future of Retail 2019

expect fast and free shipping, and they no longer consider these offerings as added perks.[48]

Baymard Institute found, along with other fees, that 61% of abandoned carts are motivated by shipping costs being too high.[49]

Usability Science conducted a study which revealed the average number of items in a cart is 3.4, and the average ticket price is $118.29 on sites without a free shipping option, while free shipping raised these numbers to an average of 3.7 items, and an average ticket price of $142.93.[50] Thus, aside from capturing more customers with free shipping, you'll make more from the customers you already have.

In terms of how free shipping impacts consumer expectations of delivery speed, research has shown that 86% of customers are willing to wait 4-7 days for free shipping.[51]

How to Offer Free Shipping

Making sure you can afford to offer free shipping while remaining profitable is a major concern for eCommerce merchants. Luckily, there are several strategies to make it work.

First, you can, of course, offer free shipping on everything in your store. Typically, this option still comes with certain restrictions. For instance, you may only offer it within your home country, or it may be a slower delivery method. Having free shipping across the board makes things simple for the customer, and you can cover costs by baking the shipping fee into the item price or instituting an incremental price increase on all items. This can be risky depending on your category, however. While item price is no longer the main area of competition between eCommerce retailers, cost remains the initial decision point. However, if the baked-in price is a faster shipping option, like 1- or 2-day delivery, many customers are willing to spend more.

A very popular option to help you cover shipping costs is only offering a free option once the order value reaches a certain threshold. This is a particularly effective upsell technique as it gives customers the option between ordering more items and paying a shipping fee. Psychologically, this makes customers feel in control of how much they spend, and it typically leads to customers adding more items to their cart.

The Impact of Free Shipping

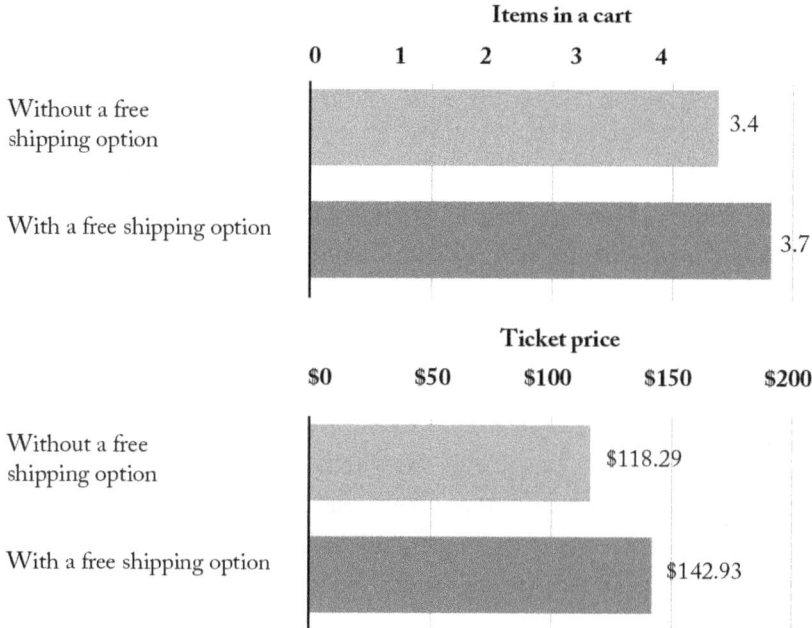

Items in a cart

| | 0 | 1 | 2 | 3 | 4 |

Without a free shipping option — 3.4

With a free shipping option — 3.7

Ticket price

| | $0 | $50 | $100 | $150 | $200 |

Without a free shipping option — $118.29

With a free shipping option — $142.93

Source: Rejoiner.com

Confining free shipping to certain times of the year is another popular tactic. Holidays and events like Black Friday and Cyber Monday are natural options, but the higher competition at this time when margins are already thin may wipe out your profits. More effective times for limited free shipping include Valentine's Day and Mother's Day.

Finally, not unlike Amazon's Prime membership, you can set up a member or loyalty program for which free shipping is a benefit. Repeat customers are not only more valuable in terms of profit but also data, and the long-term business this kind of program generates may make the cost of free shipping worth its weight in gold.

Summary, Free Shipping

There's no question that to offer free shipping, you will incur a significant cost. However, the option has proven and powerful benefits to your revenue. With the right strategy to make it affordable, free shipping can contribute to your long-term success and a happy, loyal customer base.

Product Reviews

Research consistently cites peer recommendations, personal research, and product reviews as the most influential content that affects purchase decisions and featuring them on your site can significantly increase conversions.

There's no faster way to build consumer trust than collecting and showcasing reviews. Reviews help consumers imagine themselves using your products and genuine reviews add depth and insight to product details.

Product Reviews by the Numbers:

Research shows that *95%* of consumers report they read reviews before making a purchase decision.[52] In fact, only 3% of buyers say reviews have no bearing on their buying behavior.[53] Given these impressive numbers, it's possibly no surprise that the Spiegel Research Center found displaying reviews on product pages can increase conversions by 270%. On pages for higher-priced items, conversions jump by 380%.[54] Also, the more reviews you have, the better, as five or more reviews increase the likelihood of purchase by *almost 4 times.*[55]

57% of American consumers say they only feel comfortable doing business with a brand that has a *minimum* star rating of four out of five

The Financial Impact of Displaying Reviews

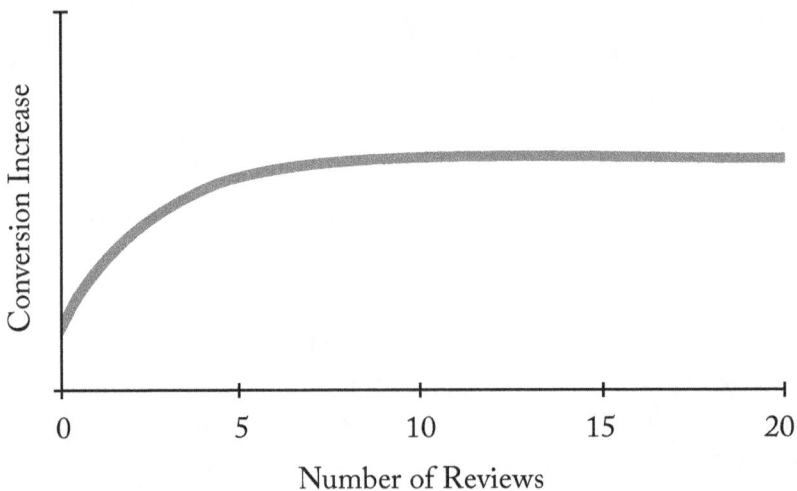

Source: Spiegel Research Center

stars.[56] However, that doesn't mean you should fret over negative reviews. An astonishing 82% of customers say they specifically seek out negative reviews, and on average, consumers spend 4 times longer engaging with negative reviews, and they lead to a 67% increase in conversions.[57] The sweet spot for the highest conversions ranges between 4.0-4.7 stars, and conversions then *decrease* as your rating gets closer to 5.[58]

Getting the Most from Product Reviews

Most eCommerce platforms do have a native ability to post reviews, but consider using a third-party platform for reviews that you cannot personally moderate: this will ensure all reviews are written by real customers. These companies also add their trust logo to reviews to advertise the impartiality of what's posted.

Each review should include:

1. The customer's name
2. Their location
3. A title for the review
4. The review itself
5. A yes/no statement as to whether customers would recommend the product.

Reviews should be positioned near the bottom of the page under the details of the product but do include the average star rating and the number of reviews in the main item description, near the price.

To get more reviews, start an email campaign that follows-up with customers after purchase. Approximately 80% of reviews originate from these kinds of follow-up emails.[59] In these emails, ask customers politely for feedback. Above all, it's critical to ensure that leaving a review is easy. The more accessible the process, the more reviews you'll get.

To further incentivize reviews, consider offering a discount or benefit like free shipping on the next purchase in exchange for a customer's thoughts.

Summary, Product Reviews

Product reviews are powerful social proof for your brand and products. Featuring reviews on your product pages significantly increases conversions and builds brand trust. Make sure that you're transparent about which reviews you publish and include negative feedback. Reply to reviews to thank customers or address any concerns.

Reducing Cart Abandonment

Any eCommerce merchant can tell you that one of their largest sources of lost revenue is abandoned shopping carts. On average, the abandoned cart rate in retail is 74.2%.[60]

There are many reasons consumers leave a purchase incomplete, including surprise fees or shipping costs, untrustworthy sites, or a complex checkout process. Some consumers simply aren't ready to buy or just get distracted.

Abandoned carts are a widespread problem, but it's possible to recover a significant portion of this lost profit by optimizing your website, checkout process, and retargeting campaigns.

Abandoned Cart Statistics

The single biggest reason people abandon their purchase, reported by a full 60% of consumers, is unexpected extra costs, including shipping fees and taxes.[61]

The second leading cause is required account creation, leading to 37% of customers abandoning their cart. 28% of customers say they've left without buying due to a long or overly complex checkout process. 23% left because they couldn't calculate their total cost upfront, while 20% experienced website crashes.[62]

Trust remains a high driver of abandonment as well, with Actual Insights finding that 61% of consumers have given up on a purchase because a trust logo wasn't present during checkout, and 75% didn't buy because a present trust logo wasn't recognized.[63]

Best Practices to Minimize Abandoned Carts

There are several ways to reduce abandoned cart rates. When you look at the statistics above, 28% of consumers say they've abandoned a purchase because the checkout process was suboptimal. This reflects that many issues can be remedied with design changes. In fact, optimizing your checkout process alone can gain a 35% increase in conversions.[64]

Upfront, many customers are turned off by being required to create an account to complete a purchase, so offer a guest checkout option.

Next, be absolutely upfront about the full cost of a customer's order before the checkout process begins. While offering free shipping is ideal, customers are very sensitive to how these fees are communicated. Unless

Reasons for Abandonments during Checkout

"Have you abandoned any online purchases during the checkout process
in the past 3 months? If so, for what reasons?"
(4,560 responses US adults 2020 @baymard.com/research)

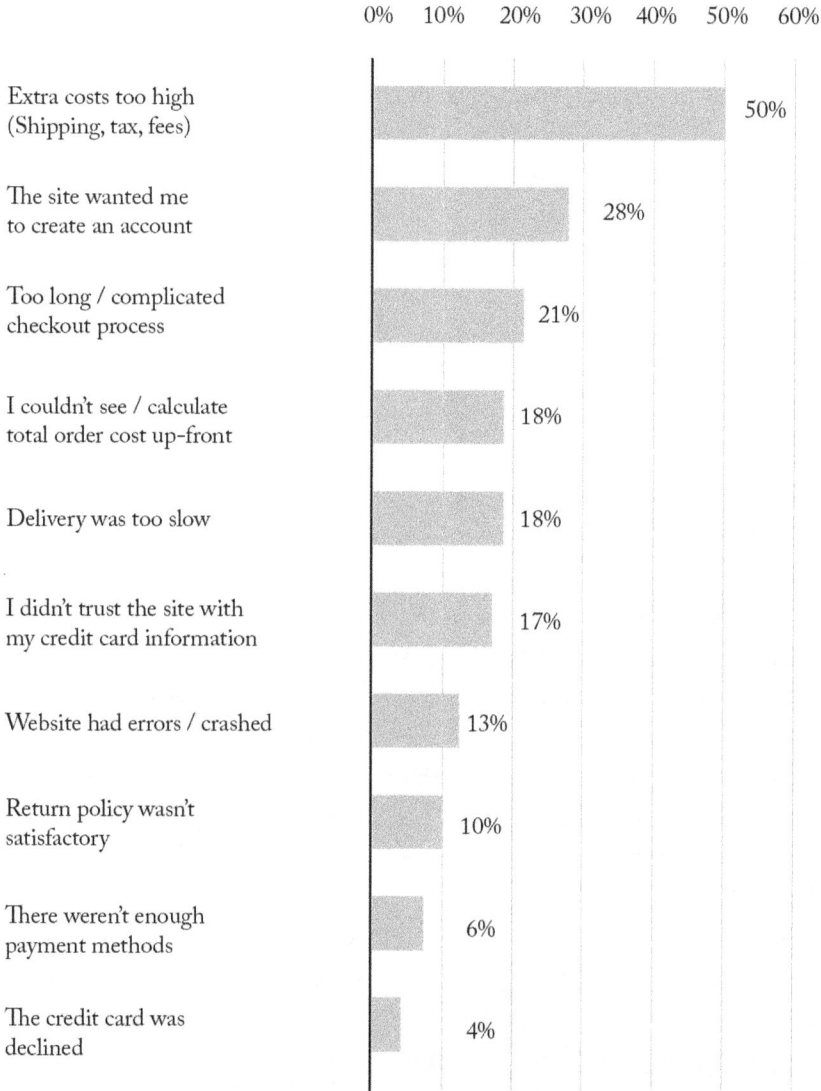

0% 10% 20% 30% 40% 50% 60%	
Extra costs too high (Shipping, tax, fees)	50%
The site wanted me to create an account	28%
Too long / complicated checkout process	21%
I couldn't see / calculate total order cost up-front	18%
Delivery was too slow	18%
I didn't trust the site with my credit card information	17%
Website had errors / crashed	13%
Return policy wasn't satisfactory	10%
There weren't enough payment methods	6%
The credit card was declined	4%

Source: Baymard Institute, 2020

you are transparent about costs, you're likely going to have a leaky checkout process.

Delivery estimates are also critical and make sure your return policy is transparent and easy to find. Like free shipping, hassle-free returns put buyer minds at ease. As customers can't see the items they're ordering upfront these assurances help customers avoid feeling like they're sending their personal information out into the void.

As for the checkout itself, testing has shown the ideal amount of form fields is seven to eight. The average US checkout has *fifteen* form fields, so this one step will put you ahead of the norm. Too many fields fuel customer suspicion, even if there's a good reason to ask for certain details. Add short trust messages beside the field, explaining why you're asking for certain items.

It's also a good idea to have these kinds of trust messages throughout the process. Give customers as much clarity as you can. Make sure there's an estimated shipping time associated with each shipping option, and if your company requires additional processing or production time in advance of shipping, add a note about this and tell customers what they can expect. Also, include a message under the "Place Your Order" button explaining their payment method will not be charged until the items are shipped.

Give customers the ability to navigate between their cart and the store easily (other than the "Back" button). The ability to save a cart for later is also especially helpful for consumers who are still comparing products.

Featuring a progress bar is another reassuring tactic. This tells consumers they're almost done and that you will not require too much of their time. If you can, fitting your checkout process onto a single page is ideal and less intimidating to consumers.

Finally, accept that you are going to lose some customers no matter how perfect your checkout design. This is where retargeting campaigns come in, and we will cover it in a later section. You can remind customers to return and complete their purchase with either retargeting ads or email. Cart abandonment emails are opened 45% of the time, and the average conversion rate for email reminders is almost 20%.[65]

The ideal email timeline:

- The first email should arrive within an hour of an abandoned cart,
- A second email 24 hours later, and,
- A third email 72 hours after their cart was left.

Emails should be personalized and include the customer's name and a list of what was left in their cart.

Summary: Reducing Abandoned Carts

There's no way to avoid cart abandonment altogether. However, it doesn't have to cut too deeply into your profits. By optimizing your checkout process, building trust, and using an effective retargeting campaign, you can recapture many of the sales you might otherwise have lost.

The Importance of Mobile eCommerce

In 2011, only 35% of Americans owned a smartphone. Today, however, 77% have a smartphone in their pocket.[66] With this mobile-centric way of life, more consumers are using their mobile devices to browse, shop, and purchase than ever before. eCommerce merchants must, therefore, offer a seamless shopping experience on mobile.

Mobile Shopping by the Numbers

While mobile traffic now represents almost 51% of all eCommerce traffic, this activity doesn't result in half of a site's sales.[67] Mobile visitor numbers increase annually, but mobile conversions remain relatively low.

By device, the average conversion rate (ACR) on desktop is 2%, and the average revenue per visit (ARPV) is $4.11; on tablet, the ACR is 1.5%, and the ARPV is $2.58; meanwhile, on mobile, the ACR is 0.6%, and the ARPV is $0.87.[68] Unsurprisingly, mobile also has a significantly higher cart abandonment rate at 85.65% versus 73.07% on desktop.[69] The pattern would appear to be that as screen size decreases, conversion becomes more difficult.

Despite this, mobile represents 19% of eCommerce sales, and this number is predicted to reach 54% by the end of 2021.[70] Overall, consumers prefer shopping on mobile apps versus mobile websites. In the US alone, 88% of mobile minutes in all markets are spent on apps.[71]

One of the most significant changes the shift to mobile has made is in how consumers reach purchase decisions while shopping in-store. About one-third of consumers say they have looked up additional information and reviews of items via their mobile device while in a brick-and-mortar store. In this group of consumers, 20% have decided to complete their purchase elsewhere, 22% decided to buy the item online, while 19% completed their purchase in-store, and 20% decided against the purchase altogether.[72]

Optimizing Your Brand for Mobile

Conversions tend to be lower on mobile because few eCommerce sites are optimized for mobile browsing and shopping. Many mobile eCommerce stores are plagued by slow loading times and unresponsive sites leading to frustrating site navigation that requires zooming in and out. In 2016, Google announced their algorithm would now run off mobile sites instead

ACR & ARPV (by Device Type)

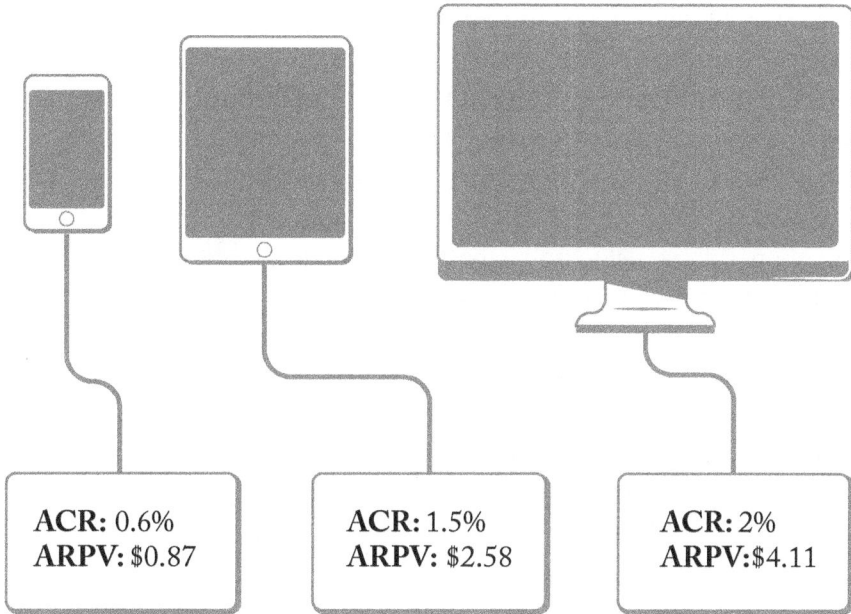

| ACR: 0.6% | ACR: 1.5% | ACR: 2% |
| ARPV: $0.87 | ARPV: $2.58 | ARPV:$4.11 |

Source: invespcro.com

of desktop. This means eCommerce merchants have to think mobile-first to stay relevant to consumers. Retailers now need to intentionally design their mobile experience.

Consumers tend to use their mobile devices in short, frequent bursts. In order to make sure a consumer completes a purchase journey in a single visit, mobile sites need to require fewer steps to complete each action. For instance, any phone number listed on your mobile site should be text rather than an image, allowing mobile users to tap-to-call. Due to the smaller screen, which makes reading large swaths of text difficult, visual content is also more important.

You'll still need main navigation but increase the padding around each menu item making options easier to read and accurately tap.

Form fields need to be larger on mobile, so they're easier to read, tap, and input. It's particularly important to have a touch-optimized form fields where the keyboard that pops up is customized to match the type of information being asked for. For example, in a field asking for a phone number, the keyboard should automatically display a number pad only, making input easier and minimizing mistakes.

On your product pages, mobile users expect smartphone gestures like double-tap and pinch-to-zoom to work. Be sure these abilities are allowed on your pages and enable swipe on product images. Keeping your site experience as close to the user's general mobile experience will help it feel seamless.

When it comes to your checkout, 80% of mobile purchases are made through guest checkout,[73] so don't hide this option. Our eyes are attracted to large open form fields, so it's best to keep the sign-in option collapsed and place the guest option on top, so its visibility is maximized.

You'll also want all of your call-to-action and progress buttons kept in the "thumb zone" of smartphones; generally, the lower-left half of the screen.

Finally, there is always the question of whether you're better off focusing on optimizing a mobile responsive website or developing a native mobile app. The advantages of websites include easier indexing by search engines, higher visitation rates than apps, added ease of design and maintenance, all leading to added cost-effectiveness. In addition, you can more easily track analytics. The downside, however, means that while you get more visitors, it's more difficult to convert on a mobile site. Customers are less likely to sign-in while viewing your site and so there's less data and fewer opportunities for personalization.

Native apps have much higher engagement levels than sites, and they have better conversion rates. Consumers are more likely to sign in and opt into other offers and loyalty programs. Since consumers need to specifically download the app, their identity is more likely to be attached, so you'll have better data and more opportunities for personalization. Apps also provide the ability for push notifications, and they load faster and don't require a web connection. However, since consumers need to intentionally download your app, you'll need to market its availability. Apps are also more expensive to design and develop, particularly as you'll need two primary versions: iOS and Android.

Summary, Mobile eCommerce

While most online traffic is coming from mobile, consumers typically switch to desktop to complete their orders, but this doesn't mean you should neglect the importance of your mobile site. Every channel should be optimized for providing a great experience and to increase conversions.

Customer Service

Offering comprehensive and trustworthy customer service is critical to your brand's success as it will be a consumer's direct touchpoint. A negative experience makes a lasting impression as, according to BI Intelligence, 60% of US consumers report they have failed to complete an intended purchase due to poor customer service.[74]

Customer service is especially challenging for eCommerce merchants since online doesn't offer the same in-person service as in-store shopping. However, there are many things you can do to build consumer confidence.

Chatbots

Of course, it would be ideal to employ live agents to handle all of your service requests, but this can be costly, especially because customers expect 24/7 service online. Chatbots are, therefore, an accessible option for even smaller eCommerce companies. A chatbot is a form of artificial intelligence that can simulate a conversation with live users either through text or speech. By simulating how a live person would respond, chatbots can do many of the jobs a human customer service agent does, but with more cost and time efficiency.

As more and more shoppers are using mobile devices to shop, chatbots can help mobile customers complete purchases, answer basic questions, and offer personalized recommendations.

Chatbots can also address customer service complaints and get the process started for more complex concerns. Chatbots are available at all hours and on holidays, and they can engage multiple customers at once, so no one's ever left waiting.

Chatbots By the Numbers

Chatbots are a relatively new phenomenon in the eCommerce world, but they are catching on quickly.

In fact, Statista found that the online retail sector has the widest acceptance of AI-enabled service out of any industry, with 34% of customers reporting they are comfortable engaging with a chatbot.[75]

They also offer a significant opportunity to improve the overall customer service experience. While no more than a 5-minute delay in response to an inquiry is ideal, a 10-minute or more delay reduces a company's chances

Acceptance of Artificial Intelligence Chatbots
(by customers worldwide, as of 2017, by service: 6,000 Respondents, 18 years and older)

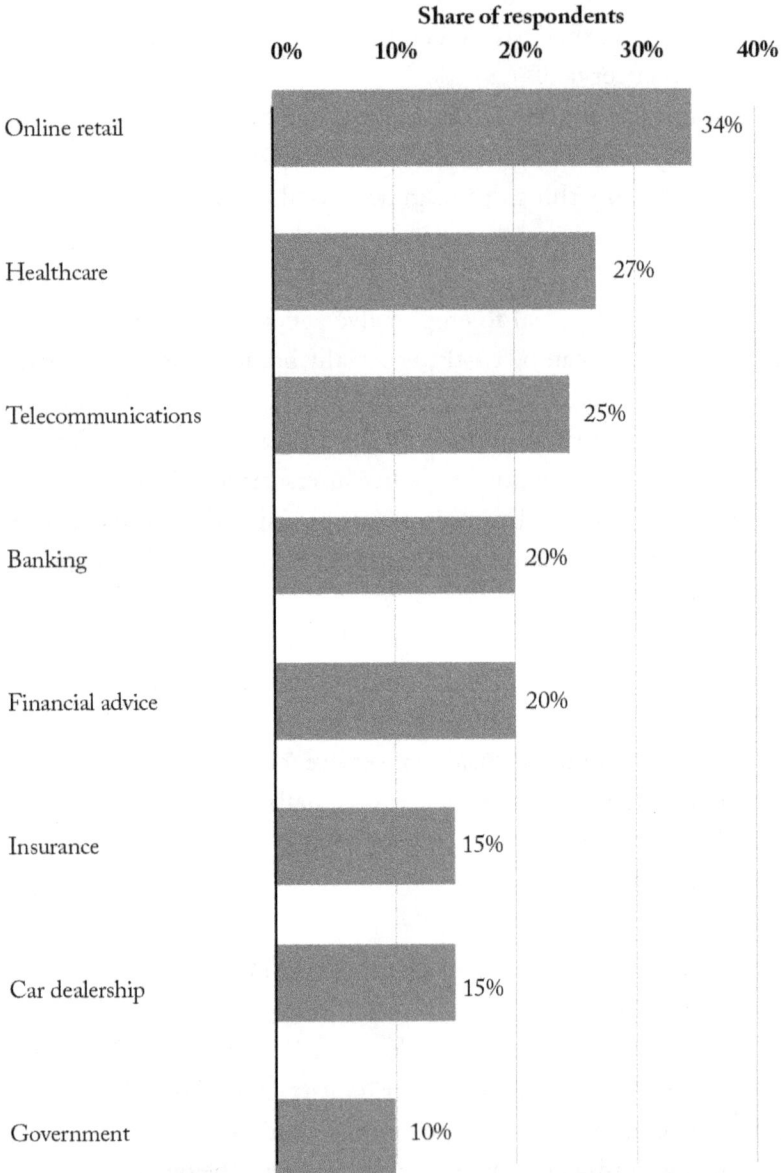

Share of respondents

0%	10%	20%	30%	40%

Online retail — 34%

Healthcare — 27%

Telecommunications — 25%

Banking — 20%

Financial advice — 20%

Insurance — 15%

Car dealership — 15%

Government — 10%

Source: Statista 2017

of attracting a lead by up to 400%.[76] By having a chatbot that can reply instantaneously, you, therefore, capture a greater percentage of leads.

Best Practices for a Great Chatbot

The baseline requirement for a good chatbot is a professional, bug-free experience. It must work on a variety of devices, have good linguistic skills, and accurately perform tasks.

Truly great chatbots bring your brand's voice to life and help foster an emotional connection with customers. They also can adapt a tone to match the situation. For example, if the customer has a complaint, it should speak with empathy.

To make sure your chatbot gives customers a seamless, on-brand experience, you want your chatbot to closely approximate a real conversation. To achieve this, give your bot multiple welcome messages to avoid repetition. Most importantly, however, is to use a chatbot that's aware of dialect, meaning the customer can speak with their voice and word choice, instead of being restricted to pre-packaged answers and inquiries. Chatbots that ask for the customer's name and ask how they're doing today also help things move along, and if a request takes a few minutes for your chatbot to process, give your chatbot the ability to make small talk to keep the customer engaged.

Summary, Chatbots

While most customers still prefer to speak to live agents for their service concerns, chatbots are an increasingly important aspect of offering the best customer service for your eCommerce store. Chatbots can assist customers along their purchase journey, provide a positive, personal brand experience, and get service complaints either resolved or expedited.

Email Marketing

Email marketing is simply the process of using email to increase traffic and ultimately boost sales for your store, and it's one of the most powerful tools at your disposal.

Email works because it reaches prospects who have already shown an interest in your brand and products.

There's no shortage of approaches to email marketing, for instance, you may set up an automated email to follow up on abandoned shopping carts, or you might use email for a drip campaign, where you send personalized content straight to customers. But email marketing truly shines in its ability to build relationships with consumers.

Why an eCommerce Store Should Invest in Email Marketing

Email marketing has a phenomenal ROI. From a $100 investment in email marketing, companies earn an average of $4,425.[77] Email is also forty times more effective at acquiring new customers than social channels like Facebook and Twitter.[78]

In addition, email marketing is also the cheapest marketing option. There are several free tools and services to help you set up and run an email marketing campaign, like Klaviyo, Active Campaign, and Mailchimp.

Despite the proliferation of social channels and options, email remains the default communication tool for most consumers. There are 2.9 billion email accounts in the world, so chances are your consumers are using email daily.

In general, email is the only direct line of communication to consumers. Consider that consumers are far more likely to at least read the subject line of a branded email because they have an inbox to clear. On social media, by contrast, users either see a post or they don't. Email also works on your terms. Whereas Facebook's algorithms, for instance, largely determine who can see your posts, email lets you reliably reach out to customers.

On social, you're just another user with a profile. With email, more factors are under your control, most importantly, your access to your audience as you own your email list. There are also fewer regulations about when you can send an email and what you can say. You must, however, still offer value in your emails. Whatever form of campaign you choose, whether it's a weekly newsletter of valuable insights or announcements of new products and promotions, you want to be sending the right message about your brand and your values to ensure your emails are building long-term relationships. These campaigns can again be inspired by the eBrandBuilders' Content Creation Framework, where each weekly email can be related to a particular "C."

Finally, one of email's most powerful benefits is the ability to segment your email list and further target specific sections of your audience. This will allow you to offer more personalized and relevant content, which will be more effective in retaining customers.

Crafting Your Store's Email Strategy

Building an email list needs to be a priority for your business. It's as easy as asking visitors to your site for their email address, and you can incentivize a response by offering a one-time discount or other benefits like free shipping or access to special content. According to Accenture, 54% of customers say they'd share their emails in exchange for a discount.[79] Another tactic is to offer exclusive content like a free download, a quiz, or entry into a contest: these lead magnets are proven to work.

Once you have a list, you'll need to set up your campaigns and start automating your emails. Then send regular emails with valuable content or consumers will quickly opt-out. You'll see the most returns if you intertwine your email marketing with your content strategy since more people will sign up for your emails if you offer something unique.

The 6 specific email campaigns you need to run:

1. *Welcome emails:* These are the initial, introductory emails customers receive after first signing up. Consider including information about your brand values and introduce your brand story. If you offered a coupon or download for signing-up, include it here.

2. *Brand awareness:* Reach out to recent subscribers to generate leads, deliver new content, and nurture an ongoing relationship with your brand.

3. *Purchase:* These emails are sent automatically after a customer has completed a purchase. They confirm the order, summarize the purchase, and offer support if needed.

4. *Post-purchase:* These emails go out roughly 2 weeks after an order. The customer has most likely received their order and had a chance to start using it. Use these emails to ask for a quick review or feedback on the

SIX ECOMMERCE EMAIL CAMPAIGNS

01 • **Welcome:**
Initial, introductory emails customers receive after first signing up.

02 • **Brand Awareness:**
Emails to recent subscribers to generate leads, deliver new content, and nurture an ongoing relationship with your brand.

03 • **Purchase:**
Emails sent automatically after a customer has completed a purchase: order confirmation, purchase summary, and support offers.

04 • **Post-Purchase:**
Emails sent roughly 2 weeks after an order: quick review or feedback to net social proof.

05 • **Cart Abandonment:**
Emails, retargeting consumers who left your site without purchasing after putting items in their cart.

06 • **Win-Back:**
Emails sent to re-engage a month and a half after a purchase if the customer hasn't returned to your site.

products to net the social proof of reviews, and help your brand stay top-of-mind.

5. *Cart abandonment:* These emails, as mentioned, retarget consumers who left your site without purchasing after putting items in their cart. The best approach is a series of emails which gently remind customers they never finished their order.

6. *Win-back:* Send these emails about a month and a half after purchase if the customer hasn't returned to your site. Re-engage customers with your brand and remind them how easy it is to order with you.

Summary, Email Marketing

Email marketing has been a great investment for decades, and it remains one of the most profitable marketing options. Not only does email marketing promise the highest ROI, but it also keeps you in full control of your email list and messaging, making email the most direct and effective line of communication with your customers.

Retail Space

The Growing Trend of Retail Space for eCommerce Brands

Despite countless eulogies for the death of retail, many eCommerce brands are discovering that the in-store experience still has life. Opening a brick-and-mortar location allows digitally native brands to create a physical touchpoint that aligns with the brand's persona and creates an immersive, high-end experience that integrates seamlessly with their online channel.

Many previously online-only brands are now opening brick-and-mortar stores like Casper, Boll & Branch, ModCloth, Glossier, Greats, Amerisleep, and MM.Lafleur. While other online brands like Warby Parker, Zappos, and Bonobos have also launched their first retail locations in the past decade, the rate at which eCommerce brands are moving to traditional retail has skyrocketed in the past few years. About 67% of the largest eCommerce brands have made the leap to physical retail in the past 36 months alone.[80]

This may seem counterintuitive as, according to CNBC, as of early March 2019, 4,810 stores have already announced they're closing this year.[81] Yet, many retail experts argue that the issue isn't in-person shopping losing appeal, rather traditional retailers are failing to update their business model.

eCommerce merchants, meanwhile, see physical locations as part of an omnichannel approach to sales.

In addition, unlike traditional retailers, eCommerce brick-and-mortar stores and pop-ups are heavily touted as events, and the marketing efforts include influencer campaigns, strategic content, and promotions.

Physical Retail Options for eCommerce

Many brands, particularly luxury brands, use retail space as a showroom to allow customers to interact directly with products and also be immersed in the brand's culture. These are larger, standalone stores that give brands enough space to be creative. While these kinds of locations typically come with the highest cost in terms of rent, they can be a smart option if you've tested the market with another option first.

Pop-ups are a cost-effective way to test your local market as "pop to permanent" has been the evolution of many brands. Pop-ups offer versatile designs and experiences. Casper, for example, set up a "Sleep Shop" in New York that offered 45-minute naps on their mattresses for $25, and they have recently begun opening permanent showrooms.

Co-retail is another option. These stores-within-stores see online brands pair with big-box retailers and set up inside a chain store. This gets your products in front of a larger audience and helps give consumers another reason to visit a local chain. Greats and Allbirds have partnered with Nordstrom, for instance. In a unique online-to-offline partnership, Quip, a Brooklyn-based electric toothbrush company, partnered with Target. Quip sells starter kits for $25 at all 1,800 Target stores and Target. com, but consumers can only buy refill brushes from Quip's site. This arrangement helps Quip scale but keeps customers coming back to their own site. Target, meanwhile, can explore how their customers convert on an external online store while providing a new type of product for its younger customer base.

The Benefits of a Physical Location

In the interest of creating a truly omnichannel journey, the brands finding success with physical retail are creating an immersive atmosphere in-store. While eCommerce retailers can deliver the convenience of 24/7 shopping as well as lots of choices and a good price, it's difficult to create a brand experience through a screen. Using the in-store experience to showcase your brand's personality and culture can bring your brand alive for consumers in a way that isn't possible online. And the possibilities are only limited by your imagination:

- Away Luggage offers events that include concerts and yoga classes.
- Greats, the sneaker brand, offers exclusive products at their New York location.
- MM.LaFleur offers appointments with a personal stylist who curates a selection of clothing items and looks for customers to try on.

When the in-store experience aligns with and complements the online one, the brand is powerfully reinforced in the minds of customers. Rather than being sales-focused, your location should lead customers through a holistic, unique journey that draws consumers into a relationship with your brand.

In general, physical stores have much higher conversion rates with online shops and offer a more personal approach to getting help from an associate. TimeTrade's State of Retail Report found that a third of customers like receiving advice from in-store associates and a full 90% of consumers are likely to buy after getting this kind of help. A customer's average order value also tends to increase once they've spoken to a staff member.[82]

Among the other financial benefits of a physical store is a boost for online sales as well. L2's Intelligence Report found that brands with a brick-and-mortar location see an increase of brand mentions and organic searches online. These retailers also have a significantly lower customer acquisition cost via paid search and email.[83]

Physical stores can also serve as warehouses and distribution centers, solving many of eCommerce's logistic challenges. This also allows brands to offer "click and collect" options, a smart move as UPS research revealed 45% of customers picking up an online order will buy extra products while in-store.[84]

Finally, another major benefit of a retail location is the ability to do market research. Observing your customers as they move through the purchase journey can give you deep insights not available in any focus group. In-store you can notice what customers are drawn to, discover their reasoning for why they decide to buy or not buy, and so on, helping you more accurately make business decisions and develop new products. You may even discover a new audience to tap into.

Conclusion

There's no question eCommerce has revolutionized traditional retail. But instead of spelling the end of brick-and-mortar shopping, eCommerce has triggered its evolution into a true omnichannel experience. The eCommerce merchants making the most of what in-person shopping has to offer are those that are blending the digital and the physical in new and unexpected ways.

Shared Channels

Shared channels include marketplaces, crowdfunding, and partnerships. Marketplaces are where eCommerce sellers generate a large part of their revenue, primarily due to the low barriers to entry, a ready market, and a global customer base. Crowdfunding forms another first entry point for eCommerce sellers, in particular to those that offer something truly unique and appealing to early adopters for funding. Finally, partnerships are an opportunity for more mature eCommerce properties.

Marketplaces

What has been labeled as "The Great Retail Apocalypse" for three consecutive years (2017-2019), is on pace to break the record for retail door closures per annum, from Sears to Toys R Us. This trend has left malls deserted, and they now find themselves at an inflection point. While the retail real-estate industry figures out how to fill these sky-high vacancy rates, customers are turning to online marketplaces. According to Juniper Research, the growth of the marketplace economy led by sharing economy companies is set to double between 2017 and 2022, growing from $19 billion to $40 billion.[85]

Total Sharing Economy Revenues, Split by Key Regions by 2022

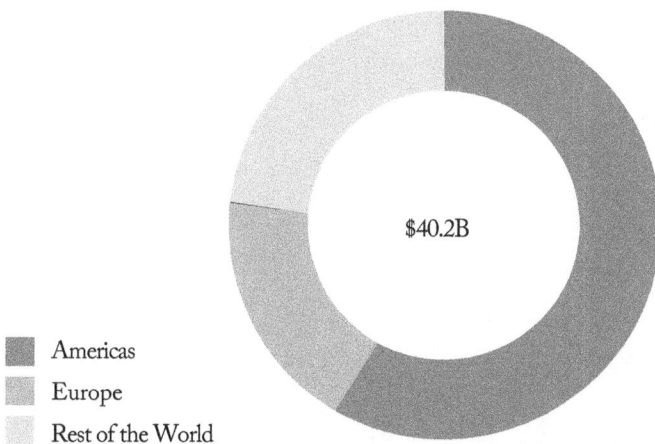

$40.2B

- ▮ Americas
- ▨ Europe
- ▢ Rest of the World

Source: Juniper Research Sharing Economy: Opportunities, Impacts & Disruptors 2017-2022

<u>**Amazon**</u>

<u>*Amazon by the Numbers*</u>

Founded in 1994, Amazon began as an online bookstore, and today has grown into the world's largest online retailer. As of 2020, Amazon's share of the retail eCommerce market is 38.7%.[86]

Top 10 US Companies, Ranked by Retail eCommerce Sales Share, 2020

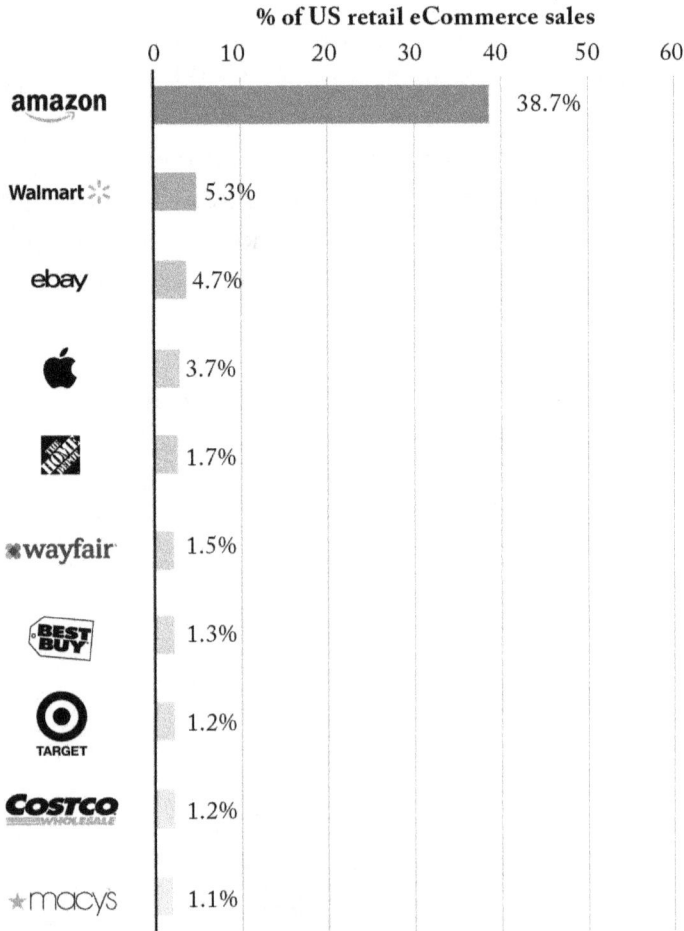

% of US retail eCommerce sales

amazon	38.7%
Walmart	5.3%
ebay	4.7%
Apple	3.7%
Home Depot	1.7%
wayfair	1.5%
Best Buy	1.3%
Target	1.2%
Costco Wholesale	1.2%
macy's	1.1%

Source: eMarketer 2020

While the largest segment of Amazon's revenue comes from its retail sales, the second largest section comes through its third-party seller services. As of the last reported quarter, 53% of units purchased were sold by third-party sellers.[87] This platform allows eCommerce merchants to

Percentage of Paid Units sold by 3rd Party Sellers on Amazon
(as of 1nd quarter 2020)

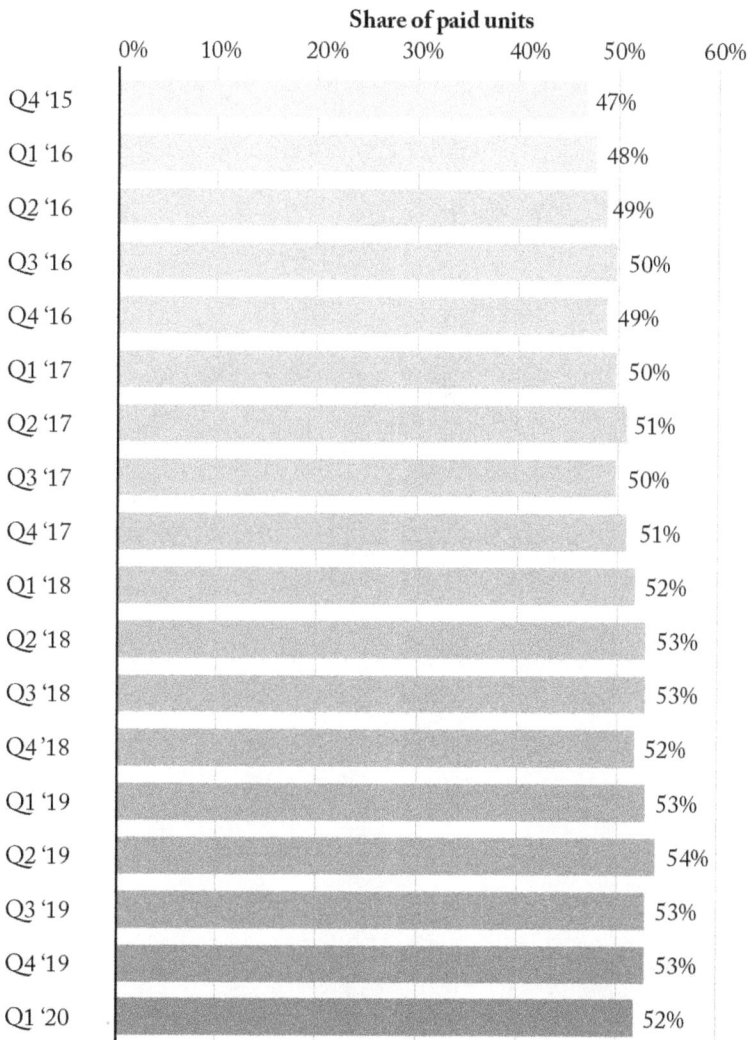

Share of paid units

Q4 '15	47%
Q1 '16	48%
Q2 '16	49%
Q3 '16	50%
Q4 '16	49%
Q1 '17	50%
Q2 '17	51%
Q3 '17	50%
Q4 '17	51%
Q1 '18	52%
Q2 '18	53%
Q3 '18	53%
Q4 '18	52%
Q1 '19	53%
Q2 '19	54%
Q3 '19	53%
Q4 '19	53%
Q1 '20	52%

Source: Statista 2020

reach Amazon's 310 million global users. Sellers can list, promote, and advertise products.

In 2019 third-party sellers, made up of a number of small to medium-size businesses (SMBs), about half (50.7%) of Amazon sellers make from $1,000-$25,000/month, which could mean annual sales from $12,000-$300,000 and one in five made $25,000-$250,000/month, amounting to annual sales between $300,000 and $3,000,000.[88]

Average Monthly Sales for Amazon Sellers

(recent survey of thousands of Amazon sellers conducted by Jungle Scout)

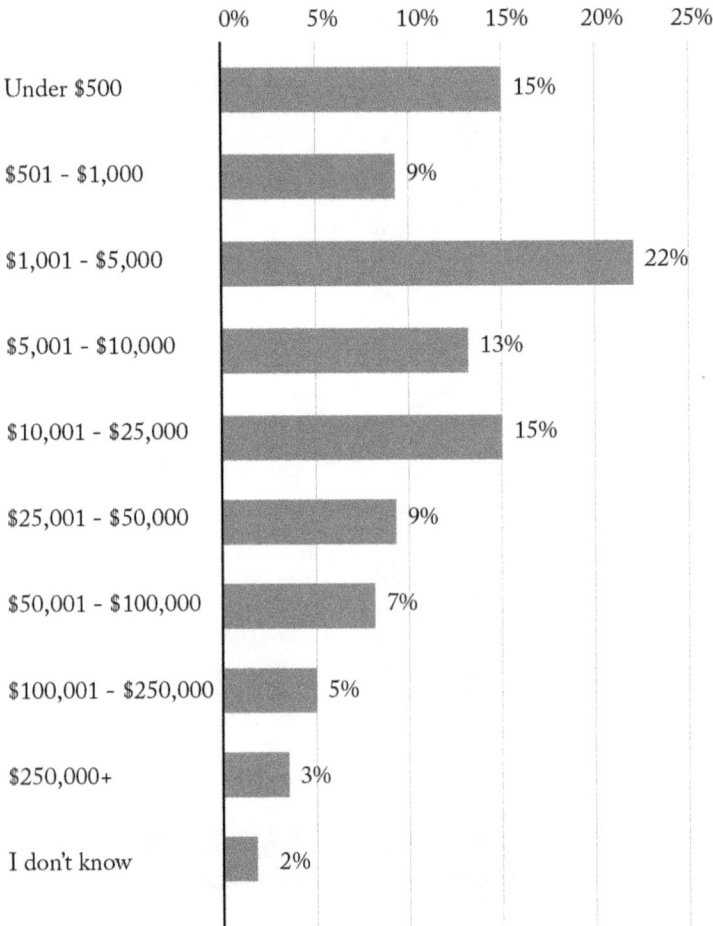

Category	Percentage
Under $500	15%
$501 - $1,000	9%
$1,001 - $5,000	22%
$5,001 - $10,000	13%
$10,001 - $25,000	15%
$25,001 - $50,000	9%
$50,001 - $100,000	7%
$100,001 - $250,000	5%
$250,000+	3%
I don't know	2%

Source: Jungle Scout

The Advantages of Amazon

Due to the sheer number of active users on Amazon's platform, Amazon represents an exceptional entry point for new eCommerce entrepreneurs.

While there are fees associated with selling through Amazon, the platform allows merchants to set up shop and begin selling quickly with very little risk, as most fees are incurred upon selling. Aside from exposure to Amazon's tremendous customer base, selling on Amazon gives your brand a level of credibility. Consumers feel safe buying from unknown sellers on Amazon because they trust Amazon's promise of exceptional customer service.

Sellers, meanwhile, have the option to use Amazon's 'Fulfillment by Amazon' service in which you ship in bulk to Amazon's fulfillment centers, and Amazon then manages your inventory and shipping. A major advantage of this approach is that your products will automatically qualify for Prime shipping and Buy Box priority, which can impact your overall sales positively.

Another major advantage of selling through Amazon is the ease with which you can expand internationally. By creating listings on local Amazon sites, there's no need to adapt your checkout process and listings to multiple languages since this is done automatically. The headaches of setting up local payment systems, logistics and operations are also managed by Amazon, taking much of the risk out of testing new markets.

The Disadvantages of Amazon

Sellers now run the risk of competing with Amazon itself and its increasing number of private-label brands. In fact, 38% of surveyed sellers report their biggest concern is competition from Amazon.[89] Amazon has a growing list of more than 130 private label products, including kitchen goods, batteries, clothing, and electronic accessories. To further compound matters, according to a new report by the Wall Street Journal,[90] Amazon is no longer focused on product development, and instead, it wants other, more established brand manufacturers to do the heavy lifting. The eCommerce giant launched an accelerator program through which companies could develop new Amazon-only products last year. So far, they include a line of sweeteners from the sugar substitute brand Equal, a mattress brand from the startup Tuft & Needle, and two supplement brands from GNC. This move is part of Amazon's greater strategy to cut costs and boost profits for Prime.

There's also growing competition with other sellers, as Amazon added 1,029,528 new sellers in 2018. And these sellers have added a new layer of heightened rivalry, with hijacked listings, counterfeit goods, black-hat and grey-hat techniques to circumvent Amazon's algorithm and rank more highly. On top of this, sellers are left to fend for themselves with no concrete actions taken by Amazon.

To compound matters, the staff at Seller Central, the portal from which Amazon sellers manage all aspects of their sales, is not equipped to properly handle the complexities of patent infringement. This results in listings that are taken down or sellers being banned for no reason, and with no recourse options.

In addition, Amazon owns powerful data such as customer email addresses, which they do not share with sellers. This prohibits sellers from directly engaging with customers and building a relationship with buyers.

Is Amazon Worth It?

Based on this analysis, it may seem like the drawbacks of building a presence on Amazon's marketplace outweigh the positives, but this is not the case. In addition to your store, adding another sales channel into your overall mix, like Amazon or Walmart, can increase revenue by 38%, 120%, and 190% for each channel added. However, the key to understanding is that Amazon can serve as a powerful launchpad and seriously boost sales and revenue, but it should not be a place to build a brand. Brand building starts when you can engage customers with your story, bring them to your eCommerce store, build a relationship that leads to a sale, and encourage repeat purchases. While there's nothing wrong with leveraging Amazon's brand when you're starting out, eventually, you need to become a brand in your own right if you want longevity.

Walmart.com

Founded in 1962, Walmart is the largest publicly owned retailer with more than 11,000 stores worldwide, and in 2019 their global net sales hit $514.41 billion US.[91]

Walmart's Net Sales Worldwide from 2006 to 2019
(billion USD)

Year	Net Sales
2006	$308.95
2007	$344.76
2008	$373.82
2009	$401.09
2010	$404.74
2011	$418.5
2012	$443.42
2013	$465.6
2014	$473.08
2015	$482.23
2016	$478.61
2017	$485.87
2018	$500.34
2019	$514.41

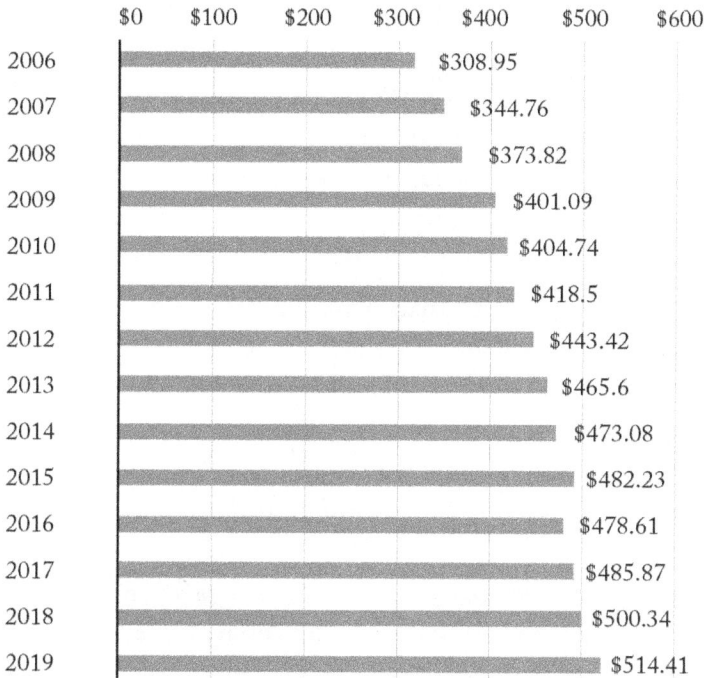

Source: Statista 2019

Despite this overwhelming success in traditional retail, Walmart has been relatively late to the eCommerce party. Not willing to concede dominance to Amazon, Walmart has recently made aggressive moves to position themselves as Amazon's direct competition. As of late 2018, Walmart passed Apple to become the No. 3 eCommerce retailer in the U.S. Although still at a fraction of Amazon's 49.1% share of the online market, after a 43% increase in their eCommerce sales last year, Walmart now represents 4% of all sales made online.[92]

Walmart's Budding Marketplace

One of the major differences between Walmart and Amazon's approach is that Walmart requires third-party sellers to apply to participate. In particular, Walmart prioritizes sellers who price their products competitively, have a good customer service record, a unique product assortment, and have fast and reliable fulfillment processes. They also want partners who share their values.

Walmart is a much smaller third-party platform, and according to Feedvisor's "State of the Amazon Marketplace 2018" report, 25% of Amazon sellers are now selling on Walmart in addition to eBay and their own website.[93] The pattern was extremely clear: getting your products on Walmart offers a tremendous opportunity to increase sales.

The Advantages of Selling with Walmart

Wider Customer Base

It may be a smaller platform than Amazon, but Walmart still gets 110 million visitors, many of whom are unlikely to be Prime members and are therefore more open to buying from another marketplace.

No Monthly or Initial Set Up Fees

For sellers, there are no monthly or set up fees either, and most fees are deducted from sales. These fees range from 6-20%.

Fewer Sellers

Another serious advantage is that Walmart's platform is much less competitive than Amazon and other sites like eBay, helped in part by the application process needed to join. Walmart, therefore, gives early adopters a significant opportunity to grab market share.

The Disadvantages of Walmart's Marketplace

Extreme Exclusivity

While the lower levels of competition are a significant draw, the application process can create too high of a bar for many smaller eCommerce brands to join as Walmart prefers brands with established reputations.

Potential Listing Issues

Walmart also uses a unified catalog system, meaning they use single UPCs. Therefore, the first seller to offer certain products will become the home base for other sellers providing the same item.

Delayed Seller Support

While many Amazon sellers bemoan that support leaves a lot to be desired, sellers on Walmart's marketplace report the situation is worse, and the seller-support team just isn't prepared to deal with many of their concerns.

The Bottom Line

There are pros and cons to Walmart's budding third party seller platform, but it can't be ignored. Once your brand is through the application process, Walmart represents an important opportunity, and getting in early can give you a significant advantage, especially if your products are not already available on their marketplace.

Crowdfunding

Crowdfunding is a cultural phenomenon that has become a viable way for entrepreneurs to secure funding for their developing products and services by pitching their product or service to an online community. This audience may then invest a small or large amount of money to help the company reach its financial goals. By raising small amounts from a wide number of people, businesses have the opportunity to avoid seed funding, bank loans, and to keep control of their business while getting their offerings to market. In 2019 the transaction value of crowdfunding amounts to almost $7 billion, with the average funding per campaign amounting to $794.[94]

Crowdfunding Platforms

The two largest and most popular crowdfunding platforms for physical products are Kickstarter and Indiegogo. While they offer similar services, each platform has different rules about whether you're required to raise your entire financial goal in order to have access to funds.

Kickstarter

Probably the most well-known crowdfunding platform, Kickstarter has seen over 450,000 successfully funded projects with over $4.3 billion pledged since they launched and have an estimated success rate of 37%.[95] This higher success rate is partially due to their quality control and a selective process that determines which campaigns can fund on the platform.

Overview of Projects and Dollars on Kickstarter
(as of October 2019)

Projects and dollars	Projects, million US dollars success rate in percent
Launched projects	461,628
Total dollars pledged (billion US dollars)	4.56
Successful dollars (billion US dollars)	4.07
Unsuccessful dollars (million US dollars)	447
Live dollars (million US dollars)	41
Live projects	3,872
Success rate (%)	37.3

Source: Statista 2019

Kickstarter is, however, an all-or-nothing system. Funds are only released if the campaign hits its goal. If your campaign fails, all money is returned to backers. Kickstarter charges a 5% fee on funds raised and a 3-5% transaction fee.

Indiegogo

Since its founding in 2009, Indiegogo has raised $3.2 billion for successful projects. Smaller than Kickstarter, Indiegogo has an estimated 9 million unique monthly visitors to its site and an estimated success rate of 17%.[96] While this rate seems low, it's mainly because the platform doesn't have the same gatekeeping function Kickstarter does for new campaigns.

Indiegogo charges similar fees as Kickstarter, 5% of campaign funds and transaction fees in addition to 3% + 30 cents. However, Indiegogo offers flexible funding, meaning you can keep all funds raised, even if you don't meet your goal.

Which Platform Is Right for You?

While both platforms offer similar services, the companies are very different. Recently, for example, Kickstarter was worried they were being seen as an eCommerce platform and published a blog post titled 'Kickstarter is Not a Store.' Meanwhile, Indiegogo opened an online store on its platform that sells their successfully funded products.

In terms of analytics, Indiegogo offers a deeper wealth of data and enables you to track the success of Facebook and Google ads. Kickstarter provides data as well, but there are limitations, for instance, you can't distinguish whether your traffic is coming from mobile. In addition, Indiegogo allows you to see a list of your backers as they pledge, while Kickstarter withholds this list until your campaign ends. This early access to backers can help you optimize your ad strategy and attract more funders to your campaign.

The Benefits of Crowdfunding

Getting Funding

Paramount to all benefits is the ability to procure funding with no need to pester your family, seek seed funding, or a bank loan. You remain in control of your company without having to give away huge stakes to get started.

Build an Evergreen Audience

A properly run crowdfunding campaign can help you build a loyal and engaged audience, making sure your business gets off on the right foot. Posting on a platform like Kickstarter or Indiegogo gives you access to an enthusiastic community who want to get on board early and stick with you.

Conduct Market Research

Crowdfunding can also decrease business risk as you can test the market and determine if your products are viable. In addition, input and feedback from this engaged community can help you further develop your products.

Leverage the Power of Pre-Sales

Pre-selling products mean you avoid buying large quantities of inventory. In turn, if you do have a lot of pre-sales, you can place larger orders with manufacturers and decrease your cost-per-unit while increasing margins.

Key Success Factors

Choosing the Right Product

The basis of a successful crowdfunding campaign is also one of the biggest challenges: choosing the right product. The products that do best are those that powerfully appeal to a niche audience and offer an innovation not currently on the market.

Build the Initial Audience

Once you have a product in mind, focus on building your initial audience. Reach out to your existing audience, leverage shareable content on social media, and consider running a contest or giveaway that relates to the product you're looking to fund. This foundation can give you a powerful advantage: according to Fundly, campaigns that meet their goal raise 30% of their pledged amount within the first week.[97]

Share Your Story

It's now time to make your appeal to potential backers. Engage the story of your brand, your purpose, and your values: it all comes back to the C's of Core and Customer. Share where the idea came from, and why you're passionate about this project. Create a sense of bonding with your customers over a common cause. On your physical page, make sure you have an attractive project-header image as well as a compelling video. This video pitch should cover the concept, Soleness, and a demonstration of its benefits to consumers. A personal story regarding the product is a great approach. Fundly found that personal videos raise 105% more than campaigns without a video pitch.[98]

Be in Project Mode

- Projects have definitive start and end dates, are anticipated, and promoted in advance to get initial buy-in.
- Projects define deliverables, and decide on people, resources, and budget.
- Projects require all stakeholders to understand the requirements and involve tracking and reporting as the project progresses.
- Projects have opportunities for people to participate a lot or a little, and to support a small or larger level of commitment.

<u>*Summing Up*</u>

The cultural phenomenon of crowdfunding is emerging as one of the best ways for brands to develop and secure funding for their products and ideas, without losing control over their business. With the right strategy, the right product, and a commitment to follow through, crowdfunding offers a tremendous opportunity for eCommerce merchants to establish their brand, prove the potential of their products, and build a loyal following.

Partnerships

Partnership marketing is a great way to grow your brand by tapping into another brand's audience. Whether you help promote each other's brands or work on a shared project, partnerships can be an effective way to market your business. A partnership marketing strategy can help reduce marketing costs as you both help one another grow using your own channels. By choosing the right partner, you can grow your customer base, increase your sales and offer great product selection to your customers.

<u>Brand Collaboration</u>

<u>*What is Brand Collaboration?*</u>

Brand collaboration describes when two or more brands partner via strategic marketing campaigns to support each other in achieving greater brand awareness, sales, and other goals. These kinds of arrangements can be tremendously beneficial for both brands and customers, and it's a great, cost-effective way to grow your eCommerce store.

<u>*The Benefits of Brand Collaboration*</u>

Empower Your Customers

The fact is, most customers prefer to buy from the brands they already know and trust. The invitation to visit another site to buy a product can feel intimidating if the brand is relatively unfamiliar. With a brand partnership, you open the door to being able to offer your products on another brand's site, and vice versa. In this case, purchasing your products on a preferred retailer's site can feel more inviting and safer, particularly if the customer is trying your products for the first time.

Extend Your Customer Reach and Attract New Customers

By leveraging the audience of your partner brand, you can expose your products to new markets and customers who might otherwise never have discovered you. If you partner with the right brands that have a relevant audience, these kinds of promotions can help you find more loyal customers.

Increase Sales and Conversion Rates

And of course, the more sales channels you have, the greater convenience for customers, and the easier you make your products to find and purchase, the more you'll sell. It will also give you greater financial security as you won't be depending on a single revenue stream.

Who Should You Collaborate With?

Perhaps the most important decision in the collaboration process is choosing which brands to partner with. In order to work, the collaboration must make sense for both parties and your respective customers. You must, therefore, have a good grasp of who your customers are and who comprises the audience of your prospective partner. Consider how old your audience is, their interests, what their lifestyle is like, and their level of disposable income. How do your potential partners fit into this picture? Does this brand offer something of value to your target customers?

Consider, too, this is a partnership, not a takeover, so you want to make sure your brand's identity and values aren't compromised for the sake of a larger audience. Does your prospective partner have similar brand values as you? How about their brand voice, does it complement or clash with yours? Messaging needs to stay consistent, regardless of collaboration, and two conflicting styles threaten to dilute your brand identity and come off as confusing to customers which can damage your brand in the long run.

Of course, if your prospective partner has done any formal branding, sharing your brand documentation, including persona work, etc. is also an easy way to "compare" side-by-side for fit.

Remember, you want to partner with a brand that complements your product line without being in direct competition with it. For instance, if you sell protein bars, partnering with a brand that offers health supplements might be perfect.

WAYS TO COLLABORATE

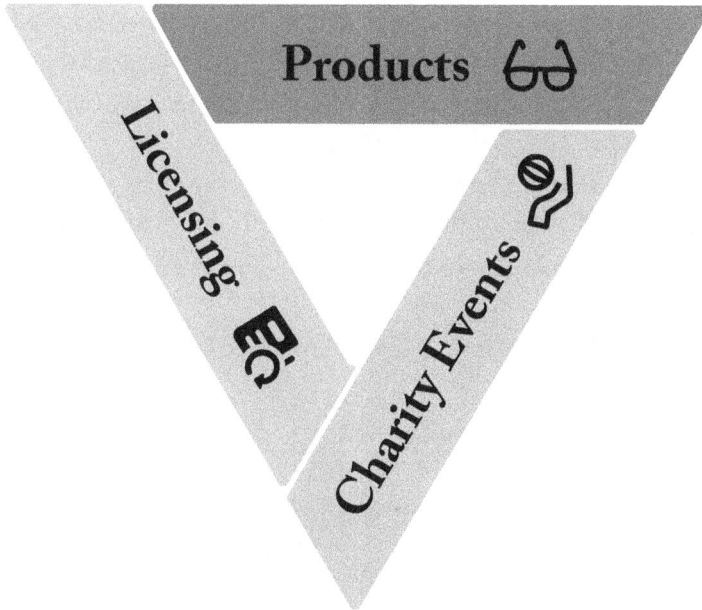

Partnership for Products

In this case, partner brands agree to either cross-market or bundle each other's products in their respective distribution channels. Offering a bundle with a mix of both of your products can be an effective way to bring new customers to your store to see what else you sell.

This also lends the impression of higher value to your products. Both brands involved should also already be trusted by their respective audiences and have an identity that resonates with customers. This way, both brands are in the best position possible to encourage loyalty and retain any new customers the partnership creates. Another option is to create a subscription box with a mix of your products or reach out to a subscription service to be included.

Partnership for Charity Events

Here, brands collaborate with charitable organizations. While this approach isn't sales focused, it still offers great benefits as brand awareness is increased, and positive associations are made with your brand. A partnership may take the form of a sponsored exhibition, a public event, an award show, sponsorships, raffle contributions, or news stories. Just like partnering with another brand, you want to choose an organization that shares your values and addresses the social issues and initiatives that fit with your brand purpose.

This is a particularly powerful strategy as customers are increasingly looking for brands that align with their values and whose business decisions are made ethically and transparently. By collaborating with charities and causes that are natural extensions of your brand purpose and values, you prove to consumers you're a caring company that's willing to take a stand on important issues.

Licensing

A partnership may also take the form of a licensing agreement. Licensing describes when one brand allows another to manufacture products bearing its brand image and property in exchange for an agreed payment. PopSockets, for instance, a company that makes cell phone accessories, has several licensing agreements, including a license to produce official Pokémon PopSockets. While most of their products cost $10, the licensed PopSockets are priced at $15, likely to cover the cost they owe to their partner brand or artist. But this price increase also makes the products seem more valuable, and many consumers are willing to pay extra for licensed items of brands they recognize and love.

Summary

In branding, it can be tempting to believe it's you against the world but taking the leap to partner with another brand or charitable organization can bring significant benefits. From tapping into a new audience, increasing awareness, and reinforcing your values, brand collaborations can be a powerful strategy for growing your store.

Affiliate Marketing

Through affiliate marketing, brands partner with affiliates, who might be individuals or organizations, who independently promote the brand's products or services. In return, brands pay affiliates a commission of the sales generated by the affiliate's efforts.

Typically there are three parties involved: the affiliate, an affiliate network, and the merchant.

The Affiliate

Affiliates are essentially marketers, or "publishers" of content who are willing to promote your products and services, either through blog posts, reviews, how-to videos, feature articles, and other content marketing through some form of online real estate, whether a blog, YouTube channel or website. In most cases, affiliates are provided with hyperlinks that automatically track any sales secured through their efforts. Based on the performance of these hyperlinks, affiliates are then paid a commission. Depending on the specific affiliate program, affiliates may be paid for traffic generated (usually per 1,000-page visits), form submission, email sign-up, or any other action the merchant desires, though sales is the most popular option in eCommerce. It's relatively low-risk for affiliates as they don't carry the burden of developing, manufacturing, storing, shipping, and selling products. Instead, they are directly helping consumers with helpful advice and tips.

Brands certainly carry more of the business-risk, but affiliates are a more cost-effective approach to marketing as you only pay for success, and it does take out the resources required for content creation. Since affiliates want the highest income possible and don't want to erode trust with their audience, they're motivated only to promote products they believe in and that fits their profile, resulting in high-quality leads. Consumers, meanwhile, feel like they're getting trusted advice, and they don't pay a higher price for the items through affiliates.

The Affiliate Networks

While you don't need to join an affiliate marketing network, it is the easiest and fastest way to get started. Through your network's tools and software, you can track, report, and manage payments to affiliates. Networks also resolve many of the trust issues in this breed of marketing. Affiliates are sometimes wary about partnering with businesses, as they're unsure if they're being paid for every sale or lead their content generates.

HOW AFFILIATE MARKETING WORKS

AFFILIATE

Places ad on Owned Media and receives $

AFFILIATE NETWORK

Facilitates transaction

MERCHANT

Sale for eCommerce store and
incentivizes affiliates

Using a network puts their minds at ease that everything is being tracked automatically and transparently.

Here are some of the most popular networks:

Amazon Associates: this network is best to promote products listed on Amazon. If you are already selling anything on Amazon, you're considered an Amazon Merchant. Affiliates have the option of advertising any product found on the site.

CJ Affiliate: formerly Commission Junction. Publishers, or affiliates, go through a rigorous application process to ensure retailers are partnering with the most sophisticated marketers. Their service includes several publishing and (pay-per-action) PPA models as well as various affiliate marketing tools to track and manage your campaigns.

Rakuten: formerly known as LinkShare. Rakuten tends to work with bigger companies that have large marketing budgets. They have an intuitive interface and offer several innovative tools like the ability to create rotating ad banners, deep linking, and access to thousands of plug-ins for affiliates.

ShareASale: is particularly popular with affiliates, and many of them use ShareASale exclusively. Affiliates can search for programs by sector, brand, and keyword to find the best match for them. There are also several options for text links, widgets, and product feeds.

Remember, these networks are *not* free, and will either take a cut of sales generated, or will charge a flat fee, so consider this extra cost when deciding which network is right for you. It's also ideal to sign up with several networks to give yourself a wider selection of marketing models and for the greatest exposure to affiliates.

The Merchant

This is you: the merchant or brand that's selling products and wants to partner with people who have marketing skills and equity with the right audience. Based on your current goals, you can pay for sales, email sign-ups or increased traffic to your site.

Affiliate marketing is an especially advantageous option because although pay-per-click advertising is also performance-based, those clicks may not produce actual leads or sales. Whereas affiliates are speaking directly to your relevant audience and can provide real-world, trusted context for your products that leads to consumers with higher intention to buy.

Blogger Outreach

Blogger outreach is a type of influencer marketing strategy, except you work with popular bloggers. Bloggers make ideal brand partners as they have significant influence over their audience's purchase decisions. Getting a reputable, high-authority blogger on board can thus powerfully impact sales.

Types of Blogger Outreach

Blogger outreach is a process to help you achieve measurable success in your business. Here's how you can use blogger outreach to drive traffic and sales for your store:

1. *Product Reviews*

In this case, brands typically send free products to bloggers in exchange for a review. The blogger is free to write their honest opinion, good or bad, though these kinds of \requests rarely result in anything worse than a neutral review, but you need to have high confidence in your products.

Product Reviews

Affiliate Programs

Guest Post

Gift Guides

2. *Guest Post*

Guest posting gives you a way to get in front of someone else's audience. Not only does this drive traffic back to your website, but the links back to your website will help with SEO. It will raise awareness of your brand, and you will reach out to more potential consumers.

3. *Gift Guides*

Many blogs also post gift guides, typically related to various holidays like Christmas, Mother's Day, and Father's Day. Getting your products included on this kind of list can be extremely successful because you're getting exposure to the blogger's audience and gaining traffic with purchase intent.

4. *Affiliate Programs*

Finally, bloggers make exceptional affiliates, so starting a program can help incentivize bloggers to drive traffic to your site by offering them a cut of the sales their links generate.

Blogger Outreach Campaign Process

The key to blogger outreach is to get organized and create a good process you can follow:

1. *Research Target Audience*

In order to get the most out of this process, look for bloggers whose audience is made up of your target customers. The ideal blogger will also depend on your goals: you might want a blogger who's a niche authority or considered an expert in your industry or product category. You may want to target bloggers based on their social authority, or, if engagement is more important to your goals, seek out relevant bloggers with more regular visitors, subscribers, and comments. Several tools can help you with this process, including BuzzSumo, Ninja Outreach and Tomoson.

2. *Take Advantage of Editorial Calendars*

Many blogs will have an editorial calendar listing the topics they're currently interested in. If your brand or product allows for it, making a direct pitch related to the current calendar can boost your outreach.

3. *Engage and Contact Bloggers*

When reaching out to bloggers, don't just send a cold email. A pitch will be better received if there's familiarity between you and the blogger. Look up your target bloggers and engage with them through their social channels. Leave comments on their blog posts and nurture a connection over shared interests. This might also involve liking/favoriting and sharing/retweeting blogger's posts through their various social accounts. This engagement on your part will demonstrate to the blogger you care about their mission and are interested in a relationship beyond a simple transaction.

An Effective Email Script Template

Introduce Yourself:

Begin by introducing yourself and include a quick description of who you are and the brand you're associated with. You don't want to send bloggers to Google to look you up and remind them of who you are.

> *Hey NAME, I run an eCommerce store called COMPANY, or I am the Founder of... Our PRODUCT is...*

Build a Connection:

Then, make it clear that you follow them on their various channels. Explain what you like about their content and what appeals to you about their work. Our example here is general, but the more specific you can be in your email, the better. You want to demonstrate that you are genuinely interested in and engaged with their content.

> *I follow you on Twitter regularly, and I appreciate the valuable insights that you provide daily!*

Go for the Ask:

Now, what do you want? These days everyone is busy, so get to the point quickly.

> *I noticed that you focus on this PRODUCT category. As such, I'd love to have you give an honest review of the PRODUCT.*

Make it Rewarding:

Once you've set this groundwork, quickly and concisely ask for what you want. Are you looking for a review in exchange for a free product? An affiliate relationship? Make it clear and then explain the benefit this partnership provides to them and their audience.

> *Here is an exclusive offer, a promo code, or other compelling content.*

Go for the Close:

Respect the time of the blogger you're contacting by closing your email with a simple, direct question to which they can respond 'yes' or 'no.'

> *Would it be fine if I sent you this product for free?*

Sign Off:

Then sign off with your name and resist the temptation to add more. You don't want to distract from the question, which makes it easier for bloggers to reply right away.

This is just a template that you should adapt to your specific needs and your brand's personality and voice.

Follow Up:

If you're reaching out to bloggers with a significant following, it's always possible for your email to get lost in the inbox-shuffle. After waiting 3-4 days with no response, you can send a follow-up message. You want the tone to be approachable, low pressure, and keep it limited to one or two sentences. Reiterate your 'yes' or 'no' question and send it as a reply to your original message, so the blogger doesn't have to go searching for it for more context. If the blogger is interested, they'll get back to you.

> *Hey NAME, I'd still love to send you a free sample of PRODUCT if you're interested. Just reply yes to this email to let me know.*

If they don't respond, move on.

Summary, Blogger Outreach

Blogger outreach has tremendous potential to attract new customers and boost sales, but it does require an investment of time and energy to make it work. The payoffs, however, are well worth the effort as the right partnership can seriously raise the profile of your products and your brand.

A similar strategy can be adopted for media outreach, where the personnel changes, but the pitch, tools, and process remains the same.

Paid Channels

Paid platforms like Facebook, Instagram, and Google Shopping make it easy for advertisers to get started, and the simplicity of their platforms makes them a very appealing option for many brands.

This section, as mentioned, has been written to offer a strategic overview of the various socials and other platforms available as advertising tools. Your particular choice for one or more of the tools will largely be a function of who your customer is and which social platforms your customers are on.

Social Media

Today's customer is driven by research: they are well ahead in their shopping journey and as a result, are empowered in their decision making. This change in behavior needs to be recognized as brands engage with their consumers on the socials.

We will start by first looking at the top 7 social network sites relevant to eCommerce advertisers, ranked by the number of users.

Most Famous Social Network Sites Worldwide
(Number of active users in millions, as of July 2020)

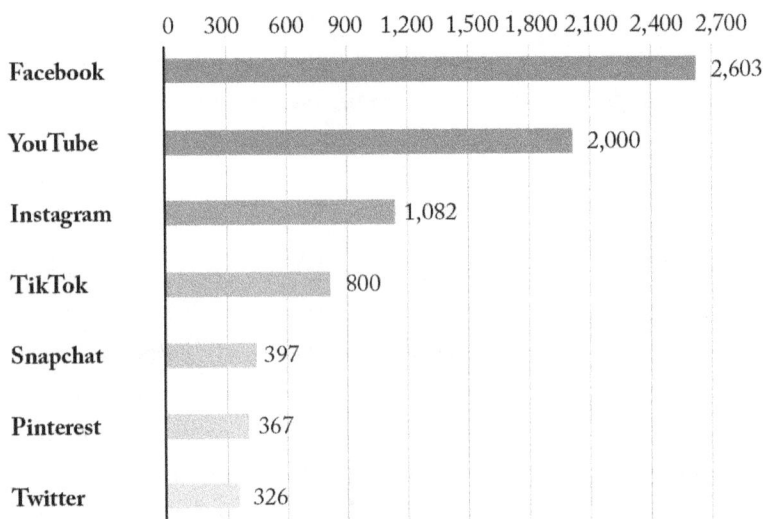

Platform	Users (millions)
Facebook	2,603
YouTube	2,000
Instagram	1,082
TikTok	800
Snapchat	397
Pinterest	367
Twitter	326

Source: Statista 2020

In 2020, it is estimated that there will be around 3.08 billion social media users around the globe, up from 2.95 billion in 2019 that will be available to potential eCommerce advertisers to promote their products.[99]

Number of Social Media Users Worldwide from 2010 to 2023

(Number of users in billions)

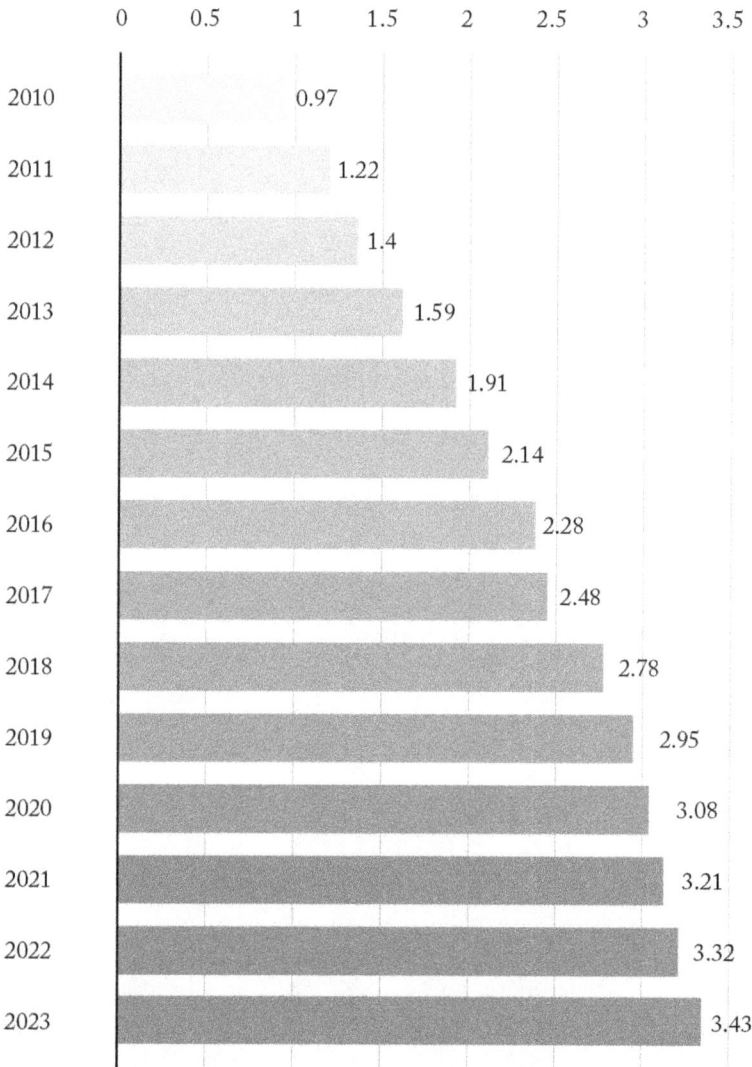

Year	Users
2010	0.97
2011	1.22
2012	1.4
2013	1.59
2014	1.91
2015	2.14
2016	2.28
2017	2.48
2018	2.78
2019	2.95
2020	3.08
2021	3.21
2022	3.32
2023	3.43

Source: Statista 2020

Facebook still dominates in paid, with 94% of all U.S. self-identified professional marketers having used Facebook Ads. Followed by Instagram at 44%, Twitter at 26%, and YouTube at 10%.[100]

Also when respondents were asked how effective social media marketing has been for their business, 43 percent said "somewhat effective" and a further 29 percent believed that social media marketing had been "very effective."[101]

How effective has Social Media Marketing been for your business?

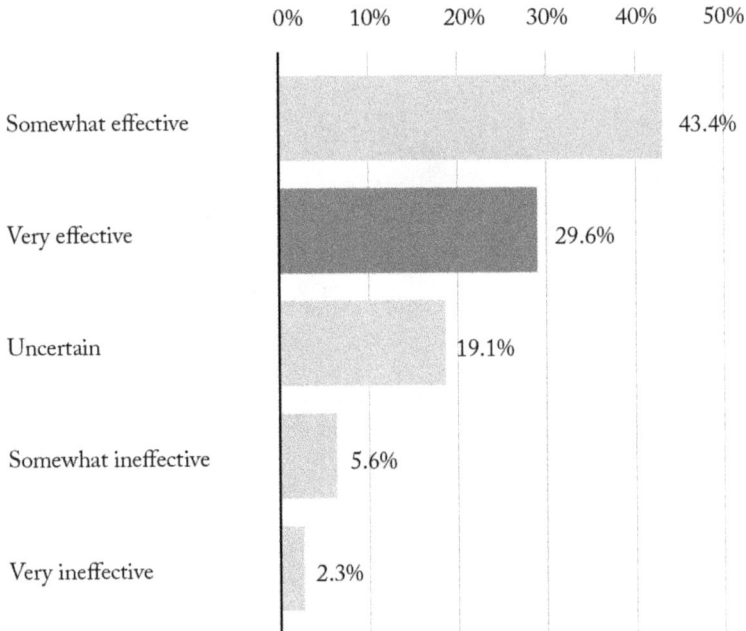

Category	Percentage
Somewhat effective	43.4%
Very effective	29.6%
Uncertain	19.1%
Somewhat ineffective	5.6%
Very ineffective	2.3%

Source: The State of Social 2019

Now that we have established the growing importance of paid advertising on social networks, we'll look at each one of the platforms individually from a strategic perspective.

Facebook Advertising

Founded in 2004, Facebook is easily the biggest and most popular social network, with *2.6 billion monthly active* users worldwide.

Despite being a social network, Facebook offers eCommerce brands an important way to connect with customers as well as a robust advertising platform.

Facebook is the second largest digital publisher behind only Google, and their second-to-none targeting abilities allow advertisers to specifically attract your most relevant and ideal customers. As the most popular social network, the ads that run on the site also have significant social proof behind them. It's no surprise then that about 3 million businesses are on Facebook, and 96% of all media marketers still consider Facebook the most effective social advertising platform.[102]

Compared with other social networks, Facebook's sheer audience size makes it indispensable. With 2.6 billion users worldwide and 22 billion ad clicks per year, Facebook is providing businesses with the largest advertising opportunity since search. Their closest competitor is YouTube, which has 1.9 billion users.

With seemingly endless demographics, behaviors, and interests, the most powerful feature of Facebook's advertising platform is its targeting capabilities. Options extend to connections, education, work, age ranges, languages, or locations, actions on your website, engagement in your app – all allowing you to layer targeting capability on each other to ensure you're getting rid of any out-of-market clickers.

Facebook users are also especially engaged: the average user accesses Facebook 8 times a day. Instagram, by comparison, is accessed an average of 6 times a day, Twitter 5 times, and Facebook Messenger 3 times daily. Users spend an average of 35 minutes per day on the site as well.[103]

Facebook's eCommerce Focus

In May 2020, Facebook announced the launch of a new eCommerce feature: Facebook Shops.[104] For a network that already holds so much of the world's attention, it's a potential watershed moment that will reposition Facebook as an eCommerce marketplace, allowing it to compete seriously with giants like Amazon and Walmart. Releasing at the height of the COVID pandemic, Shops is being positioned as a solution for small business owners to reach customers and maintain a revenue stream in the era of social distancing. Of course, the pandemic has not only boosted eCommerce overall – online sales skyrocketed from 15% of all retail sales to 27% in a matter of weeks[105] – Facebook also saw an increase of usage across their family of apps.

Longer-term, Facebook is betting that consumer behavior has effectively shifted, and that customers are now comfortable with the idea of shopping and ordering from retailers through a social network.

Shops will allow business owners to create a storefront directly on their Facebook profile. Users will see a "View Shop" button under the business's cover image, a link that will take them to a list of the brand's products and collections, all without leaving Facebook. Consumers will be able to save items, add them to a shopping cart, and in the US, checkout. Outside the US, for now, shoppers will be redirected to the brand's website to complete their transaction. Shops is therefore not going to manage transactions directly but will be a new way for brands to connect with customers.

Brands will also be given control over the look of their Shop. You'll be able to customize your cover image and accent colors, including the look of call-to-action buttons. Merchants will be able to manually enter their products and create collections, or they can opt to upload a catalog via XML file.

With a store integrated into your Facebook profile, customers will be able to directly contact brands for more information about products, seek support, or track an order. In the future, Facebook plans to also add live video chat, as well as the option for live broadcasts, turning your Facebook profile into a branded home shopping network. Augmented reality applications to try on clothing, cosmetics, and glasses may follow as well.[106]

Facebook is also currently testing ways for businesses to integrate loyalty programs, allowing customers to track rewards by linking their membership to their personal profile. Likewise, store owners will be able to manage their loyalty programs through Shops as well.

This level of integration between social, commerce, and customer service seems poised to offer consumers a complete shopping experience. Best of all for merchants, is that you can create a storefront on Shops for free. This news may spell out trouble for Amazon's current business model, especially if Shops takes off. Unlike Amazon, Shops allows sellers to set up, list, and sell without fees, and they'll also retain full control over their store and the customer relationship. Not to mention the fact that Facebook also offers exposure to half the world's internet users.

However, there's potential danger for platforms like Shopify and BigCommerce. Although they're currently partnered with Facebook to support the new tool's backend, it could ultimately eat into their revenue. Another important distinction Shops is banking on, is that a marketplace like Amazon is the better option when customers already know what they're looking for. Whereas the more organic qualities of Facebook will make it a superior platform for discovering new products and brands. And given that the full transaction can now happen in one place – conversions are likely to increase.

Seeing as the overwhelming majority of Facebook's revenue comes from ads, there's little doubt the move is also inspired by the desire to keep their advertising platform attractive to marketers. Another effect of the pandemic was a dip in ad buying, which has since stalled. Facebook is betting that if Shops proves to be a lucrative tool for entrepreneurs, that it will make Facebook ads more appealing and valuable.

For entrepreneurs, jumping on board with Shops seems like an low-risk, potentially high-reward gamble.

Instagram

Founded in 2010, Instagram is a sharing network that allows users to share photos and videos and was bought by Facebook in 2012. Since its acquisition, Instagram has grown from 50 million users to 1 billion users.

Unlike other social networks, Instagram is relatively unsaturated compared to other channels, making now the best time to take advantage of the opportunity.

Instagram is attractive to brands because it offers a unique way to engage and connect with consumers as the site is based on *visual content*, meaning the most creative brands win. In addition, Instagram users are especially open to forming relationships with brands. About 70% of Instagram users have looked up a company on the platform, while 62% of users follow at least one brand.[107]

A Snapshot of Instagram's User Base

Instagram is a decidedly young platform, as 70% of its users are under the age of 35. It's most popular with 25-34 year-olds, and 55% of this age group is active on the site.[108]

Distribution of Instagram Users Worldwide

(as of July 2020, by age and gender)

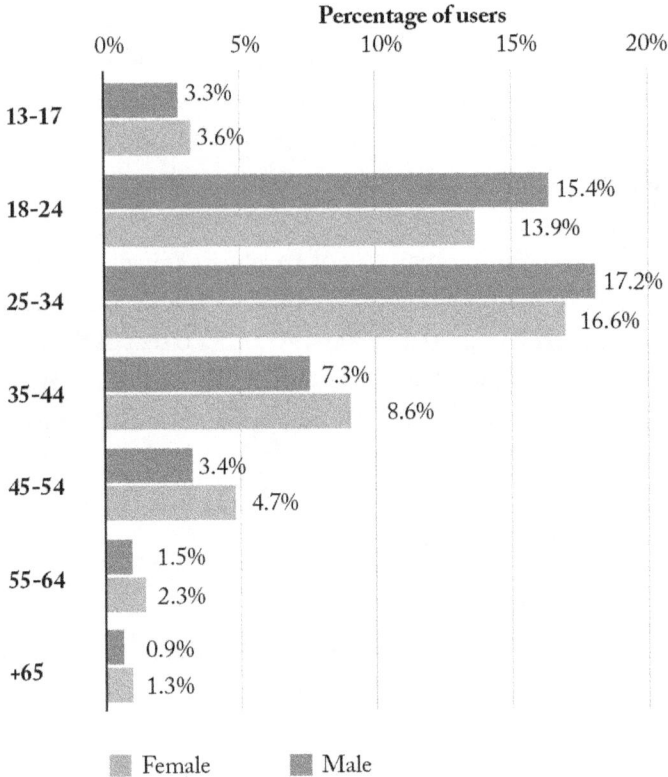

Percentage of users

Age	Male	Female
13-17	3.3%	3.6%
18-24	15.4%	13.9%
25-34	17.2%	16.6%
35-44	7.3%	8.6%
45-54	3.4%	4.7%
55-64	1.5%	2.3%
+65	0.9%	1.3%

■ Female　　■ Male

Source: Statista 2020

Instagram States: Decision Control

Instagram users are far more likely to engage with brands, and per-follower engagement rate is 4.21%, which is 58 times greater than engagement on Facebook, and 120 times higher than Twitter.[109]

Instagram's eCommerce Friendly (eFF) Features

You don't have to choose *between* Facebook and Instagram because their ad systems are managed with the same interface.

The basic options for posting on Instagram are between photo and video. You can post a single photo in landscape or square format or feature up to 4 photos in a carousel ad that allows users to swipe between images. You can also post videos up to 60 seconds long. Instagram also offers Stories, which are ads that can contain a photo or video content. Brands can add one product tag sticker per story, and users can tap it to see more information, such as price. Recently, however, Instagram has added several eCommerce features. Here's a quick run-down of the features available to business accounts.

Tagging Products: This feature allows merchants to tag products in photos, just like tagging people. Tags instantly turn your account into a sales channel, with tags that offer a call-to-action, simplifying the buying process for customers. Brands can tag up to 5 products in a single post, and up to 20 in carousels. Tags can provide more information about the product like price, special offers, and descriptions.

Shoppable Photos and Videos: These allow you to add a 'Shop Now' feature to your images, which direct users to your site for purchase. Currently, in the US, Instagram has a native payment system allowing users to purchase items directly on the platform. Shoppable photos and videos make browsing and shopping more streamlined, saving customers time and boosting conversion rates.

Swipeable Links: You're now able to add links and calls-to-action to Stories, for example, "Swipe Up to See More." Previously, Instagram banned all links anywhere other than in your bio section, making this an important new development. These links encourage followers to visit your site and do some more research into your product line.

Saved Stories: Instagram now allows you to save stories to your profile. With Story Highlights, you can group and display stories in a new section right below your bio. This new feature lets you keep your best content, show off your products, and save all the most important information about your brand in one spot. You can save up to 100 stories.

Instagram Checkout

Instagram's newest eCommerce-friendly feature is 'Checkout with Instagram.' Checkout with Instagram is a button that will be available on organic posts. It can be featured on feeds, Stories, and Explore content, but paid ads are ineligible. Essentially, Checkout will replace the current "View on Website" button, and users will be able to access it once they've tapped on a post to reveal product tags.

As the name suggests, Checkout will allow users to make product purchases directly on Instagram, and they'll no longer need to redirect to the brand's website to buy. Once a user clicks to Checkout, they're prompted to enter their shipping and payment information. Instagram then stores this info, so users don't have to re-enter their details for future purchases.

In addition, users will be able to track and manage their orders through Instagram, including tracking shipments, and tools to cancel orders, initiate a return, or contact customer support. These options are especially attractive to customers frustrated with trying to keep up with emails from multiple brands, giving them a central hub from which they can control their experience.

Of course, the major advantage of Checkout with Instagram is a better, more seamless shopping experience for consumers. Without redirections, less friction means fewer abandoned shopping carts and higher conversions.

However, like any eCommerce tool, entrepreneurs need to go in with their eyes open. Checkout will, of course, include a seller fee. And to use the new feature effectively, it's important to realize that Checkout transforms Instagram into a kind of marketplace like Amazon, so it comes with similar pitfalls. Checkout users will be, essentially, Instagram customers, as individual brands will only have access to a customer's shipping information.

For now, it's not even guaranteed that brands will get the email addresses of purchasers. It's also unclear what kind of metrics Instagram will share, even basic numbers like AOV. This means Instagram will control the customer experience on its platform. Coupled with limited ability to nurture customer relationships, having a strong brand outside of Instagram will be invaluable.

Although at the time of this writing, it's in a limited release with 20 top brands and only available in the US, the feature is expected to be widely available soon.

Summary, Instagram

While brands have always been welcome among Instagram's user base, the platform itself has become friendlier to eCommerce merchants in recent years. From one-tap shopping to native payment systems, Instagram offers a wide range of eCommerce features that can seriously boost your business.

TikTok

Launched in 2016 by ByteDance, TikTok is a video-sharing platform with 800 million monthly active users, although security concerns have prompted a partnership of its US operations with Oracle and Walmart, pending approval from the Chinese and American governments, as we go to press.[110] While it's the 6th largest social network overall,[111] it's the most downloaded app of 2020 so far.[112] The app, best known for its lip-syncing and dance routine videos, allows users to create and share 15-second long videos featuring filters, custom music, and stickers.

TikTok's User Base

69% of TikTok's user base is 13-24 years old, with only 15% over the age of 36.[113] So it's probably not a surprise that while only 9% of all internet users say they've tried TikTok, 49% of teenagers have.[114] TikTok was mainly popular in China until 2017, when ByteDance acquired Musical.ly, a similar app popular with North American teenagers. Most Musical.ly users migrated to TikTok, making it a top social network in both China and the US.

Advertising on TikTok

TikTok has one of the highest engagement rates on social media. For instance, for accounts with less than 10,000 followers, engagement per post on Twitter averages 0.6%, 3.7% on Instagram, but 8.13% on TikTok.[115]

And its users are open to brands: 63% say they're brand conscious, and 52% of users say they'd buy a product just to be part of the community.[116]

There are emerging advertising opportunities on TikTok, although paid ads are still in their infancy. First, in order to be able to create campaigns, you need to apply and qualify. The only exception is for In-Feed video ads.

TikTok offers the usual audience targeting tools, but it comes at a price. The average ad price ranges from $50-150,000.[117] There are four primary ad types to choose from:

Brand Takeover: either an image, GIF, or video ad that "takes over" a topic for the day across the platform. It will run you $50,000 a day, but TikTok guarantees 5 million daily impressions.[118]

Hashtag Challenge: brands create a sponsored hashtag to inspire user-generated content and engagement, it can also help you attract influencers. 35% of TikTok users report participating in a challenge. These campaigns cost $150,000 for 6 days.[119]

Branded Lenses: this augmented reality content created for your brand, either 2D or 3D overlays users can feature in their videos. 64% of users say they've tried a brand lens.[120] Here the cost varies, between $80,000-120,000.[121]

In-Feed Video: basically sponsored video posts, and you won't need a qualified ad account to create them. These are vertical, 9-15 second videos, and they show up on the "For You" page. TikTok requires a minimum $25,000 a day per campaign, with a daily max of $30,000.[122]

Content that Works

TikTok's culture revolves around trends, and the best performing content is often heavily replicated and recreated by other users. For example, choreography from Megan Three Stallion's "Savage" spawned over 16 million videos on TikTok.[123] Participating in a cultural moment is a big part of TikTok's appeal.

This trendy nature of TikTok means you need to be extremely sensitive to your audience's tastes and perspectives. One way to stay informed is to learn how to use TikTok the same way users do: by using the discover page and carefully reviewing what's trending.Because the video format is so short, TikTok tends to draw heavy inspiration from meme culture, which evolves incredibly quickly. This makes it nearly impossible to fake, even being a week behind will flag you as irrelevant. Being constantly connected to your audience is thus essential to make TikTok work.

Music is also incredibly important and is often the common thread that identifies trends. Spoof videos of creators dancing to brand jingles is a recent trend that highlights how brands can leverage their creative assets. The original viral video featured music from an old Home Depot commercial and was totally organic. Following this, several brands, like Oreo, created their own songs for the platform.[124]

The Bottom Line:

Paid advertising is still a new concept on TikTok. It's also significantly more costly, at an average of $10 per click,[125] than other platforms, making it out of reach for many smaller brands. However, some of the best results can still be gained from organic methods. Product placement, branding, and soft-selling techniques all fit in well. Whichever way you decide to go, the key to success with TikTok is understanding the type of content your target audience likes. As the platform's ad opportunities mature, you'll know when and how to jump in.

Pinterest

Pinterest, a visual platform where users save and share images referred to as "Pins," is primarily used as a kind of visual search engine. Because of this, Pinners have a higher likelihood of buying the products they find on Pinterest since they're actively searching, rather than reactively scrolling through a feed. This intent gives the platform exceptional selling power, despite its smaller user base.

Brands tend to do well on Pinterest as Pins featuring products fit perfectly into the organic content created on and saved to the site. Unique or particularly visually appealing products easily capture attention and generate interest. Brands can also build a community on Pinterest by organizing their posts under themed boards, create a lifestyle image around their products, show off their brand's personality, and reinforce the brand's visual identity.

A Look at Pinterest's User Base

As of July 2020, Pinterest had 367 million monthly active users worldwide, up from 175 million users in April 2017. According to Statista, roughly 68% of respondents aged 18-49 stated that they use the visual blogging site.

The most popular categories on the platform are:[126]

- DIY projects
- Fashion, clothing, and apparel
- Exercise and fitness
- Home décor
- Health and beauty
- Photography
- Food, beverage, and kitchenware
- Wedding inspiration
- Travel
- Technology

Among all internet users, 59% of women have a Pinterest account. While Pinterest is still primarily used by women, the number of men with accounts is growing. Approximately 40% of new signups are men, and they now make up 33% of Pinterest's user base.[127]

The eCommerce-Friendly Features of Pinterest

If the platform is right for you, Pinterest users are particularly valuable: Pinterest found that while Pinners are just as likely as other social users to convert on an ad, they spend 50% more on average. They even outspend buyers from non-social funnels like search engines by an average of 20%.[128] When it comes to promoted Pins, the best categories include home décor, cooking, fashion, beauty, and handmade goods. These Pins are worth considering because 1 out of 2 Pinners has purchased after seeing a promoted Pin and 67% of users report discovering a new brand due to promoted Pins. On average, these Pins earn $2 for every dollar spent.[129]

Noticing a growing interest among its users for greater eCommerce support, Pinterest has introduced several new features, again shortening the buyer journey, especially in comparison to other channels. Many Pinners use the network to plan their purchases, so with a more seamless eCommerce experience, conversions through Pinterest are going up. For merchants, advanced targeting tools ensure your Pins only appear on relevant pages and search results.

Among the new features is "Shop the Brand." Product Pins will now include a link to see "More from [brand]." This will show users your brand's

Most Popular Pinterest Categories

(in the US as of February 2017, by gender)

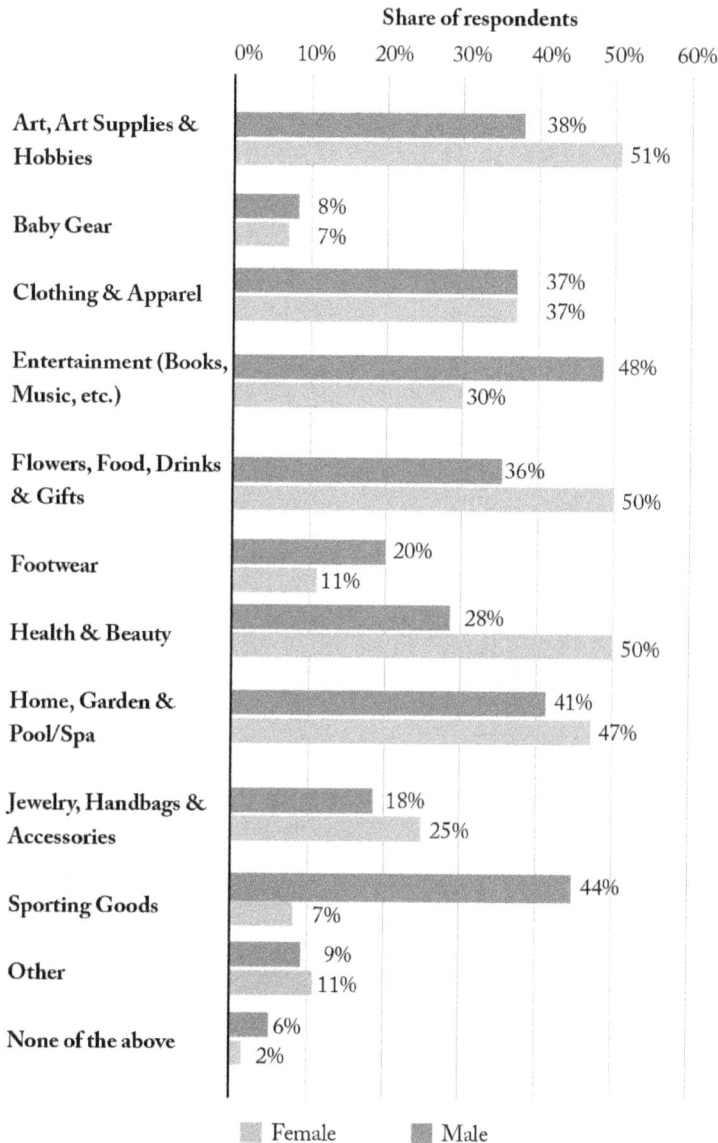

Share of respondents

Art, Art Supplies & Hobbies	Male	38%
	Female	51%
Baby Gear	Male	8%
	Female	7%
Clothing & Apparel	Male	37%
	Female	37%
Entertainment (Books, Music, etc.)	Male	48%
	Female	30%
Flowers, Food, Drinks & Gifts	Male	36%
	Female	50%
Footwear	Male	20%
	Female	11%
Health & Beauty	Male	28%
	Female	50%
Home, Garden & Pool/Spa	Male	41%
	Female	47%
Jewelry, Handbags & Accessories	Male	18%
	Female	25%
Sporting Goods	Male	44%
	Female	7%
Other	Male	9%
	Female	11%
None of the above	Male	6%
	Female	2%

Female   Male

Source: Statista 2017

full catalog on Pinterest. Even if a user only saves 1 Pin, your full range is still only a click away. It's also easier for brands to upload their whole catalog as Pinterest will create Product Pins automatically. In search results, Product Pins will now be shown at the top of the page to increase visibility. These features are available to anyone with a business account.

Pinterest is also offering users greater personalization with a "Picked For You" category. Based on the Pins and boards a user has saved or is following, Pinterest will recommend products in home, beauty, and DIY. These recommended Pins can be saved as usual or clicked to access the checkout page on the retailer's website.

Finally, while "Shop the Look" has been on Pinterest for some time, it's only been available to limited brands. It's now available to all retailers. This feature allows brands to place dots over the individual products shown in a Pin. When a user clicks on one of the dots, they can browse similar and related products.

The Bottom Line with Pinterest

If you're in the right niche for Pinterest's audience, the platform is easily one of the smartest investments of your time and resources. Because Pinterest is used primarily as a search engine, consumers visit the platform with purchase intent. Pinterest is also less susceptible to frequent algorithmic changes, and so long as your content and products are visually appealing, you'll do well. Pinterest's visual nature is a great way to showcase your brand's personality and build your visual identity. And features like promoted and buyable Pins also help boost sales, making Pinterest one of the best all-round social networks for eCommerce.

Twitter

As of July of 2020, Twitter has 326 million monthly active users. According to Pew Research, 24% of all internet users have an account on the platform: 23% of male users, and 24% of female users. Despite the fairly even gender divide, men tend to be more active on Twitter: 64% of their active users are male, with 36% being female.[130]

Like other social platforms, Twitter is especially popular with younger age groups. 40% of those aged 18-29 and 27% of those aged 30-49 have an account.[131]

Twitter's Soleness

Twitter allows users to listen to and connect with different voices from all over the globe. It's, therefore, not a particularly strong sales channel for brands, but it does provide an excellent platform for showing off your brand's personality and voice. Twitter is especially adept at helping brands build a network with other brands, journalists, as well as potential and existing customers.

Twitter as eCommerce Sales Driver

Twitter holds its weight in the social channel mix as an eCommerce sales driver, occupying the 3rd/4th position, after the heavyweights of Facebook and Instagram, and sharing its position with YouTube. It's an ideal platform to start topical conversations, address issues in real-time, and ultimately act as a brand voice.[132]

There are several important features to consider to get the most from your Twitter presence.

Leverage Organic Features

Engage with Influencers: First, learn how to leverage Twitter's organic features. Like other social platforms, look for and engage with the most relevant influencers in your space. Much of the same wisdom applies on Twitter, as does any other influencer marketing campaign, so use these tips to find and build relationships with influencers in your niche.

Make Good Use of Hashtags: Hashtags are the currency of Twitter and the key to your visibility in searches. Studies have shown that posts with more hashtags have higher engagement levels, and you ideally want to use a mix of popular or trending hashtags, medium level hashtags (around 50k shares), and niche hashtags. Also, be sure your hashtags are grounded in your brand's personality and demonstrate your brand values.

Use Twitter Chat to Engage with Buyers: Twitter chat is another great way to engage with customers and fans. Not only can you support real conversations by actively participating, but you also provide compelling social proof that your brand is responsive and willing to listen to consumers. These chats also offer you exceptional insight into the potential pain-points of consumers, what they want and need most, and lets you answer questions and customer service issues (social media is increasingly the dominant channel through which customers are seeking to have problems addressed).

Social Media Platforms used by B2C Marketers

(Worldwide as of January 2020)

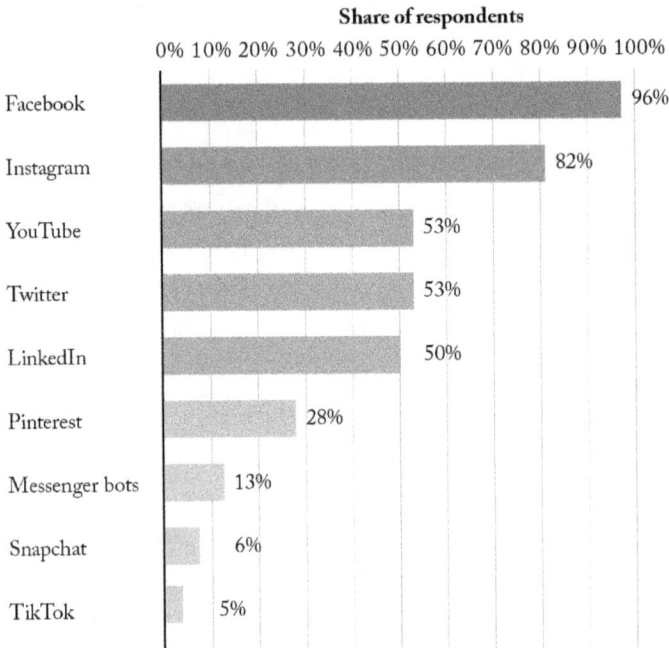

Share of respondents

Platform	Share
Facebook	96%
Instagram	82%
YouTube	53%
Twitter	53%
LinkedIn	50%
Pinterest	28%
Messenger bots	13%
Snapchat	6%
TikTok	5%

Source: Statista 2020

Twitter Advertising

There are also advertising capabilities on Twitter, including promoted Tweets, promoted accounts, and promoted trends.

Promoted Tweets: Promoted tweets allow brands to create tweet-sized billboards targeted to a specific audience based on shared interests and/or location. These are standard tweets that can be retweeted, commented on, and liked, except they have a "Promoted" label on them. These tweets aim to develop your brand's following by displaying these tweets to users that aren't already following your brand.

Promoted Accounts: This type of ad places your brand in your relevant audience's "Who to Follow" section as well as in search results and potential followers' timelines. These ads also target users who aren't following you currently. Like promoted tweets, they are clearly labeled as 'Promoted' and can also be targeted based on similar interests and geo-location.

Promoted Trends: Basically, these are branded hashtags that are pushed to the top of trending topics and can help increase awareness for your brand. Trending topics are the most talked about subjects on the platform, and they can be found under the "Explore" tab on users' timelines. These hashtags are an effective way to start conversations about your brand or generate interest in your company and products. These hashtags are a great way to build mass awareness or leverage the buzz of a product launch, announcement, or event.

Summary, Twitter

Twitter is second-to-none when it comes to speaking directly with your audience and sustaining a meaningful dialogue. Many brands find Twitter is central to their brand-building goals, if not sales. This is the platform to showcase and reinforce your brand's personality, point-of-view, and values.

YouTube

Founded in 2005, YouTube is a video hosting and search service which boasts 2 billion worldwide users making it the largest online video platform in the world. The sheer size of its user base and the presence of so many niche communities make YouTube a powerful advertising tool.

YouTube's Male-To-Female Ratio is 1:1

While accepted wisdom holds there are more male users on YouTube, research shows there's an even gender divide among users: 51% being male and 49% female.[133]

However, men make up the majority of viewers in 90% of YouTube's content categories. The most popular categories with men are gaming, sports, and virtual worlds. Categories dominated by female viewers include make-up and cosmetics, skin and nail care, and weight loss.[134]

Distribution of YouTube Users

(in the US as of Fall 2015, by gender)

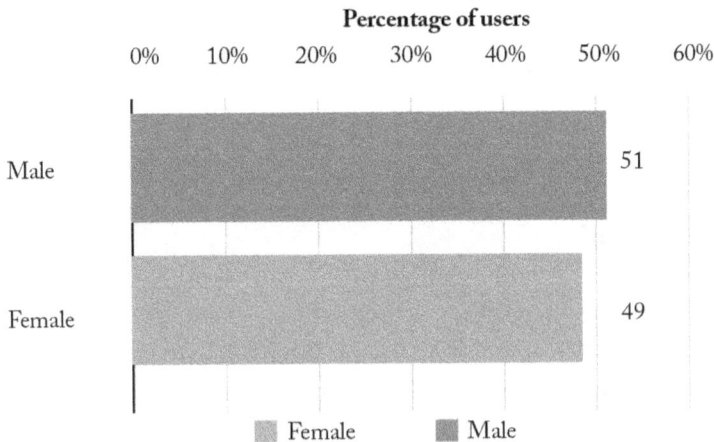

Percentage of users

Male	51
Female	49

Female Male

Source: Statista 2018

What's Special About YouTube?

As an eCommerce store owner, YouTube may be one of the most underrated yet efficient marketing tools at your disposal. It might not seem as sexy as advertising on FB, IG, or Pinterest, but video is an ideal advertising medium. It offers better engagement than any other content type, and it's the fastest and clearest way to present your message.

If you are selling a product that requires step-by-step instructions, for example, video is a much better way to ensure customers understand how to use your products correctly. In addition, having a video strategy in your marketing mix will also boost your SEO, as videos on YouTube will get your content ranked more highly by Google.

Driving eCommerce Sales: Content First Approach

Because YouTube is the primary search engine for content, marketers with a content-first approach are well-advised to consider the potential of video marketing. Not only do videos allow you to demonstrate the real-life benefits of your products, but video is also the ideal medium to proceed with our content marketing strategy, which as you remember consists of:

1. *The Story of Your Brand:* Tell your origin story. If your company was founded on an idea that was written on a cocktail napkin at a conference you paid your last $50 to attend, then share a video that captures that story. If your most recent product was discovered after you accidentally mixed the wrong chemicals, dramatize it.

2. *Brand Storytelling:* A great approach is to convert your blog posts, guides etc. to videos. If you are creating videos first, you can then reformat those to other text-based content.

3. *How-To Videos:* More and more consumers are turning to YouTube to search for solutions to their problems and dilemmas. In 2015, for instance, Google reported that 'how-to' searches were up 70%.[135] To best leverage this trend, figure out the problems and pain-points facing your target customers, then tailor your videos to offer solutions and meet their needs. By posting regular, predictably great content, you position your brand as top-of-mind when consumers are ready to make a purchase.

4. *Video Case Studies/Testimonials:* Another video form to advance brand storytelling is to feature the experiences of customers with your products. These kinds of videos are not only powerful social proof, but they also allow real customers to explain why they chose your brand instead of the competition and how your products are relevant in their lives.

5. *Providing Product Demos:* Among the few eCommerce brands that are posting video content on YouTube, many of them are only displaying photos and descriptions of their products. By offering in-depth demonstrations and tests, you can effectively differentiate your brand from others. Demonstration videos help consumers determine whether your products are right for them and details how to use them properly. These videos add perceived value to your products by bringing their features to life.

6. *Showcasing Your Team:* Capture your employees going about their everyday work and daily operations in the office, field, or lab. This approach helps consumers feel like they know you and can be a valuable way to start building consumer relationships. Most customers also appreciate the feeling of transparency, and trust is built when they're able to see how your products are developed and created.

Paid Advertising

You can also produce ads that will be featured across YouTube as consumers watch the content they're interested in. There are three types of video ads:

Skippable Video Ads (a.k.a TrueView Ads): TrueView ads are the best way to drive brand engagement on YouTube. These ads can be manually skipped after 5 seconds, making your opening critical to capturing viewer attention, and the advertiser only pays if the user watches at least 30 seconds of the ad. There are two types of TrueView ads:

Discovery Ads are those that show up on YouTube video apps, games and other videos in the Google Display Network. The maximum length of these videos is 3 minutes.

In-Stream Ads show within YouTube videos and search results. There is no limit to video length.

Preroll Ads: Non-skippable videos that display in-stream. They can play before, mid-roll, or at the end of the video. They can be 15 to 20 seconds long.

Bumper Ads: Bumpers are the third and shortest type of YouTube video ad and they just last 6 seconds. They are perfect for mobile viewers.

Summary, YouTube

With the dizzying changes happening on other social networks like Facebook, eCommerce merchants would do well to explore different avenues to build brand awareness, promote their products, and start building relationships with consumers. By focusing on content that will highlight your product features and address the needs of your customers, you can seriously support your marketing efforts on YouTube.

Google Shopping

Google Shopping is a platform that allows retailers to advertise their products in Google's search results, as well as under their "Shopping" tab. The ads that Shopping generates are also known as Product Listing Ads or PLAs, and they appear at the top of search results or in the top-right corner of the results page. While they appear to be like other ads, Shopping ads include more product information like its photo, name, price, color, size, availability, and seller name. Shopping is managed through Google Merchant Center and Google Adwords.

Launched in Spring of 2020, Google recently expanded its Shopping platform to include a new, free option. Now, any online merchant can list their entire inventory for free through Merchant Center. Placement as a promoted listing still requires keyword bidding, but these costs are performance based, meaning you only pay when consumers click-through on your ads. In combination with the free option, this makes Shopping one of the most cost-effective marketing options online, especially because it also has one of the highest click-through rates.

Once you've created your ads, Google determines where your ads show up in results based on your product feed, your website, and in the case of paid ads, your bid amounts. Coupled with the particular search terms used by a consumer, your ads may be triggered to appear.

When it comes to the paid route, you don't, however, need to promote every product you offer. The free option ensures you'll continue to capture the largest number of customers, making the best candidates for paid ads the products that will introduce your brand to consumers and get them hooked. Consider focusing on your core products. These may be your most profitable or the lower-priced items your customers order the most often. Consumables or products with low competition but good demand are also ideal choices for paid Shopping ads.

The Two Platforms at the Centre of Google Shopping

Google Merchant Center and Google Adwords are the dual platforms needed to start a Google Shopping campaign.

You'll need accounts for both, and they will need to be linked:

Google Merchant Center is where you host and manage your product inventory and feed. You enter the details of the products you want to advertise through Shopping and format them to Google's requirements. You have two options for creating your feed: a manual option and an automatic option. You can manually create your feed by entering the relevant product list and details into a spreadsheet that's formatted to Google's preference. For automatic options, there are several extensions, plugins, apps, and services that will pull the needed information directly from your website and format product details for you.

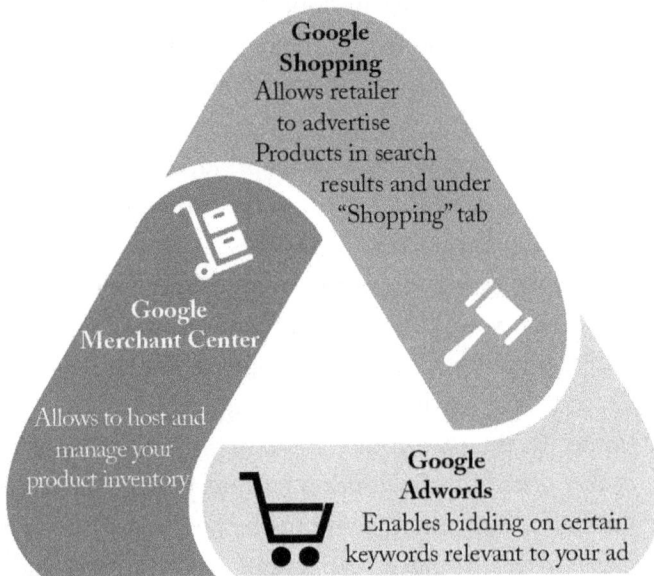

Google Shopping
Allows retailer to advertise Products in search results and under "Shopping" tab

Google Merchant Center
Allows to host and manage your product inventory

Google Adwords
Enables bidding on certain keywords relevant to your ad

Google Adwords is the platform where you'll bid on certain keywords associated with your ads. Here you'll set and manage your bid amounts and choose keywords associated with your products. You'll also set which locations and demographics to target with your ads, set your ad schedule, and be able to access a wealth of data to get insights into the performance of various ads and keywords. While Adwords is straightforward, there is a fair learning curve to getting the most from it.

Summary, Google Shopping

eCommerce retail success is rooted in search engine queries. It's critical to keep an eye on what the competition is doing, and how the search landscape is changing to ensure you're getting the most from your Shopping campaigns. And as more brands adopt PLA campaigns, more marketers will optimize and increase their spend-to-click ratio to stand out. This doesn't mean you can ignore Google Shopping, in fact, quite the opposite: it's more important than ever for merchants to continually adapt to new advertising formats and look for new opportunities.

Retargeting

Very few first-time visitors to your website are going to complete a purchase, in fact, only about 2% will.[136] Retargeting is a marketing strategy that specifically targets the remaining 98% of visitors who bounce from your site, as well as past customers, with personalized, relevant ads. These ads typically appear on other sites as they browse the web. Retargeting can also be used to re-engage customers you already have contact information for, like past buyers or those who've signed up to your email list.

To retarget, merchants place a piece of code, often called a "pixel," to their website to track visitor behavior: this code notices what products customers browse, if they add anything to their cart, what they buy, and so on. Then, after they leave your site, retargeting ads featuring your products are shown to them on other websites and social channels. For customers whose contact information you already have, you can use triggered emails to reach out to them directly, for instance, to remind them of items left in their cart or that they've looked at multiple times.

Retargeting is particularly effective because many times, consumers fail to purchase due to an interruption, distraction, or a desire to do more research. If they've found your site and browsed your products, they are likely interested even if they're not, for whatever reason, ready to buy right now. By retargeting with relevant ads, you keep your brand in front of customers across their devices. This presence makes your brand more likely to be top-of-mind when they do decide to make a purchase.

The Benefits of Retargeting

There are two main benefits to retargeting campaigns: it's a powerful way to increase brand awareness, and it helps you maximize your advertising ROI.

Because retargeting is thought of primarily as an advertising strategy, its potential as a brand-building tool is often overlooked. Traditionally, retargeting is used to influence customer behavior by enticing consumers to return to your site, sign up for an email list, or complete a purchase. However, retargeting is quite good at building brand familiarity among your target audience. In turn, this increased awareness makes consumers more likely to take indirect actions like making a Google search for your brand or organically visiting your site. In fact, research by comScore found that retargeting led to a 1046% increase in branded searches, and boosted site visits by 726% four weeks after exposure to a retargeting ad.[137]

You can further increase the success of retargeting campaigns by matching up consumer behavior with their clear next step in the sales funnel. For instance, a consumer who's visited your site once can be targeted with an ad leading to a landing page that invites them to sign up to your email list. Someone who has visited your site several times can be linked to a landing page showing them the products they're interested in with a call to action to "Add to Cart" or "Get it Now."

Summary, Retargeting

Retargeting is an incredible way to get more conversions out of your online traffic. If you approach it right, you can use retargeting to get more conversions from both the people who are *already* ready to convert *and* the ones who aren't quite there yet. Because retargeting offers such compelling benefits, making sure you set aside a percentage of your marketing budget for retargeting has become table stakes for eCommerce brands.

Influencer Marketing

As consumers become increasingly suspicious of traditional sales pitches and advertising, influencer marketing is quickly becoming a critical marketing tool. The popularity of social media has created a generation of new "digital stars" who have developed a significant online following despite being regular people. These "stars" are popular in particular niches, and many consumers see them as category and industry experts. They're called influencers because their opinions and recommendations have the power to shape the purchase decisions of their followers. This consumer trust has led many brands to approach influencers with sponsorship and affiliation opportunities.

Typically, brands pay an influencer to post a picture featuring your product along with a promo code. Often, influencers make video reviews or recommendations or provide tips and how-to guides. These kinds of partnerships may be ongoing campaigns that involve a series of posts as well. It's a great way to introduce your brand to a captive audience and increase a product's desirability. As influencers tend to be popular in a particular niche or category, it's a highly effective way for brands to reach a relevant audience. This maximizes the chances of conversion and generates higher quality leads.

Influencer marketing is a proven strategy, and it's quickly becoming the most viable tool to drive sales for your brand. It's estimated that for every dollar spent on influencer marketing, campaigns generate $6.50, and some studies place this amount above $7.[138]

22% of marketers believe influencer marketing is on par with email as providing the best ROI for acquiring customers[139] and more than 57% of consumers over 16 years old say they've made a purchase based on the recommendation of an influencer.[140]

According to a study by Linqia, the most important social platforms for influencer marketing are:[141]

- Instagram (92%)
- Facebook (77%)
- Blogs/bloggers (71%)
- YouTube (42%)
- Pinterest (39%)
- Twitter (26%)

Goals for Influencer Marketing

Influencers can be immensely helpful to your eCommerce business in 3 critical ways:

Increased Brand Awareness

By building a relationship with an influencer, you create a direct channel for your content that will reach a relevant audience. Since consumers are increasingly ignoring traditional marketing, an influencer's endorsement can give greater credibility to your brand. Brand awareness increases as they spread the word about your products. Although hard to quantify, you can track your success by creating a branded hashtag.

Improved Brand Advocacy

Because influencers have established credibility in their particular niche, they're naturally strong advocates for your brand. Their opinion carries a lot of weight with their followers, meaning they more directly influence buying behavior.

Improved Sales Conversion

Influencers can give context to your products and expand on the benefits of its features in a way that will convince more people to give your brand a try, leading to improved conversion. To track the impact on sales, use UTM parameters to track campaign performance, or consider giving influencers a unique promo code to help you identify where your traffic and sales are coming from.

Identifying the Right Influencers for Your Brand

Influencers can be broken down into three main categories:

1. *Micro-Influencers:* these influencers have fewer than 1,000 followers, but it's a tight-knit community and their fans are highly engaged. Because of this closeness, recommendations are taken more seriously, so partnering with micro-influencers tends to show higher conversion rates. They are also typically more affordable to work with than influencers with bigger followings.

2. *Macro-Influencers:* they have an audience of fewer than 100,000 followers. They operate in a well-defined and established niche and have a healthy community around them. Their followers tend to be more diverse, as well. They are more expensive than micro-influencers but have more experience working with brands.

3 Types of Social Media Influencers

Micro-influencers

> 1,000 FOLLOWERS

PROS:

Have a tight-knit relationship with their audience

Cover a wide range of niches

Have higher engagement and conversion rates*

Are often cheaper than big influencers

Macro-influencers

> 100,000 FOLLOWERS

PROS:

Have a large, diverse audience

Have a well-established position

Are experienced in working with brands

Celebrities

> 1.000.000 FOLLOWERS

PROS:

Can achieve great reach

Are highly professional

Can help you grow brand awareness

Already have a large marketing

3. *Celebrities:* have up to 1 million followers. At this level, influencers are highly professional and have valuable insight into how to best grow brand awareness and position your product with their audience. They tend to be the most expensive option but have a large marketing potential you can tap into.

If you are using an influencer program, work with multiple influencers across different platforms to create a multiplier effect. You'll also want a healthy mix of influencer levels that aren't all celebrities or macro-influencers. In fact, it's usually more beneficial to partner with up-and-coming influencers because they're often eager to work with you and cooperate more closely than some of the more professional influencers. Keep in mind, too, that many influencers have a following across several social sites but will tend to have higher prices on the influencer-heavy platforms like Instagram and YouTube versus Pinterest or Snapchat. These smaller channels may be better for your brand and help you afford a bigger influencer.

Influencer Marketing Pricing

$25 / 1000 followers
An influencer with 1,000,000 followers could charge $25,000 per post

$10 / 1000 followers
An influencer with 1,000,000 followers could charge $10,000 per post

$2 / 1000 followers
An influencer with 1,000,000 followers could charge $2000 per post

$20 / 1000 subscribers
A YouTuber with 1,000,000 subscribers could charge $20,000 per video

$10 / 1000 followers or views
An influencer with 1,000,000 followers could charge $10,000 per post

$60 / 1000 views

Source: webfx.com

On average influencers on the following platforms will charge:

- Facebook: $25,000 per 1,000,000 followers
- Instagram: $10,000 per 1,000,000 followers
- Snapchat: $10,000 per 1,000,000 followers
- YouTube: $20,000 per 1,000,000 followers

Reaching Out to Influencers

Once you've found the influencers you'd like to partner with, it's time to reach out. As mentioned, the easiest way is to use a management platform like AspireIQ, TapInfluencer, Upfluence, or Famebit for YouTube.

You can also send a pitch email or message through social media, though you'll have a harder time getting noticed with influencers that have bigger followings. In your correspondence, be sure to make it clear you're interested in collaborating, why you believe your brand would make a productive partnership, and what the influencer stands to gain from the relationship.

Be sure you personalize your message, there are egos at play here; if your pitch looks like spam, it will likely be ignored.

The *best way* is to organically build a relationship with an influencer before pitching them. Follow them on their social channels and take an interest in what they're doing. Engage them by leaving comments on their blog and posts. This way, when you do approach them, they'll likely already be familiar with your brand. Having a real relationship as the foundation of a campaign will also lead to more powerful results. The recommendation will feel more natural and genuine, and the influencer will likely be more enthusiastic about working with you.

Summary, Influencer Marketing

Whatever approach you take to reach out initially, to get the most out of this strategy, you should be focusing on the relationship, not a transaction. Having longer-term ties with influencers will help them feel like you're invested in their success and make them more loyal to your brand and their promotions more authentic. Influencer marketing is still new territory, but its unprecedented potential to impact people's purchasing decisions means it's an important strategic asset to include in your marketing budget.

Emerging Technologies

Augmented Reality and Virtual Reality for eCommerce

Augmented and Virtual Reality (AR and VR, respectively) technology offers new and exciting opportunities for eCommerce retailers. As an eCommerce merchant, you know well that one of the main drawbacks to purchasing online is that consumers typically don't have the opportunity to see, touch, and interact with the items they're interested in before buying. AR and VR promise to close this confidence gap.

For instance, let's say your online store sells high-end, unique furniture and other home décor accents. A consumer might find a coffee table online that they fall in love with, but they are unsure if it will work well in their living room. If you have an app that's AR-enabled, the customer would now be able to use the camera on their phone, point it into the space they hope to place the table, and the app would place a 3D model of the coffee table as an overlay on the live image of the room, giving the customer a clearer idea of how the table will look in their space.

In some ways, this ability to integrate virtual objects and the real world surpasses what customers can imagine even in a brick-and-mortar store. In the case of furniture, for example, the customer can visualize the new piece in their home without the hassle of visiting the store, let alone delivery.

As for VR, with a VR headset, consumers will instantly find themselves with a 3D view of your virtual store where they can walk around and interact with items. As an added feature, if a customer finds a lamp that she likes, as they fix their gaze on the item, it details the price, dimensions, and description. Where AR allows customers to visualize products in their own space, VR creates an immersive environment that can transport users into a totally new reality.

AR and VR by the Numbers

According to research by IDC, the AR/VR market increased 78.5% to reach $18.8 billion in 2020, and it is predicted to continue to grow by a five-year compound annual growth rate of 77%.[142]

AR/VR Market Size
(all figures in billion USD)

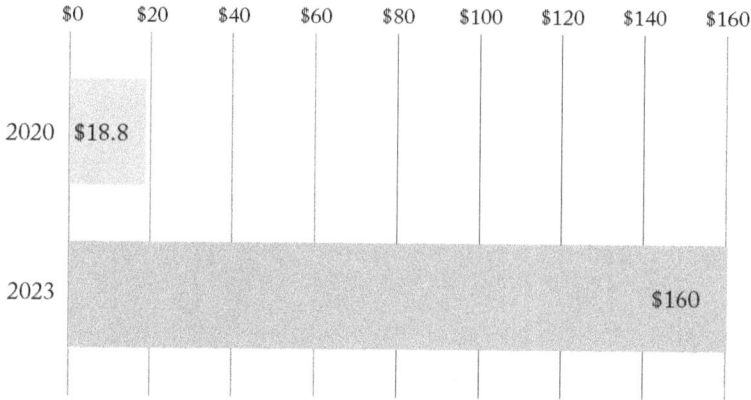

	$0	$20	$40	$60	$80	$100	$120	$140	$160
2020	$18.8								
2023									$160

Source: IDC

Benefits of AR/VR

As previously discussed, nearly 73% of online retail carts are abandoned before the purchase is completed. eCommerce has an average conversion rate of 2%-4% compared to traditional retail which boasts a 20%-40% conversion rate, and in light of these numbers, the sensory limits of eCommerce can't be ignored. AR and VR technologies offer online retailers the chance to give their customers a shopping experience comparable to being in-store.

In addition, AR and VR can increase an eCommerce merchant's ability to tailor and personalize a customer's shopping experience. AR and VR technologies can now act as a kind of virtual assistant. Not only is a higher level of personalization enabled by VR, but it's also easier for technology than it is for an in-store assistant.

It is, therefore, no surprise that Retail Perceptions found the use of AR and VR technology raises conversion rates, increases store traffic, and allows retailers to increase prices.

This technology has also been shown to decrease abandoned carts, and among the eCommerce brands that have already implemented AR features in their app or site, there's been a drop in return rates. AR and VR technology

The Impact of Augmented Reality on Retail

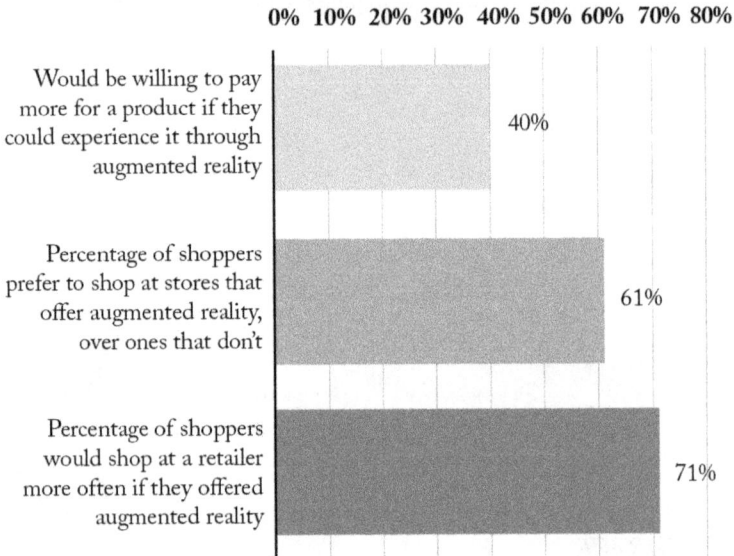

0% 10% 20% 30% 40% 50% 60% 70% 80%

Would be willing to pay more for a product if they could experience it through augmented reality
40%

Percentage of shoppers prefer to shop at stores that offer augmented reality, over ones that don't
61%

Percentage of shoppers would shop at a retailer more often if they offered augmented reality
71%

Source: Retail Perceptions

takes a lot of the guesswork out of online shopping and customers are therefore more confident about their purchases before they're even delivered.

Summary, New Realities for eCommerce

The marriage of AR-VR with eCommerce is inevitable. Though the use of AR and VR in eCommerce is still in its infancy in terms of its implementation within the market, this immersive technology is already upon us, and it is only set to grow from here.

With this technology, online shopping has the opportunity to grow from casual browsing to a fully immersive and engaging experience. In-person shopping isn't just mimicked, it can be improved upon with greater personalization and by empowering customers to make confident decisions.

eCommerce merchants would do well to take this technology seriously and realize they may soon be needed to gain a competitive edge in an already hyper-competitive market. It won't be long before consumers are actively doing business with those brands that offer AR and VR enabled experiences, leaving those who don't behind.

Voice Search

There are many forms of voice search, the most widely known being Apple's Siri and Google's Bixby, both now included by default in Apple and Android devices, respectively. Siri and Bixby allow you to carry out a variety of functions on your smartphone, like "Call George," and "Open the YouTube app," using nothing but your voice. Google Chrome also allows you to skip the keyboard inputs using a microphone to tell Google what to search for. And of course, perhaps the most popular and recognizable form of voice search is powered by smart speakers like Amazon's Echo and Google Home. The Echo, or Alexa, in particular, is the popular choice of consumers and represents 72% of the market share.[143] With the popularity of smart speakers growing, voice search is no longer a niche, empowering a shift towards conversational commerce.

According to surveys conducted by VoiceBot.ai, 25% of participants said that household items are its most commonly purchased items through voice-assistants. Apparel and entertainment were the second most commonly ordered items.[144]

Whether you've used a voice assistant to search also largely depends on your age. About 40% of millennials say they've started a search through voice before making a purchase decision. BI Intelligence also found that the younger you are, the more likely you are to take advantage of voice search as opposed to keyboard or touch screen entry. While 31% of 14-17-year-olds reported they were interested in voice search, only 7% of those aged 55+ were interested. In fact, 50% of those 55+ were not interested at all.[145]

How to Make Voice Commerce Work for Your eCommerce Business

For Amazon Sellers: The Amazon Choice Badge: Amazon's Choice was developed precisely to make voice searches with Alexa easier. The algorithm behind the badge identifies the "best fit" product based on a customer's search query. Typically, the first product Alexa recommends will be a product with Amazon's Choice badge. These products tend to have higher sales, positive ratings, are reasonably priced, and have favorable shipping options and conditions. For merchants, the ability to get an Amazon's Choice Badge for certain keywords will make the biggest difference to your sales. If a customer uses certain keywords associated with your product in their search, you'll likely be the first item Alexa offers.

Consumer Usage and Interest in Using Voice Assistants

(Are you currently using embedded voice-enabled digital assistants?)

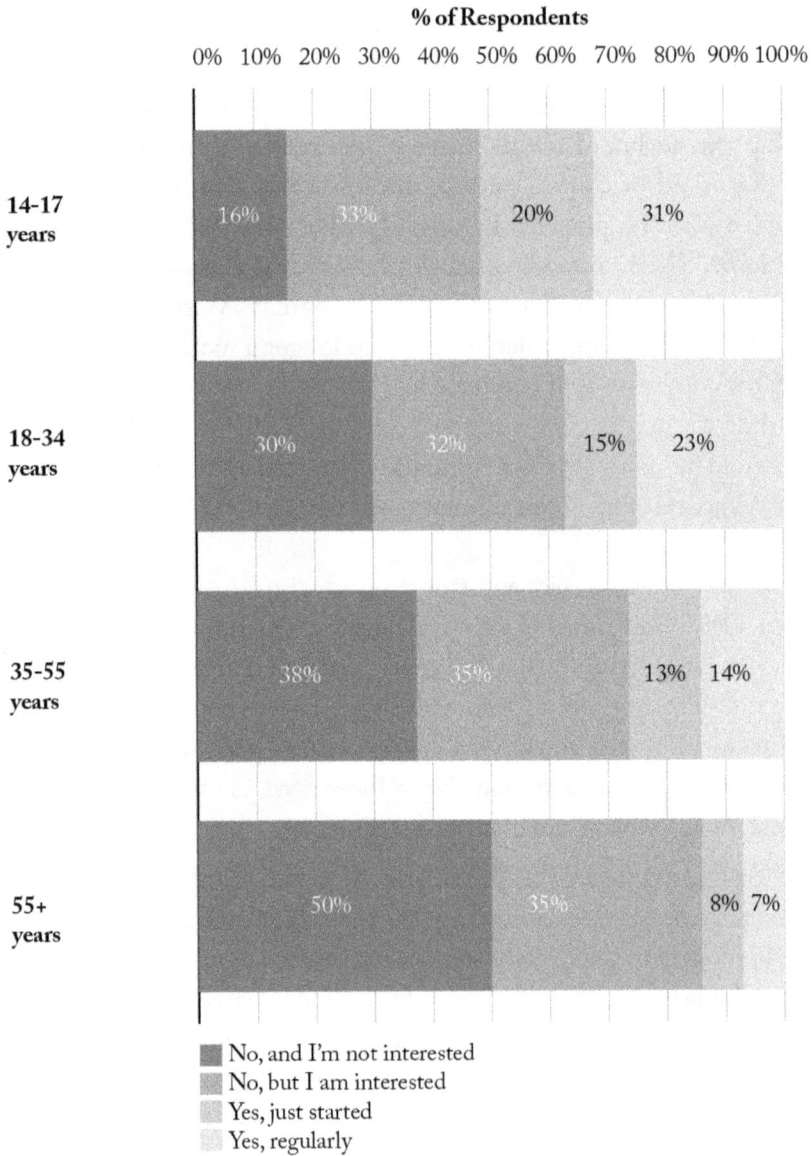

% of Respondents

0% 10% 20% 30% 40% 50% 60% 70% 80% 90% 100%

14-17 years
16% | 33% | 20% | 31%

18-34 years
30% | 32% | 15% | 23%

35-55 years
38% | 35% | 13% | 14%

55+ years
50% | 35% | 8% | 7%

■ No, and I'm not interested
■ No, but I am interested
■ Yes, just started
■ Yes, regularly

Source: Accenture

Pay Attention to Your Product Content: When someone searches with Alexa, she'll initially share the product title and price. When asked, "Tell me more," she'll then relate the average rating, the number of customer reviews, and then launch into the bullet points. To improve your voice-powered performance, make sure your product descriptions are concise, conversational, and informative.

Optimize Long-Tail Keywords: comScore predicts that half of all searches will be made with voice by 2020.[146] But there are significant differences between how consumers search with Siri, Alexa, and Google. Search queries made aloud are often more conversational, aligning with people's natural speech patterns. They're more likely to be in question format, too. For instance, instead of asking Google for "travel backpack" consumers tend to ask, "What's the best backpack for traveling?" Voice searches are thus more expressive, so you'll need to use NLP (Natural Language Processing) and natural phrasing in your content. In addition, you'll get the most out of voice searches by including these more natural phrases and questions as long-tail keywords within your listings or website.

Summary, Voice Search

While voice search has come a long way in recent years, it remains a nascent market. Its potential, however, is wide-reaching. Right now, voice search is best for purchasing unbranded basics where price, options, and comparisons have a small role to play in deciding to buy. Voice also works exceptionally well for subscription-based items or re-orders where the initial research and decision making has already been done.

Voice search has limitations when it comes to purchasing items like clothing and more involved purchases like big-ticket items that require a lot of research that is more easily done with text as text can easily be arranged side-by-side to directly compare.

Voice, therefore, still has a way to go before it takes over the eCommerce market and can offer an ideal experience, but brands would do well to begin investing in optimizing for voice to have the fundamentals in place once the technology catches up to customer needs.

Meniml's Channel Strategy

Now that we have completed an overview of the Multichannel strategy approach, and to further explain its adoption, we will head back to Meniml and craft its channel strategy based on its completed 6C's:

- Core: Purpose, Values, and Essence
- Customer: Audience and how does it elevate?
- Community: What cultural group do we identify with?
- Competition: Positioning
- Creatives: Naming, Colors, Typography, Logo, and Packaging
- Content: Story of the Brand and Brand Storytelling

Setting the foundation of the first 6C's has allowed us to zero-in on the optimal multichannel mix, and we'll break down Meniml's strategy and revenue projections, under the categories of Owned, Shared, and Paid channels, for the first full year of operation.

Owned Channels

1. Website/Mobile: As mentioned, the website serves as the cornerstone of all our marketing activities. The website will have 2 main sections:

a. "Inside Meniml:" which takes the visitor behind the scenes of Meniml.

> *Goal: Explore the brand's origin; emphasize the brand essence of "Dashing" by showcasing some of our urban scavenger hunts etc.*

A blog titled "Menual:" the eBrandBuilders' Content Creation Framework has inspired content that's mapped to TOFU, MOFU, and BOFU search queries.

> *Goal: One 2,500+ word cornerstone posts per week to drive website traffic based on rotating long–tail keywords initially.*

b. The Meniml Store: all aspects of the website are optimized to turn visitors into buyers.

> *Goal: Reach 50k monthly visitors by Q4. At a conversion rate of 2% and an AOV of $90, the website is projected to contribute to $354,600 in annual revenues.*

2. Customer Service:

a. Chatbot (Menny): We will use a chatbot for queries arising from website traffic. The objective of the bot is to reduce wait times for customers by responding to routine questions through a built-in knowledge base on skin-related topics, before involving live representatives if needed.

> *Goal: Answer all questions within 2 minutes and all emails within 12 hours.*

b. Customer Service: Phone: ensures we offer all modes of interaction and get insights on customer buying behavior, especially in the first year of launch. A toll-free number is listed on the site.

> *Goal: Answer 80% of calls in 20 seconds or less.*

3. Email Marketing: speaking in the tone of our Rebel Royal target audience, email marketing constitutes daily emails that include skincare tips as well as tools of seduction in our evening "shemails."

> *Goal: Based on an open rate of 15%, CTR of 8%, a conversion rate of 9%, AOV of $90, the targeted annual revenue through email marketing is $34K, based on a subscriber base of 3k average subscribers per month.*

4. Retail Pop-Up: similar to offering customers a phone number to call-in, having a smaller retailer presence through a pop-up will help us stay close to our customers. Based on our audience's commonalities with retail establishments, we have identified Nordstrom as a storefront that's synonymous with our brand.

> *Goal: By Q4, depending on approvals, the pop-up is projected to contribute a modest $42k in annual revenues.*

Shared Channels

1. Amazon: since we are experienced eCom sellers, Amazon will be part of the channel mix and not the sole sales lever. With the intent of building a brand, Amazon is planned for Q2 launch with a significant push with Sponsored Ads.

> *Goal: Forecasted revenue from Amazon, in the first year of operation, is $172k.*

2. Walmart: We will keep an eye on how Walmart is evolving as a platform and after evaluating its favorability have a presence on the platform the following year.

> *Goal: Evaluate and have a presence in the marketplace the following year.*

3. Crowdfunding: Kickstarter: Kickstarter catches our fancy for all its positive attributes that we discussed before.

> *Goal: Though we have not assigned any revenues at this stage, we would start to scope any new product launched through this crowdfunding platform.*

4. Partnerships: Outreach: Based on Meniml's Soleness statement, we've developed messaging to conduct outreach based on editorial calendars, of various men's magazines, specifically GQ, Men's Health, and Men's Journal.

> *Goal: Secure placements in two of three leading magazines, with an objective to drive awareness and traffic to the website.*

5. Partnerships: Affiliates: Due to the very nature of the audience, building an affiliate network will be a priority. Having partnered with an affiliate agency in the past, we'll extend this arrangement for Meniml. Managing affiliates is resource-intensive and better left to the specialists.

> *Goal: Contribute approximately a quarter of our revenue totaling $158K.*

Paid Channels

1. Facebook: Despite Facebook's privacy concerns, general algorithm, and minimal inventory, the platform will be at the forefront of our paid traffic campaigns.

Goal: The channel should drive another quarter of revenue at $207K.

2. YouTube: Based on YouTube's audience demographic, the Meniml man should be an avid subscriber to our channel.

Goal: Produce 2 videos per week, with 100-500 subscribers/month from Q1-Q4, resulting in projected revenues of $103k for the year.

3. Retargeting: strongly tied to our FB approach, retargeting audiences is composed of video views, product page visits, abandoned carts, and checkout hits.

Goal: The incremental revenue should contribute to 20% of FB contribution, resulting in sales of $41K.

4. Influencer Marketing: Finally, adding to the channel mix is influencer outreach. Rather than targeting the big guns, our strategy will be limited to building relationships with 10 micro-influencers and 2 macro-influencers.

Goal: The referral sales target is to drive 10-12 sales per influencer/month at AOV at $90. Leading to a contribution of $100k towards the annual target.

We understand that there are a lot of channels in the mix, and the reasoning for such a mix is two-fold:

First, if we were to launch Meniml, it would not be our first rodeo. With our prior expertise and resources on hand, it makes it easier to test a number of channels at the onset and scale what works quickly. Furthermore, we would be leveraging external agency support to execute on various channels.

Second, we wanted to demonstrate the thought process of including various channels and the individual financial contributions it would make.

However, if you were just entering the eCommerce space, I would strongly recommend that whatever platform you're the most obsessed with is the one you should plug into. And then quadruple down on it to still realize similar financial payback based on the 7C Method.

This marks the last entry to the 7C Canvas, with placing the various Brand Touchpoints that have been earmarked for Meniml.

Now that you can see the 7C Canvas in its completed state, I hope it demonstrates the merits of being:

- Focussed on the inherent strengths of building a brand that arises from the fundamentals and then works its way to the brand touchpoints.
- A building block approach where every C serves as a stepping stone to the next and the entire process ensures simplicity, coherence, and success.
- A method that provides confidence that you are not going to be side-tracked while minimizing shiny object syndrome.
- The common ground that engages your team and facilitates onboarding of new hires and easily communicates brand expectations.

And overall, a strategic roadmap that steers your brand's future direction.

MENIML 7C CANVAS

◈ CORE

WHY DO YOU EXIST? PURPOSE.

To offer a new, complete model for today's man. Meniml seeks to bring together thousands of factionalized "men," providing examples and models that their own fathers, social peers, and role models could not.

essence DASHING

WHAT DO YOU STAND FOR? VALUES.

- Independence
- Style – Cleanliness
- Self-Respect

☺ CUSTOMER

WHO'S YOUR AUDIENCE?

Jack is an 80's baby yet born with a timeless cool. Raised in Connecticut, always independent and curious, he engaged deeply with anything that interested him, from a stint one summer with a local circus, to busting and traveling his way across Europe each summer in between his English studies at Brown University. Since college, he's blogged, cheffed, worked as a journalist, boxing trainer, and even tried his hand at motorcycle racing after dropping in at a local contest and winning its $1,000 prize.

HOW DOES YOUR PRODUCT ELEVATE?

I am confident, stylish, self-reliant, handsome (or well-groomed). I care about having quality tools for all of my daily needs, including grooming, and like them to be well-organized and essential.

⚒ COMMUNITY

WHAT CULTURAL GROUP DO WE IDENTIFY WITH?

Our community of men see our brand as a cultural rallying point. Unsatisfied with the combative tribes of lumbersexuals, metrosexuals, or aggro-jock warriors, but knowing they're more than sterilized stallions in corporate suits and ties, they look for relationships with other "modern classic" men, who are self-reliant, tough but fun, curious but principled, confident but vulnerable. In other words, "virile men." They don't want to sit around a sweat lodge hugging other men and crying, but they do want to feel a connection to others.

◎ COMPETITION

HOW ARE YOU UNIQUE?

Meniml is the brand for today's adult Man who wants a one-stop, complete but simple grooming solution that goes beyond soap and shampoo (but below another brand). It organizes, simplifies, and displays sequential skin, hair, and body maintenance products, stocking only the necessities for maximum male grooming. UNLIKE women's beauty products that have excess SKUs to sell more to the same customers, our product simplifies while adding pride & eliminating "shame" in complete grooming for Men. Our brand guides its user's in a new, integrated but complete model of being a Man in itself.

◉ CREATIVES

NAMING
Meniml
www.meniml.com

LOGO
meniml

COLORS

TYPOGRAPHY
Futura

PACKAGING

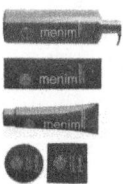

▤ CONTENT

STORY OF THE BRAND

Neil and Ren were discussing men's beauty brands and Neil remarked, "I really believe there's a place for another brand." Men are buying more beauty care products than ever before but it does not seem that there a focussed target. Men are spiritual tofu, defined by age; they're cross-generational. This made sense to Neil, and things clicked. "I get it. Something that offers a simple, but inclusive, model of masculinity and we can call it "Meniml.""

BRAND STORIES

Star: Ditch clueless slob for old-school cool.

Chain: Meniml has a clearly labeled, ordered regiment that takes the guessing out of self-care that's refilled automatically every month.

Hook: A simple routine for simply dashing. Order your kit today.

▦ CHANNEL

YOUR BRAND TOUCHPOINTS

OWNED CHANNELS
- Website/Mobile — $356,600
- Blog
- Customer Service/Phone
- Customer Service/Chatbot — $34,000
- Email Marketing
- *SUB REVENUE* — $386,600

SHARED CHANNELS
- Marketplace: Amazon — $172,000
- Marketplace: Wal-Mart
- Crowdfunding: Kickstarter — $158,060
- Partnerships: Media — $42,000
- Partnerships: Affiliates
- Partnerships: Retail
- *SUB REVENUE* — $372,000

PAID CHANNELS
- Facebook — $209,200
- YouTube — $155,000
- Retargeting — $100,000
- Influencer Marketing — $47,000
- *SUB REVENUE* — $451,000

TOTAL REVENUE — $1,211,660

OUTRODUCTION

Well, you've arrived at the beginning. This is a lot to digest, but at the very least, you now have a real eCommerce branding *system* that can yield predictable results for your business. You now have the same secrets that unlock the results iconic brands spend millions in brand development to achieve. While branding is both an art and a science, don't be threatened by the art side. It just means you need to give yourself and your team room to experiment and the flexibility to modify and adapt to reactions. And then you do it again, as markets and your people change.

The best advice for taking on the branding process may come from Lewis Carroll, who once said, "Begin at the beginning and go on till you come to the end; then stop." And no matter where you are in the branding journey, it's always a "brand new day" for you to start. But we want to give you a sense of your next steps, so we'll leave you with some broader, "big picture" branding advice, as well as a quick summary of the key points of this book.

eCommerce and digital branding have their own learning curve, but our hope is this comprehensive study has provided you with everything you need to take your brand to the next level. But tackling this learning curve is necessary if you want to serve your brand well and provide value to the consumers with whom you'd like to do business. It means gaining a working knowledge of the eCommerce space in which you, competitors, and consumers are playing. To do this, you'll need to take the time to experiment and engage with the technical tools you're already familiar with, as well as the new branding tools we've provided. Combining widgets and applications (craft) with meaningful brand creative (art) is where the magic will happen for you.

To be perceived as a credible brand it's essential that you can demonstrate that you know what you're doing, and while we've given you professional branding tools matched with digital implementation tips and tricks, you *must* give yourself and your team some flexibility and play space for your early endeavors. This includes asking yourself if it's brand-appropriate to use a specific digital tool or channel to make consumer actions easier, more convenient, or more fun— whether it's shopping, buying airline tickets, getting product reviews, or setting up a community for new moms. Is this channel a relevant place for your brand to be and does your brand have any business being there? By now, you know the answer depends specifically on your target customer, that person you want to convert to a brand fanatic. Once you know who they are, the next step is simply following them, looking at how they act, what they say, how they want to receive value, and what their primary channels and platforms are.

Induce, don't assume.

To become a brand that customers actively search for and choose to interact with, you've got to take advantage of all the innovative new ways you can gain *insights* about the consumers you want to reach. The need to watch what your customers and prospects are doing, and to listen to *what matters to them*, is more important than ever. Luckily, it's also now easier than ever to do. While gaining insight about what's important to consumers has always been a key factor in a brand's success, consumers today can signal what they want before you deliver it, so look for these signals. If you don't zero in quickly on what matters most to the people you most want to attract, a new entrant brand will.

Consumers now have so many more brand choices and so many more ways to see what's out there. It's therefore critical for consumers to be able to discern immediately what makes one brand different from another. Differentiating your brand based on some functional benefit is becoming harder to do, so it's increasingly necessary to take the benefit "up the ladder" to an emotional rung, ideally creating new meaning for your brand.

Anyone responsible for your branding (*including you*) must be able to quickly and intuitively understand what the brand stands for and recognize how to bring it to life. Marketing is no longer for masses to ask if what they're doing is right. Second, if your brand's meaning isn't clearly and simply defined before going to market, the market will define it for you—and you probably won't like the definition.

In addition, brand signals, those *energy with meaning* spots that emanate through your touchpoints, come in a wider assortment than ever before, and some are simply more influential with one target group than another. Therefore, it's critical to determine *which* touchpoints will have the greatest influence on the specific audience you want to reach. You can reinforce what makes your brand different and relevant by taking advantage of the right tools in your branding toolbox, digital and otherwise.

The eCommerce and digital world is an "always interactive" world. To be noticed in this noise, you need a clear brand voice that personifies your brand and clearly defines your brand's values, beliefs, and character traits. To be perceived as credible, the brand's voice must be conveyed *consistently across all touchpoints*, and *each expression must be appropriate to the interaction*. Yes, we've covered this ad nauseam, but having just completed a section on channel messaging and value, it's important to double-back and remind you to consider what the embedded value within your brand messaging is.

It's a truism of digital marketing, but a core tenet of digital branding, that you must engage with customers on *their terms*. The digital marketplace, *your* market space as an eCommerce entrepreneur, is *made* for relationship building. And success will follow anyone who's able to engage customers in a way that adds genuine value to the conversations or activities taking place. Better yet, if you're able to make the value of these brand interactions so obvious and compelling, consumers will actively seek you out.

Trust is of the essence when creating valuable brand interactions, so you need to invest in content that people want, content that is functional and/or entertaining. If you create something that is fun to watch, people will send it to their friends. This doesn't mean you can't also embed a more important brand message, but it's important to remember that *fun transports function*. By creating a website with useful information, people will return to it time and again and spend more time with it. Giving away content for free is another huge brand-building investment that should be considered part of the marketing or branding budget. Because consumers now have the tools to pass along information and content they find interesting, original, and engaging, the value of great creative work has literally never been greater. Free content can spawn spontaneous distribution, which can be a boon to the bottom line. To be successful, however, the creative work must be considered interesting, ingenious, and engaging by the consumers you want to attract, and not just to the people who created it.

Branding for eCommerce is about Big Data. Your brand will be defined in the hearts and minds of your customers by the sum of every interaction and individual touchpoint with your brand. To succeed, then you need to understand how each channel and touchpoint add to a meaningful whole.

This synergy of identity and information is at the heart of eCommerce Branding Big Data.

Chapter Summaries

Take the time to review any sections where you still have lingering questions, even if you, personally, won't be directly managing the work described. As a leader, you must close the gap between knowing and understanding, because it's only when you understand that you can teach and guide. To help you make this transition to understanding, we'll now provide you with an overview of everything you've read to help solidify that learning and build those neural pathway grooves. As cultural change-agent and neuroscientist A. Powers said: "It's Groovy Baby," as all useful learning should be.

Core: The Purpose of Having a Why

Consumers today value brands that care about social welfare, fair trade, and higher-purpose based work. When customers say they're looking for healthier choices, they aren't just talking about more natural ingredients in food; they're talking about brands that offer benefits and value good for *all* brand stakeholders: customers, employees, vendors, and the environment. Consumers want to contribute to ethical businesses and vote with their wallets. This means the most successful brands share values with their target customers and strive to use their brand levers to make a positive and meaningful social impact. Brands that can embody these qualities will be trusted, considered authentic, and become dominant in their categories.

A brand purpose is its "Why," and a purpose-driven brand understands why it exists, for whom it exists, and what it will do. Defining this purpose is an *inside-out strategy,* and your "why" will be the most significant part of a brand to its constituents, as consumers today are more concerned with why a brand exists than what it does. Purpose is, therefore, an important difference between brand and product.

We reviewed the "Golden Circle," created by business writer Simon Sinek, to illustrate why every person and brand should start with their purpose, their "why."

We then shifted our focus to brand values. *Your brand's values are the foundation of your company's identity. These values define who you serve, the problems you solve, and the principles which guide your decision making in the pursuit of your purpose. These are the core, bottom-line beliefs that your brand stands for and defends.* We then went on to provide numerous eCom examples from Chubbies to Tortuga, and demonstrate how brand values can, and should, guide the overall direction of your brand.

Finally, we explored brand essence. *Essence is the core value, idea, or emotional benefit that consumers associate with your products and services. Your essence thus defines the role your brand plays in the lives of consumers: it's the emotional experience consumers can count on your brand to deliver with every interaction.* Capturing the totality of your brand in 1-3 words is a significant challenge, so we offered the tool of "laddering" to give you a process to move from product function, through emotion, to meaning: your brand essence.

Customer

It's paramount that you understand the hearts and minds of your customers. Use the persona tool to build a guiding prototype of your ideal target customer. It can be helpful to think of your brand as a consumer insights company, but designed to serve a specific, niche segment of consumers.

In the teachings of Judaism, there is an anecdote about individuals and audiences that's relevant to branding and target customers: "If there are ten people, one will be someone who criticizes you no matter what you do. This person will come to dislike you, and you will not learn to like him either. Then, there will be two others who accept everything about you and whom you accept, too, and you will become close friends with them. The remaining seven people will be neither of these types. Now, do you focus on the one person who dislikes you? Do you pay more attention to the two who love you? Or would you focus on the crowd, the other seven? A person who is lacking in harmony will see only the one person he dislikes and will make a judgment of the world from that."[147]

Top performers and speakers also use this mindset when they're in front of an audience: they find *one* person in the audience they connect with and then focus on them the entire time. This audience member is the person who gets them. This focus results in inspiring an entire tribe of other "ones" who deeply connect with one another around the performer's message. Likewise, most successful PR agencies and YouTube bloggers would advise you that "there is no bad PR," and "haters are good." *Because the more polarizing a brand is, the more emotional commitment and support a brand gets from its tribal supporters.*

The most important tool in your brander's toolbox is, therefore, figuring out your customer, finding that "one" person amidst the rabble and noise who loves your brand. Going beyond "marketing" into "branding" means, in part, moving from a demographic view of markets and the world (gender, age, income) to a psychological, or psychographic view of the world: what people feel, imagine, identify with, and want. All of these elements are included in your customer persona, and these deeper insights will help your brand find and connect with the individual tribe that shares those ways of thinking and feeling.

Once you have built your customer persona, answering one additional and critical question - what do your customers *aspire* to be? - will deepen your understanding of your customer and reveal their true motives for purchasing your product. The answer to this question is usually emotional, and will help you understand the business you are really in. In turn, this insight can effectively shape your brand voice, messaging, and ensure your assets are in perfect alignment with your customer.

Community

The strength of your brand is directly proportional to the strength and connectedness of your community.

Forget this at your peril.

In such a crowded, competitive marketplace, it's critical to focus on brand community building. To be heard through all of this noise, brands need to demonstrate that they care more about nurturing relationships than sales. Being willing to listen and respond as a *human* brand is essential to creating a valuable, authentic community for your customers to interact within.

We all want to be a part of a tribe where we feel welcome and safe to contribute. Creating this kind of online community for your customers is a powerful way to build a tribe and deeply bond customers to your brand.

Your most important first goal is building your first 1,000 true fans (as in *fanatics*). If you can generate 1,000 fans, you can make a living from your fan base. You might not make enough to pay for your own jet or mansion, but you can make a sustainable living. And the beauty of this base of 1,000 fans is its organic virality. Once you hit 1,000 fans, they'll carry your brand across the psychic mosh pit to the next 2,000, 3,000, and 10,000 fans. This is a major advantage of branding versus marketing.

Competition & (Positive) Competitive Deviance

What can you do uniquely that your competitors cannot or will not do?

Real branding is "anti-competitive" since its goal is to differentiate one brand from another and help the *right people* select and own it. With that said, the issue, and the opportunity, for you as a brander is summed up by this statistic:

"Only 25% of brands are seen as distinctive by customers."[148] The other 75? They're like *Tofu*. They blend in, take on the flavor of things around them, and thus, like a wallflower, ultimately engage no one.

Building a *unique* brand gives your fanatics something to interact with, so they're never just transacting with your company.

How do you achieve this uniqueness? Through what we call "Soleness."

The process of SOLENESS is finding and claiming a market *position* that you can own and retain. With this kind of distinctive brand and product, you don't need to compete on price. In fact, you don't need to compete in any of the traditional and tangible marketing comparables: you just need to compete for attention.

Employing the eBrandBuilders' Option Planning Quadrant Matrix, the four primary ways of creating Soleness are:

1. Use of Intangibles
2. Disruption
3. Category of 1
4. Positioning

For the sake of brevity, as this is a summary, review Chapter 4 if you need a refresher on the details of any one of these methods for creating Soleness.

Creatives

Your creative strategy should *follow* your brand strategy, as creative assets are *symbols* of your brand's core, not just design for its own sake. The major points of meaningful identity we focused on are:

- Brand name
- Logo
- Colors/Palette
- Typography
- Packaging (which integrates all your creative assets)

Content

Content marketing has been a tool that only larger companies have been able to use, but it has been around for decades. As of this decade, however, the entry stakes for being a publisher and distributor of content to thousands, even hundreds of thousands of individuals has decreased to virtual nil. To succeed as a publisher now, you simply need a unique perspective and the ability to deliver value through your content. The tools for doing this are also, similarly, so democratized that *not* creating content makes a brand feel lazy. The benefits of content marketing are also deep and broad, and the ROI, from both a business and brand impact perspective, is unbeatable. Creating content can and will:

- Attract customers.
- Educate your buyers about a purchase they are considering.
- Overcome resistance or address objections.
- Establish your credibility, trust, and authority in your industry.
- Tell your brand story.
- Build buzz via social networks.
- Build a base of fans and inspire customers to love you.
- Inspire impulse buys.

At the core of content marketing is storytelling. *Stories are emotion-delivery vehicles that appeal to the subconscious mind, and which assists in the buying process. Storytelling sets the tone for your brand and brings your brand purpose and values to life.*

To facilitate execution, at eBrandBuilders, we break down storytelling to two components: the brand story and brand storytelling.

The brand story is the origin story for your brand and delves into how your company came to be. It introduces the brand founder(s) and explores when, where, and most importantly, why it was started. It may also cover the brand's early challenges and the obstacles you had to overcome birthing, organizing, and growing your brand into what it is today. Brand storytelling is guided by the brand story and bridges the gap between your internally developed brand strategy and how that is conveyed and relayed to your customers.

To enable day-to-day execution, we explored the eBrandBuilders' Content Creation Framework to illustrate how to tie your content to the first 5 C's, to bring it all together. Your brand story correlates to your Core, whereas brand storytelling maps to the individual questions you answered for your Customer, Community, Competition & Creatives. We also offered a list of sample stories to help you build your editorial calendar.

Creating content geared towards a specific audience attracts qualified traffic, meaning visitors are potential customers who are more likely to buy your products since they've already shown an interest in them. Since the traffic you're receiving is laser-focused on your niche, you have a better chance of converting these visitors into customers. Engaging content also allows you to communicate with your customers on an ongoing basis. You provide information to guide consumers at every point in their buyer's journey, too. This differs from traditional marketing, which usually focuses only on content that directly sells your products. For example, you might show ads that promote backpacks with its price and where it can be bought. You show this ad to your customers several times a day and hope it reaches them when they're ready to buy.

Content marketing, on the other hand, encourages you to create all types of content that's helpful to your customer. If your company sells backpacks to travelers, start by finding a niche that's relevant to your customers. In this instance, you might feature unique travel destinations you or your extended team has visited on your blog. You might also offer special tips and local customs most tourists don't know about, or advice on how to get around on a budget and with ease. This allows you to organically include information about your products in your posts, but instead of feeling like an ad, customers will see you're offering valuable advice at their points of need.

This comes down to the master seller's insight: people don't like to be sold, but they love to buy.

Channel

The foundation of a modern eCommerce channel strategy is implementation through multichannel marketing.

Multichannel marketing is connecting with your prospects and customers wherever they like to be, whether it's on marketplaces, social media, messaging apps, or other online communities. This allows customers to buy from you on their terms, exactly when and where they prefer.

On average, it takes seven "touches" with a brand before a customer is ready to purchase. One of the core benefits of multichannel marketing is the ability to generate multiple exposure points for the brand that matches the customer's natural buying journey, that is, on the channels they prefer. In terms of social media, for an eCommerce store, this may take the shape of a buy now button on a Tweet, a sponsored post on Instagram, a buyable Pin on Pinterest, or target Facebook ads. It also means having a presence on various online marketplaces, like Amazon, Walmart/Jet, eBay, Etsy, Google Shopping, and more.

Today, your brand needs to be omnipresent to be noticed and to stay above the noise. For instance, *retailers who sell on two marketplaces see 190% more in revenue than those who only sell on just one marketplace.* Not to mention that, on average, retailers who sell on two channels have double the revenue of retailers that sell through a single channel. As such, multi-channel makes dollars and sense.

In addition, being available through a marketplace increases your brand's trust factor. Despite the evolution of eCommerce, generating trust is still a necessary process before customers are willing to buy, online and offline. Because larger marketplaces have already generated and proven their trustworthiness, which is linked to their brand equity, customers are more willing to take a chance on an unfamiliar brand through their channel. In fact, according to the largest annual national poll, 49% of consumers begin their product search on Amazon, 36% begin on a search engine like Google, and the remaining 15% begin on social media or other marketplace channels.[149] In general, however, your social media presence will primarily drive product discovery and brand awareness.

Three Primary Channels

Owned Channels are the in-house channels you create and directly control, including your store's website, blog, mobile app, email lists, and any retail presence. In eCommerce, the central hub of your brand will be your website, which showcases your essential brand and user experience. We discussed several tools, optimization points, and the impacts of optimization, from the purely technical, such as reduced graphical information at the tail end of the buying process, to the more broadly applicable, such as payment options, optimizing product descriptions, and ways to reduce cart abandonment. We also discussed the importance of customer service in eCommerce and the rise of chatbots.

Email marketing remains one of the most profitable investments for your time and marketing dollars. With the right combination of campaigns, you can nurture relationships with your most relevant customers and capture more sales. Not only does email marketing promise the highest ROI, but it also keeps you in full control of your email list and messaging, making email the most direct and the most effective line of communication with your customers. We recommended building 6 types of email campaigns: welcome, brand awareness, purchase, post-purchase, cart abandonment, and win-back.

We also discussed the trend of DTC brands opening physical stores, suggesting the apparent retail apocalypse isn't what it seems. We then presented four different options for your brand to leverage this opportunity, including standalone stores, pop-ups, co-retail, and a blended model.

Shared channels include channels that you share with other sellers. They have stipulated rules and regulations you must follow, and you have limited control over the platform itself. The list of shared channels includes marketplaces (Amazon.com, Walmart.com), crowdfunding, and brand partnerships.

Marketplaces constitute the bulk of eCommerce revenue, primarily due to the low barriers to entry and a ready-made market of global customers. This makes marketplaces an especially attractive channel for new eCommerce sellers that have yet to set up their own channels like a website.

Crowdfunding offers another first entry point for eCommerce sellers, in particular to those that offer something truly unique, appealing to early adopters, and that requires funding.

Finally, partnerships are the final type of shared channel, though most often an opportunity for more mature eCommerce properties. Generally, partnerships with other brands are more easily established when your brand has an established offering, strong sales, and media mentions.

Paid Channels are the most important for eCommerce brands. Luckily, paid platforms like Facebook, Instagram, TikTok, and Google Shopping make it easy for advertisers to get started, and the simplicity of their platforms makes them a very appealing option to many brands.

In this section, we covered the socials, Google Shopping, retargeting, and influencer marketing. The goal here was to present the options, emphasize eCommerce-ready features, highlight key trends, and provide key stats around usage and demographics.

The Big Picture

Which brings us all the way back to the end of the beginning, which means it's time to take a step back and discuss the bigger picture to help you frame everything you've learned.

Brand as Business Management

Let's take a wider view and look at *brand as business management*, a more holistic view. Great brands are built from the inside-out, starting with their core, their purpose, which is always a reflection of their target customer segment.

Remember, people love to buy, but they don't like to be sold. Branding is effective because it's a "pull" mechanism, not a "pushy" marketing tactic.

The best brands also make trends rather than following them. If they don't, chasing trends will leave you like Wylie Coyote, suddenly floating in the air with no solid ground beneath you.

The devil, and in our case, the *angel*, is in the details. Brand *masters* have "positive OCD:" they are constantly organizing, refining, augmenting, and updating.

Finally, all the above means there should be no separation between brand and business. Even in eCommerce, leaders need to focus on managing the brand and business as one. Of course, *internal branding* is all about nurturing and mastering your company's *culture*. But isn't that also a form of "bottom-up" management? Yes. Of course, culture requires a clear and defined purpose for the internal tribe, but with that, you can achieve alignment, and *mass execution* (... in a good way). The pragmatic meaning of "brand as business management" is just that simple. Simple, but not easy. Our hope, however, is that we've made it *easier* for you.

Thank you so much for reading!

Addendum

Next Steps: You Don't Have to Do This Alone

One reason you may need professional help is that sometimes your boss, your team, or your CEO is so in love with the brand that they can't see its flaws. Or, some data-driven (and smart) CEO's are too involved with their numbers-only view and strategic plan that they don't "care" about branding, or simply don't recognize it as a core part of their business. Of course, you now have some of the financial numbers which underline the importance of branding for business. If you are a CMO (and assuming your company does not have a Chief Brand Officer (CBO)), you may need to hire an outside CBO for a CEO or Founder to trust the process until you have things in motion. Either way, sometimes you need an outsider's perspective.

But bringing in an outside brand consultant is getting ahead of ourselves. First, go back and study the questions in chapters 1, 2, 3, 4, 5, and 6 of this book. Dig deep and answer those questions as precisely as you can. Then take the results and compare them to your current brand strategy. Do they match up? If so, that's great. If not, then you have some work to do. Either way, having the knowledge contained in these pages will put you way ahead of the competition in understanding the true meaning of branding and why it's so important to your future success.

But this approach isn't just for bigger, established companies. Even if you're a one-man or one-woman show, the 7C method can revolutionize your business, and we hope you have found the first steps towards your success in this book.

If you feel you need some more guidance or are ready to move beyond these beginning steps, we also offer more advanced training in the form of the eBrandcubator, our 7-week coaching program. Find out more by booking a free, 45-minute coaching call at ebrandcall.com or feel free to reach out to us via email (contact@ebrandbuilders.com). We would love to help you reach your business goals, whatever they are, and we hope to hear from you soon. Either way, we wish you the best of luck and great success on your eCommerce journey.

ECOMMERCE BRANDS MENTIONED

Alala: (alalastyle.com) Alala Style is a luxury women's activewear brand, designed for women who want the best fashion and function in their activewear.

All Birds: (allbirds.com) All Birds is a direct-to-consumer designer of environmentally friendly footwear for men and women. Made with all-natural materials, they're the world's most comfortable shoes.

Amazon: (amazon.com) With a range of 3 billion products and more than 300 million global customers, Amazon is the world's largest online retailer and marketplace.

Amerisleep: (amerisleep.com) Amerisleep is a direct-to-consumer mattress manufacturer. Their products are made in the USA using natural, plant-based material to reduce petroleum consumption.

Anomalie: (dressanomalie.com) Anomalie offers custom wedding dresses designed by brides in collaboration with a stylist. Their unique creations and transparent pricing help every bride realize their dream.

Asos: (asos.com) An online fashion and cosmetics retailer, ASOS believes in fashion democracy and is a proud partner with GLAAD. They also work with 200 models who represent their diverse audience.

Away: (awaytravel.com) Away designs, manufactures, and sells travel gear. Their luggage isn't just "smart" but thoughtful, with built-in phone chargers, combination locks, and polycarbonate shells.

Baby Mori: (babymori.com) Baby Mori produces the softest baby clothing and accessories. Their products are all-natural and sustainably sourced. They also offer an online community for parents.

BarkBox: (barkbox.com) BarkBox is a subscription box for dogs featuring themed treats and toys sent monthly to your favorite canine.

Barn & Willow: (barnandwillow.com) Barn & Willow produce high-quality, custom-made window treatments delivered to customers without the brand-tax and inflated cost of middlemen.

BestSelf: (bestself.co) BestSelf design and sell journals to help customers make the most of their precious time and reach their goals, all while staying focused and motivated.

BKR: (mybkr.com) BKR believes that skin-health begins with proper hydration and offers chic glass water bottles with signature small spouts and silicone sleeves inspired by fashion, art, and culture.

Boll & Branch: (bollandbranch.com) Boll & Branch are a luxury eCommerce bedding company. Their products are made with organic cotton, and they were the first bedding company to be certified by Fair Trade USA.

Bombas: (bombas.com) Bombas has created the most comfortable socks in the world: they perfectly contour the foot and feature moisture-wicking technology. And for every pair of socks sold, Bombas donates a pair to someone in need.

Bonobos: (bonobos.com) An apparel brand for men, Bonobos pride themselves on their better-fitting menswear. They're also known for their exceptional shopping experience, both online and in-store.

Bouqs: (bouqs.com) Bouqs partners with local farmers to offer fresh-cut flowers sent right to your door. Without the waste of traditional florists, Bouqs hand-crafts their arrangements and deliver in as little as 2 hours.

Burrow: (burrow.com) Burrow manufactures luxury couches and armchairs made with sustainable, durable material. Their couches are fashionable and easy to assemble and move without hiring movers.

Casper: (casper.com) A direct-to-consumer mattress manufacturer, Casper mattresses are designed by a 30+ person R&D team that hold more than 50 patents. Casper uniquely offers a 100-night trial and exceptional customer service.

Charity Water: (charitywater.org) Charity Water is a non-profit organization whose mission is to provide clean drinking water to communities in developing countries.

Chewy: (chewy.com) Chewy is an online pet-supply retailer who has partnered with more than 1,000 trusted brands, vets, and service providers.

Chubbies: (chubbiesshorts.com) Chubbies makes retro-inspired shorts for men meant to remind you of your dad and the weekend. With an unforgettable sense of humor, they believe in aloha shirts and anything with the American flag on it.

Cotopaxi: (cotopaxi.com) Cotopaxi sells outdoor products and experiences. The company was born from the founder's desire to merge his love of traveling with a business model that fights poverty. 2% of all profits are donated to alleviate poverty.

Dollar Shave Club: (dollarshaveclub.com) Dollar Shave Club is a direct-to-consumer brand that delivers razors and other personal grooming products to customers in a subscription box that seriously undercuts the prices in retail stores.

Everlane: (everlane.com) Everlane is an eCommerce clothing retailer offering timeless basics made in ethical factories with premium materials.

Fit & Fly: (fitandflygirl.com) Fit & Fly hosts travel retreats for women all over the world. Their mission is to bring women together and offer well-rounded trips that blend fitness, wellness, culture, pampering, and adventure.

Fluff & Familia: (fluffandfamilia.com) Fluff & Familia offer cloth diapers, accessories, and other baby products. You're not just a customer, you're part of the "familia" and a valued member of their community.

Free People: (freepeople.com) Free People is an American apparel and lifestyle company with a bohemian flair. Although its life began as a private label for Urban Outfitters, after several iterations it became its own mature brand in 2001.

Glossier: (glossier.com) Glossier is a direct-to-consumer beauty brand that sees makeup choice as an element of your personal style. Glossier seeks to empower customers to find the products right for them.

Greats: (greats.com) Greats creates classically inspired, luxury sneakers for men and women. Based in Brooklyn, Greats offers high-quality, high-fashion shoes for an accessible price.

Greetabl: (greetabl.com) Greetabl offers a range of creative, curated, and personalized gifts and greetings. Gifts are designed to delight and surprise for those moments a card isn't enough and flowers are too much.

Harry's: (harrys.com) Harry's is a direct-to-consumer razor company fed up with overpaying for over-designed razors in drug stores. Harry's only uses the best material to embrace the messiness of masculinity.

Huckberry: (huckberry.com) Huckberry is a lifestyle brand that curates and sells outdoor gear and apparel. They aim to inspire more active and adventurous lives.

Jack Erwin: (jackerwin.com) Jack Erwin crafts men's footwear with timeless designs. The company seeks to create well-made and well-priced men's shoes that they love but couldn't find elsewhere.

Jeni's: (jenis.com) An artisan ice cream shop, Jeni's Splendid Ice Creams, has dozens of unique flavors available in their stores and for order online. They shun emulsifiers, synthetic flavorings, and dyes, and run a fellowship business model.

Leader Bag Co.: (leaderbagco.com) Leader Bag Co. designs high-quality, fashionable diaper bags and accessories. Leader hopes you'll wear your parenthood proudly and pack the values of kindness, solidarity, wisdom, and love wherever you and your little ones go.

M.Gemi: (mgemi.com) M.Gemi is a direct-to-consumer shoe brand. They're partnered with family-owned, luxury shoe manufacturers in Italy who produce hand-crafted, high-quality shoes which M.Gemi sells online.

Madsen Cycles: (madsencycles.com) Madsen Cycles produce the "bucket bike," a unique bicycle designed for families. Madsen seeks to encourage more families to get outside and make memories.

Mahabis: (mahabis.com) Mahabis has reinvented the slipper and also offer loungewear. Mahabis is "the essence of chill" and seeks to elevate the most ordinary experiences into treasured ones.

MeUndies: (meundies.com) MeUndies is an underwear and loungewear brand with a membership model that tops up your top drawer every month.

Ministry of Supply: (ministryofsupply.com) Ministry of Supply is an apparel company creating the new category of "performance professional" clothing. They're transforming stiff, high-maintenance dress clothes into stretchable, breathable, classics that don't need to be ironed.

MM.LaFleur: (mmlafleur.com) MM.LaFleur specializes in luxury apparel and accessories for professional women. Looking to "take the work out of dressing for work," MM.LaFleur offers personal styling and a totally modern shopping experience.

ModCloth: (modcloth.com) ModCloth offers vintage-inspired, yet timeless apparel for women. Each outfit is an opportunity for self-expression, and the brand seeks to celebrate the stories of the women to serve its mission to give everyone a place to fit in.

Nisolo: (nisolo.com) Nisolo makes handmade, high-quality leather shoes and accessories, inspired by the craftsmen of Peru. Nisolo also prioritizes ethical business practices by offering producers fair trade wages, healthcare, and a positive, safe, working environment.

Oliver Cabell: (olivercabell.com) Oliver Cabell creates footwear for men and women that combines art, craft, and technology into fashionable, timeless designs. The brand prizes challenging the status quo and seeing things differently.

Patagonia: (patagonia.com) Patagonia is an outdoor clothing and gear retailer specializing in the "silent sports" of climbing, skiing, snowboarding, surfing, fly-fishing, and trail running. They seek to create the best products possible with sustainable solutions, all while causing no unnecessary harm.

Paul Evans: (paulevansny.com) Paul Evans is a direct-to-consumer designer of men's footwear. Their shoes are handmade in Naples, Italy, designed in New York. Each shoe is Blake stitched giving them maximum flexibility and strength. They are also hand-painted, making every pair totally unique.

Peloton: (onepeloton.com) Peloton is a fitness equipment and media company. They produce high-quality indoor exercise bikes with built-in tablets through which users can stream live and on-demand fitness classes.

PooPouri: (poopourri.com) Poo-Pourri is a fragrant toilet spray made of essential oils and other natural ingredients designed to hold in bad odors. The brand came to prominence with several viral YouTube videos known for their unique sense of humor.

PopSockets: (popsockets.com) PopSockets produce grips, mounts, and cases for mobile phones and devices. PopSockets began as a Kickstarter campaign, and there are more than 40 million PopSockets grips around the world today.

Pressed Juicery: (pressedjuicery.com) Pressed Juicery offers a range of cold-pressed, raw juices. The nutritional integrity of their juices has been backed up by independent research, and they go to extra lengths for food safety, using high-pressure processing for all their cold-pressed products.

Quip: (getquip.com) Quip sells oral-care products and dental services online, including their flagship electric toothbrush. Their products are designed to support healthy, lifelong habits.

Rothy's: (rothys.com) Rothy's manufactures ballet and pointed flat toe shoes. Their products combine sustainability and high fashion with woven fabric made from recycled plastic, but without sacrificing comfort.

Scarosso: (scarosso.com) Scarosso makes luxury Italian shoes for both men and women along with other leather accessories. Shoes are manufactured in Marche, Italy, with transparency and sustainable materials.

Shopify: (shopify.ca) Shopify is an eCommerce store and point-of-sale platform. Shopify offers eCommerce merchants a plethora of tools to manage every aspect of their online business easily.

SimplyGum: (simplygum.com) SimplyGum offers all-natural and refreshing chewing gum and mints. Worried about the synthetic ingredients hidden behind the FDA-approved "gum base" most other brands use, SimplyGum has transparent ingredients, all in a beautiful package.

Skullcandy: (skullcandy.com) Skullcandy manufactures headphones, earphones, and other audio-related accessories. Born on a chairlift, Skullcandy merges the worlds of sports, music, and culture, pioneering color and style in a previously monochromatic industry.

STATE Bags: (statebags.com) STATE Bags designs fashionable work, travel, and school bags for everyone. While they are a for-profit company, they have a non-profit heart who are especially passionate about supporting kids in America's most under funded neighborhoods.

StitchFix: (stitchfix.com) Stitch Fix is an online subscription and personal shopping service. Looking to revolutionize how people find clothes, they strive to combine technology and the personal style and fashion sense of style experts.

Third Love: (thirdlove.com) Third Love is a lingerie company that was frustrated with all the ill-fitting alternatives. Offering double the number of available sizes compared to other brands, Third Love uses the measurements of millions of real women, not size templates, to design their bras.

Threads: (threadsstyling.com) Threads Styling is a luxury personal shopping service that operates through messaging platforms. Threads is at the helm of conversational commerce, and looking to connect with the next generation of luxury shoppers.

Tom Bihn: (tombihn.com) Tom Bihn offers a range of luggage and travel accessories. Everything is done in-house, including manufacturing, developing new materials, website maintenance, and photography. Tom Bihn is driven by creativity and value their 47-person team.

TOMS: (toms.com) TOMS provides stylish shoes based on the Argentine alpargata design. TOMS is also well-known for their One-for-One platform, which gives to someone in need for every product sold.

Tortuga: (tortugabackpacks.com) Tortuga creates backpacks specially designed for city travel. Their carry-on sized bags are made to help you live and travel on your terms.

Tuft & Needle: (tn.com) A direct-to-consumer mattress company, Tuft & Needle seeks to restore transparency and fairness in the mattress industry. Their mattresses are high-quality, made in the USA, but are fairly priced.

Warby Parker: (warbyparker.com) Warby Parker is a direct-to-consumer retailer of prescription eyewear. Warby Parker offers stylish glasses for a fraction of the price and give a pair to someone in need for every pair purchased.

Wolf & Shephard: (wolfandshepherd.com) Wolf & Shepherd is a men's dress shoe brand that make the most comfortable dress shoes. Wolf & Shepherd's products are professional and fashionable on the outside, with the internal comfort and support of a sneaker.

Zappos: (zappos.com) Zappos is an online shoe and apparel retailer. Zappos is known for its customer-centric culture which includes a 365-day return policy and 24/7 customer service.

NOTES

1   "How Many Products Does Amazon Sell Worldwide." ScrapeHero, 27 Oct. 2017, https://www.scrapehero.com/how-many-products-does-amazon-sell-world-wide-october-2017/.

2   "Amazon takes USD 44 cents per dollar spent in US ecommerce space." The Paypers, 25 Oct. 2017, https://www.thepaypers.com/ecommerce/amazon-takes-usd-44-cents-per-dollar-spent-in-us-ecommerce-space/770593-25#.

3   "Annual Study of Intangible Asset Market Value from Ocean Tomo, LLC." Ocean Tomo, 5 Mar. 2015, http://www.oceantomo.com/2015/03/04/2015-intangible-asset-market-value-study/.

4   Magana, Greg. "New study shows consumers want seamless multichannel e-commerce." Business Insider, 21 Mar. 2019, https://www.businessinsider.com/consumers-want-seamless-multichannel-ecommerce-2019-3.

5   "Global Online Beauty and Personal Care Products Market Insights, Forecast to 2025." Analytical Research Cognizance, 10 Oct. 2018, http://www.arcognizance.com/report/global-online-beauty-and-personal-care-products-market-insights-forecast-to-2025.

6   Sinek, Simon. Start with Why. Portfolio, 2009.

7   Daniel Pink. Drive. Riverhead Books, 2015. PP 24-32.

8   Ibid, PP 31.

9   Ibid, PP 32.

10   Denning, Stephanie. "The Making of MeUndies: How to Create a Successful Subscription Model." Forbes, 28 Mar. 2018, https://www.forbes.com/sites/stephaniedenning/2018/03/28/the-making-of-meundies-how-to-create-a-successful-subscription-model/#4b471abb4683.

11   Kelly, Kevin. "1,000 True Fans." KK, 4 Mar. 2008. https://kk.org/thetechnium/1000-true-fans/.

12   Loizos, Connie. "How to Build a Brand in 2017: Tips from Glossier CEO Emily Weiss." TechCrunch, 17 Feb. 2017, https://techcrunch.com/2017/02/17/beauty-guru-emily-weiss-on-building-a-brand-from-scratch-in-2017/.

13   "What to Do When There are Too Many Product Choices on the Store Shelves?" Consumer Reports, Jan. 2014, https://www.consumerreports.org/cro/magazine/2014/03/too-many-product-choices-in-supermarkets/index.htm.

14   Swartz, Barry. The Paradox of Choice. Ecco, 2004.

15   "Understanding Brand Strategy with Mark Di Somma." On Brand with Nick Westergaard from Brand Driven Digital, 11 Jan. 2016, https://www.branddrivendigital.com/understanding-brand-strategy-with-mark-di-somma/.

16   "Percentage of paid units sold by third party sellers on Amazon platform as of 4th quarter 2019." Statista, https://www.statista.com/statistics/259782/third-party-seller-share-of-amazon-platform/. Accessed 4 Mar. 2020.

17   Dunne, Chris. "Amazon Has 1,029,528 New Sellers This Year (Plus Other Stats)." Feedback Express, https://www.feedbackexpress.com/amazon-1029528-new-sellers-year-plus-stats/. Accessed 23 Apr. 2019.

18   "Meet Shop, Your New Personal Shopping Assistant." Shopify, 28 Apr. 2020, https://news.shopify.com/meet-shop-your-new-personal-shopping-assistant#.

19   Coker, James. "Covid-19 Pandemic will speed up shift to eCommerce." EssentialRetail, 8 Apr. 2020, https://www.essentialretail.com/news/covid-19-shift-ecommerce/.

20   "Blake Mycoskie on 10 Years of Toms." The Business of Fashion, 6 May 2016, https://www.businessoffashion.com/articles/news-analysis/blake-mycoskie-on-10-years-of-toms.

21   Brucculieri, Julia. "Can Sneakers Made from Recycled Plastic Save Our Planet?" Huffington Post, 28 Feb. 2018, https://www.huffingtonpost.ca/entry/plastic-bottles-into-sneakers_us_5be9fcbbe4b0caeec2bca0b6.

22   Harold, Theresa. "Why the future of luxury fashion is on WhatsApp and WeChat, this start-up believes." South China Morning Post, 4 Dec. 2018, https://www.scmp.com/lifestyle/fashion-beauty/article/2176199/chat-commerce-pioneer-luxury-threads-styling-personalises.

23   Jarski, Verónica. "How Product Packaging Affects Buying Decisions [Infographic]." MarketingProfs, 6 Sept. 2014, http://www.marketingprofs.com/chirp/2014/25957/how-product-packaging-affects-buying-decisions-infographic.

24   Ibid.

25   Ibid.

26   Ibid.

27   Ibid.

28   Scott, David Meerman. "Marketing is Not Advertising." David Meerman Scott, 25 Aug. 2011, https://www.davidmeermanscott.com/blog/2011/08/marketing-is-not-advertising.html.

29   Rogers, Stewart. "Content Marketing is Up 300%, but Only 5% of it Matters." VentureBeat, 27 Sept. 2016, https://venturebeat.com/2016/09/27/content-marketing-is-up-by-300-but-only-5-of-it-matters/.

30   Spencer, Jean. "How to Convince Your Boss to do Content Marketing." Kapost Blog, 15 July 2014, https://marketeer.kapost.com/convince-boss-content-marketing/.

31   Donovan, Michelle. "The art of storytelling: researchers explore why we relate to characters." McMaster University, 13 Sept. 2018, https://brighterworld.mcmaster.ca/articles/the-art-of-storytelling-researchers-explore-why-we-relate-to-characters/.

32   "Thanksgiving weekend multichannel shopping up almost 40 percent over last year." <u>National Retail Federation</u>, 27 Nov. 2018, https://nrf.com/media-center/press-releases/thanksgiving-weekend-multichannel-shopping-almost-40-percent-over-last.

33   "Internet Trends Report 2018." <u>Kleiner Perkins</u>, 30 May 2018, https://www.kleinerperkins.com/perspectives/internet-trends-report-2018/.

34   Ibid.

35   "UPS Study: U.S. Online Shoppers Turning to International Retailers." <u>UPS Pressroom</u>, 7 June 2017, https://pressroom.ups.com/pressroom/ContentDetailsViewer.page?ConceptType=PressReleases&id=1496778994415-208.

36   Fain, Breena. "Stitch Data Report: Why Multichannel Selling is a Win for Retailers." <u>StitchLabs</u>, 8 July 2015, https://www.stitchlabs.com/blog/stitch-data-report-why-multichannel-selling-is-a-win-for-retailers/.

37   Ibid.

38   "Average Page Load Times for 2018 – How does yours compare?" <u>MachMetrics</u>, 25 Feb. 2018, https://www.machmetrics.com/speed-blog/average-page-load-times-websites-2018/.

39   Padychova, Zuzana. "How Page Load Time Affects Conversion Rates: 12 Case Studies [Infographic]." <u>HubSpot</u>, 23 Mar. 2017, https://blog.hubspot.com/marketing/page-load-time-conversion-rates?__hstc=138892268.2048d5a5b04d-be5e834e8d9cc4c74bb2.1552312033477.1552312033477.1552312033477.1&__hssc=138892268.1.1552312033477&__hsfp=2021768341.

40   "How to Speed up Your WordPress Site (Ultimate 2019 Guide)." <u>Kinsta</u>, 1 Mar. 2019, https://kinsta.com/learn/speed-up-wordpress/.

41   Ching, Elizabeth. "20 Visual Marketing Statistics You Need to Know [Infographic]." <u>CrowdRiff</u>, 18 Jan. 2017, https://resources.crowdriff.com/blog/visual-marketing-statistics.

42   "How Important is Product Photography in eCommerce." <u>AmeriCommerce</u>, https://www.americommerce.com/how-important-is-product-photography-in-ecommerce. Accessed 1 Oct. 2018.

43   Miller, Grace. "51 Vital Visual Commerce Statistics." <u>Annex Cloud</u>, 14 Jan. 2016, https://www.annexcloud.com/blog/51-vital-visual-commerce-statistics/.

44   King, Jennifer. "For Online Shoppers, Photos Can Influence a Purchase." <u>eMarketer</u>, 25 April 2018, https://www.emarketer.com/content/for-online-shoppers-photos-can-influence-a-purchase.

45   Wood, Cara. "Cracking the Consumer Code: How product content drives conversion [Infographic]." <u>Salsify</u>, 20 June 2016, https://www.salsify.com/blog/cracking-the-consumer-code-how-product-content-drives-conversion-infographic.

46   Feldman, Sarah. "Leading Payment Methods Used in 2018." <u>Statista</u>, 19 Feb. 2019, https://www.statista.com/chart/17072/leading-payment-methods-used-in-us/.

47   "Payment methods not used by U.S. online shoppers 2017." <u>Statista</u>, https://www.statista.com/statistics/705855/payment-methods-not-used-by-online-shoppers-in-the-us/. Accessed 2 Oct. 2018.

48   "The Future of Retail 2018" <u>WalkerSands</u>, Aug. 2018, https://www.walkersands.com/walker-sands-2018-future-of-retail-report-the-new-age-of-voice-commerce/.

49   Ibid.

50   Putnam, Joe. "What Impact Does Free Shipping Have on Online Retail Sales?" <u>Rejoiner</u>, http://rejoiner.com/resources/free-shipping-online-retail-sales/. Accessed 3 Oct. 2018.

51   Ibid.

52   McCabe, Kristen. "50+ Statistics Proving the Power of Customer Reviews." <u>Learning Hub</u>, 16 May 2018, https://learn.g2crowd.com/customer-reviews-statistics.

53   "No online customer reviews means BIG problems in 2017." <u>Fan and Fuel</u>, https://fanandfuel.com/no-online-customer-reviews-means-big-problems-2017/. Accessed 4 Oct. 2018.

54   Collinger, Tom. "How Online Reviews Influence Sales." <u>Spiegel Research Center</u>, https://spiegel.medill.northwestern.edu/online-reviews/. Accessed 4 Oct. 2018.

55   Ibid.

56   "Local Consumer Review Survey 2018." <u>BrightLocal</u>, https://www.brightlocal.com/learn/local-consumer-review-survey/. Accessed 4 Oct. 2018.

57   Collinger, Tom. "How Online Reviews Influence Sales." <u>Spiegel Research Center</u>, https://spiegel.medill.northwestern.edu/online-reviews/. Accessed 4 Oct. 2018.

58   Ibid.

59   Ibid.

60   "Shopping cart abandonment rate worldwide 2018, by industry." <u>Statista</u>, https://www.statista.com/statistics/457078/category-cart-abandonment-rate-worldwide/. Accessed 3 Oct. 2018.

61   "40 Cart Abandonment Rate Statistics." <u>Baymard Institute</u>, https://baymard.com/lists/cart-abandonment-rate. Accessed 3 Oct. 2018.

62   Ibid.

63   Walker, Tommy. "How to Reduce Shopping Cart Abandonment by Optimizing the Checkout." <u>Shopify</u>, 31 Aug. 2017, https://www.shopify.com/enterprise/44272899-how-to-reduce-shopping-cart-abandonment-by-optimizing-the-checkout.

64 "40 Cart Abandonment Rate Statistics." Baymard Institute, https://baymard.com/lists/cart-abandonment-rate. Accessed 3 Oct. 2018.

65 "Shopping Cart Abandonment Stats You'll Need for 2019." Moosend, 23 Jan. 2019, https://moosend.com/blog/cart-abandonment-stats/.

66 "Mobile Fact Sheet." Pew Research Center, 5 Feb. 2018, http://www.pewinternet.org/fact-sheet/mobile/.

67 Serrano, Stephan. "Complete List of Cart Abandonment Statistics: 2006-2018." Barilliance, 28 Feb. 2018, https://www.barilliance.com/cart-abandonment-rate-statistics/.

68 Shukairy, Ayat. "Mobile Commerce Statistics and Trends [Infographic]." Invesp, https://www.invespcro.com/blog/mobile-commerce/. Accessed 4 Oct. 2018.

69 Serrano, Stephan. "Complete List of Cart Abandonment Statistics: 2006-2018." Barilliance, 28 Feb. 2018, https://www.barilliance.com/cart-abandonment-rate-statistics/.

70 Mali, Nabeena. "You M-Commerce Deep Dive: Data, Trends and What's Next in the Mobile Retail World." BigCommerce, https://www.bigcommerce.com/blog/mobile-commerce/#understanding-mobile-payment-options. Accessed 23 Apr. 2019.

71 Chaffey, Dave. "Mobile Marketing Statistics Compilation." Smart Insights, 11 July 2018, https://www.smartinsights.com/mobile-marketing/mobile-marketing-analytics/mobile-marketing-statistics/.

72 Shukairy, Ayat. "Mobile Commerce Statistics and Trends [Infographic]." Invesp, https://www.invespcro.com/blog/mobile-commerce/. Accessed 4 Oct. 2018.

73 Appleseed, Jamie. "The State of Mobile Checkout & Form Usability." Baymard Institute, 2 Dec. 2015, https://baymard.com/blog/mobile-ecommerce-checkout-forms.

74 Nguyen, Mai-Hanh. "Customer service and virtual assistant bots will be prevalent for online businesses in many markets." Business Insider, 24 Oct. 2017, https://www.businessinsider.com/customer-service-chatbots-websites-2017-10.

75 "Customer comfort with AI chatbots service worldwide 2017, by service." Statista, https://www.statista.com/statistics/717098/worldwide-customer-chatbot-acceptance-by-industry/. Accessed 28 Sept. 2018.

76 Krogue, Ken. "Lead Response Management Best Practices." InsideSales.com, 11 June 2015, https://blog.insidesales.com/lead-response-management/infographic-2/.

77 "Why Email Marketing is Amazing." WebFX, https://www.webfx.com/data/why-email-marketing-is-amazing/. Accessed 8 Oct. 2018.

78   Aufreiter, Nora, et al. "Why marketers should keep sending you e-mails." McKinsey & Company, Jan. 2014, https://www.mckinsey.com/business-functions/marketing-and-sales/our-insights/why-marketers-should-keep-sending-you-emails.

79   "U.S. Consumers Likely to Increase Holiday Spending, Go Extra Mile for a Good Deal, Accenture Survey Reveals." Accenture, https://www.accenture.com/t20161013T212752__w__/us-en/_acnmedia/PDF-34/Accenture-Retail-2016-Holiday-Shopping-Survey-Results-Infographic-v2.pdf. Accessed 6 May 2019.

80   Lynn, Katie. "So much for the retail apocalypse." UseHero.com, 23 Aug. 2017, https://blog.usehero.com/67-of-ecommerce-brands-have-opened-physical-stores-2260c110e864.

81   Thomas, Lauren. "Gap, Tesla and Victoria's Secret are among the nearly 5,000 store closings already in 2019." CNBC, 9 Mar. 2019, https://www.cnbc.com/2019/03/08/these-retailers-have-announced-store-closures-in-2019.html.

82   "Study: 85% of Consumers Prefer to Shop at Physical Stores vs. Online." TimeTrade, https://www.timetrade.com/about/news-events/news-item/study-85-of-consumers-prefer-to-shop-at-physical-stores-vs-online/. Accessed 11 Oct. 2018.

83   "Death of PurePlay Retail." L2 Intelligence Report, 12 Jan. 2016, https://www.l2inc.com/research/death-of-pureplay-retail.

84   "UPS Online Shopping Study: Empowered Consumers Changing the Future of Retail." UPS Pressroom, 3 June 2015, https://www.pressroom.ups.com/pressroom/ContentDetailsViewer.page?ConceptType=PressReleases&id=1433180166893-264.

85   "Sharing Economy: Market Snapshot 2017." Juniper Research, https://www.juniperresearch.com/resources/infographics/sharing-economy-market-snapshot-2017. Accessed 24 Sept. 2018.

86   Perez, Sarah. "Target breaks into the top 10 list of US e-commerce retailers." TechCrunch, 24 Feb. 2020, https://techcrunch.com/2020/02/24/target-breaks-into-the-top-10-list-of-u-s-e-commerce-retailers/.

87   Clement, J. "Third-party seller share of Amazon platform 2007-2019." Statista, 9 Aug. 2019, https://www.statista.com/statistics/259782/third-party-seller-share-of-amazon-platform/.

88   Connolly, Alyssa. "How Much Money Do Amazon Sellers Make?" JungleScout, 17 Dec. 2019, https://www.junglescout.com/blog/how-much-money-amazon-sellers-make/.

89   Del Rey, Jason. "Surprise! Amazon now sells more than 70 of its own private-label brands." Recode, 7 April 2018, https://www.recode.net/2018/4/7/17208804/amazon-private-label-brands-list.

90   Gasparro, Annie, and Laura Stevens. "Brands Invent New Lines for Only Amazon to Sell." The Wall Street Journal, 25 Jan. 2019, https://www.wsj.com/articles/food-makers-invent-brands-for-only-amazon-to-sell-11548414001?mod=hp_lead_ pos3.

91   "Walmart's net sales worldwide from 2006 to 2019 (in billion U.S. dollars)." Statista, Mar. 2019, https://www.statista.com/statistics/183399/walmarts-net-sales-worldwide-since-2006/.

92   Perez, Sarah. "Walmart passes Apple to become No. 3 online retailer in U.S." TechCrunch, 16 Nov. 2018, https://techcrunch.com/2018/11/16/walmart-passes-apple-to-become-no-3-online-retailer-in-u-s/.

93   "The State of the Amazon Marketplace 2018." Feedvisor, 2018, https://fv.feedvisor.com/rs/656-BMZ-780/images/Feedvisor_The-State-of-the-Amazon-Marketplace.pdf. Accessed 24 Apr. 2019.

94   "Crowdfunding worldwide." Statista, https://www.statista.com/outlook/335/100/crowdfunding/worldwide. Accessed 11 Mar. 2018.

95   Szmigiera, M. "Kickstarter project funding success rate as of October 2019." Statista, 2 Oct. 2019, https://www.statista.com/statistics/235405/kickstarter-project-funding-success-rate/.

96   Alois, JD. "Crowdfunding 101: Kickstarter & Indiegogo (Infographic)." Crowdfund Insider, 28 Aug. 2014, https://www.crowdfundinsider.com/2014/08/47987-crowdfunding-101-kickstarter-indiegogo-infographic/.

97   "Crowdfunding Statistics [Updated for 2017!]." Fundly, https://blog.fundly.com/crowdfunding-statistics/. Accessed 24 Sept. 2018.

98   Ibid.

99   "Number of global social media users 2010-2021." Statista, https://www.statista.com/statistics/278414/number-of-worldwide-social-network-users/. Accessed 25 Sept. 2018.

100   Read, Ash. "The State of Social 2018 Report: Your Guide to Latest Social Media Marketing Research." Buffer, 18 Jan. 2018, https://buffer.com/resources/state-of-social-2018.

101   Ibid.

102   "The Beginner's Guide to Facebook Advertising." AdEspresso, https://adespresso.com/guides/facebook-ads-beginner/why-you-should-advertise-on-facebook-now/. Accessed 4 Oct. 2018.

103   "Social Media Fact Sheet." Pew Research Center, http://www.pewinternet.org/fact-sheet/social-media/. Accessed 4 Oct. 2018.

104   "Introducing Facebook Shops: Helping Small Businesses Sell Online." Facebook, 19 May 2020, https://about.fb.com/news/2020/05/introducing-facebook-shops/.

105   Del Ray, Jason. "Here's Facebook's new play to make you shop on Instagram." Vox, 19 May 2020, https://www.vox.com/recode/2020/5/19/21263898/facebook-shops-instagram-shopping-shopify-ecommerce.

106   "Facebook's Announcement Is a Long-Planned Head-On Attack on Amazon." SeekingAlpha, 24 May 2020, https://seekingalpha.com/article/4349811-facebooks-announcement-is-long-planned-head-on-attack-on-amazon.

107   Read, Ash. "A Complete Guide to Instagram Marketing: Get the Playbook that Drives Results for Instagram's Top Profiles." Buffer, 3 Dec. 2016, https://buffer.com/library/instagram-marketing.

108   Clement, J. "Instagram: distribution of global audiences 2019, by age and gender." Statista, 9 Aug. 2019, https://www.statista.com/statistics/248769/age-distribution-of-worldwide-instagram-users/.

109   Hainla, Liis. "21 Social Media Marketing Statistics You Need to Know in 2019." Dreamgrow, 5 July 2018, https://www.dreamgrow.com/21-social-media-marketing-statistics/.

110   "50 TikTok Statistics That Will Blow Your Mind." Influencer Marketing Hub, https://influencermarketinghub.com/tiktok-statistics/. Accessed 14 May 2020.

111   Sehl, Katie. "Everything Brands Need to Know About TikTok in 2020." Hootsuite, 2 Mar. 2020, https://blog.hootsuite.com/what-is-tiktok/.

112   Raj, Pritish. "TikTok Is Most Downloaded App of Q1 2020 Followed by Facebook Family." NextBigBrand, 17 Apr. 2020, https://www.nextbigbrand.in/tiktok-is-most-downloaded-app-of-q1-2020-followed-by-facebook-family/.

113   Sehl, Katie. "Everything Brands Need to Know About TikTok in 2020." Hootsuite, 2 Mar. 2020, https://blog.hootsuite.com/what-is-tiktok/.

114   "50 TikTok Statistics That Will Blow Your Mind." Influencer Marketing Hub, https://influencermarketinghub.com/tiktok-statistics/. Accessed 14 May 2020.

115   Ibid.

116   Sehl, Katie. "Everything Brands Need to Know About TikTok in 2020." Hootsuite, 2 Mar. 2020, https://blog.hootsuite.com/what-is-tiktok/.

117   Ibid.

118   Ibid.

119   Ibid.

120   Ibid.

121   Ibid.

122   Ibid.

123   Ibid.

124   Ibid.

125   Browne, Ash. "TikTok: Should You Be Advertising On It?" The Drum, 30 Jan. 2020, https://www.thedrum.com/opinion/2020/01/30/tik-tok-should-you-be-advertising-it.

126   "Most popular categories on Pinterest in the U.S. 2017." Statista, https://www.statista.com/statistics/251048/most-popular-categories-browsed-on-pinterest/.

Accessed 15 Oct. 2018.

127   "Pinterest by the Numbers: Stats, Demographics & Fun Facts." <u>Omnicore</u>, 6 Jan. 2019, https://www.omnicoreagency.com/pinterest-statistics/.

128   "3 Reasons You Need to Try Pinterest Ads." <u>WordStream</u>, 31 July 2019, https://www.wordstream.com/blog/ws/2017/05/04/pinterest-ads.

129   Lin, Casey. "$2 in profit for every $1 spent Analytic Partners' analysis shows Pinterest's impact." <u>Pinterest Business</u>, 4 Oct. 2017, https://business.pinterest.com/en/blog/2-in-profit-for-every-1-spent-analytic-partners-analysis-shows-pinterests-impact.

130   "Social Media Fact Sheet." <u>Pew Research Center</u>, http://www.pewinternet.org/fact-sheet/social-media/. Accessed 4 Oct. 2018.

131   Ibid.

132   "Most popular social networks worldwide as of July 2020, ranked by number of active users." <u>Statista</u>, https://www.statista.com/statistics/272014/global-social-networks-ranked-by-number-of-users/. Accessed 1 Sept. 2020.

133   "Social Media Fact Sheet." <u>Pew Research Center</u>, http://www.pewinternet.org/fact-sheet/social-media/. Accessed 4 Oct. 2018.

134   Blattberg, Eric. "The demographics of YouTube, in 5 charts." <u>Digiday UK</u>, 24 April 2015, https://digiday.com/media/demographics-youtube-5-charts/.

135   Gesenhues, Amy. "YouTube "How-To" Video Searches Up 70% with Over 100 Million Hours Watched in 2015." <u>Search Engine Land</u>, 13 May 2015, https://searchengineland.com/youtube-how-to-searches-up-70-yoy-with-over-100m-hours-of-how-to-videos-watched-in-2015-220773.

136   McGrath, Louisa. "A Beginner's Guide to Retargeting." <u>Funnel</u>, 30 May, https://blog.funnel.io/a-beginners-guide-to-retargeting.

137   "ComScore Study with ValueClick Media Shows Ad Retargeting Generates Strongest Lift Compared to Other Targeting Strategies." <u>ComScore</u>, 22 Sept. 2010, https://www.comscore.com/Insights/Press-Releases/2010/9/comScore-Study-with-ValueClick-Media-Shows-Ad-Retargeting-Generates-Strongest-Lift-Compared-to-Other-Targeting-Strategies.

138   Foster, Jeff. "Why Influencer Marketing is Creating Huge Returns for Businesses." <u>Convince & Convert</u>, https://www.convinceandconvert.com/digital-marketing/influencer-marketing-for-businesses/. Accessed 21 Sept. 2018.

139   "Influencer Marketing Study." <u>Tomoson</u>, https://blog.tomoson.com/influencer-marketing-study/. Accessed 21 Sept. 2018.

140   Mortimer, Natalie. "Influencer content accounts for almost 20% of consumer media consumption." <u>The Drum</u>, 25 Jan. 2017, https://www.thedrum.com/news/2017/01/25/influencer-content-accounts-almost-20-consumer-media-consumption.

141   "The State of Influencer Marketing 2018." <u>Linqia</u>, http://www.linqia.com/wp-content/uploads/2017/12/Linqia-The-State-of-Influencer-Marketing-2018.pdf.

Accessed 9 May 2019.

142 "Worldwide Spending on Augmented and Virtual Reality Expected to Reach $18.8 Billion in 2020, According to IDC." IDC, 27 Nov. 2019, https://www.idc.com/getdoc.jsp?containerId=prUS45679219#:~:text=FRAMINGHAM%2C%20Mass.%2C%20November%2027,will%20be%20spent%20in%202019.

143 Kinsella, Bret. "Amazon Echo Maintains Large Market Share Lead in U.S. Smart Speaker User Base." VoiceBot, 8 Mar. 2018, https://voicebot.ai/2018/03/08/amazon-echo-maintains-large-market-share-lead-u-s-smart-speaker-user-base/.

144 Southern, Matt. "New Study Reveals What People Are Buying Through Voice Assistants." Search Engine Journal, 17 Jan. 2019, https://www.searchenginejournal.com/new-study-reveals-what-people-are-buying-through-voice-assistants/287277/#close.

145 Smith, Jessica. "The Voice Assistant Landscape Report: How artificially intelligent voice assistants are changing the relationship between consumers and computers." Business Insider, 2 Mar. 2017, https://www.businessinsider.com/voice-assistant-report-2017-3.

146 Bentahar, Amine. "Optimizing for Voice Search is More Important than Ever." Forbes, 27 Nov. 2017, https://www.forbes.com/sites/forbesagencycouncil/2017/11/27/optimizing-for-voice-search-is-more-important-than-ever/#68a5ab0a4a7b.

147 Kishimi, Ichiro, and Fumitake Koga. The Courage to Be Disliked. Translated by Ichiro Kishimi and Fumitake Koga, Atria Books, 2017.

148 "Understanding Brand Strategy with Mark Di Somma." On Brand with Nick Westergaard from Brand Driven Digital, 11 Jan. 2016, https://www.branddrivendigital.com/understanding-brand-strategy-with-mark-di-somma/.

149 "Internet Trends Report 2017." Kleiner Perkins, 31 May 2017, https://www.kleinerperkins.com/perspectives/internet-trends-report-2017.

www.ingramcontent.com/pod-product-compliance
Lightning Source LLC
Chambersburg PA
CBHW031839200326
41597CB00012B/203